WHAT IS THE SANGHA?

Also by Sangharakshita

A Survey of Buddhism
A Guide to the Buddhist Path
The Three Jewels
What is the Dharma?
Through Buddhist Eyes
Know Your Mind
The Taste of Freedom
Peace is a Fire
Human Enlightenment
The Religion of Art
The Eternal Legacy
Travel Letters
Alternative Traditions
Who is the Buddha?
Ambedkar and Buddhism
Crossing the Stream
The History of My Going for Refuge
Flame in Darkness
The Ten Pillars of Buddhism
Vision and Transformation
New Currents in Western Buddhism
The Rainbow Road *(memoirs)*
Facing Mount Kanchenjunga *(memoirs)*
In the Sign of the Golden Wheel *(memoirs)*
The Inconceivable Emancipation
Ritual and Devotion in Buddhism

The Buddha's Victory
Tibetan Buddhism: An Introduction
The Priceless Jewel
The Bodhisattva Ideal
The Call of the Forest and Other Poems
A Stream of Stars
The Drama of Cosmic Enlightenment
The FWBO and 'Protestant Buddhism'
Wisdom Beyond Words
Forty-Three Years Ago
The Meaning of Conversion in Buddhism
Complete Poems 1941–1994
Was the Buddha a Bhikkhu?
In the Realm of the Lotus
Transforming Self and World
Buddhism for Today – and Tomorrow
The Essence of Zen

Booklets

Going for Refuge
Buddhism and the West
Great Buddhists of the Twentieth Century
The Meaning of Orthodoxy in Buddhism
Extending the Hand of Fellowship
My Relation to the Order
Mind – Reactive and Creative

SANGHARAKSHITA

WHAT IS THE SANGHA?

THE NATURE OF SPIRITUAL COMMUNITY

WINDHORSE PUBLICATIONS

Published by Windhorse Publications
11 Park Road
Birmingham
B13 8AB

© Sangharakshita 2000

The cover shows a Nepalese thangka of Avalokiteśvara
Cover design Vincent Stokes
Line drawings Varaprabha
Printed by Biddles Ltd, Guildford, Surrey

A catalogue record for this book is available from the British Library

ISBN 1 899579 31 1

The right of Sangharakshita to be identified as the author of this work has been asserted by him in accordance with the Copyright, Designs and Patents Act 1988

CONTENTS

About the Author   vii
Editor's Preface   1

Part 1 The Group and the Spiritual Community
    Introduction   9
  1   The Sangha Jewel   13
  2   The Traditional Sangha   23
  3   Individuality: The Essence of Sangha   35
  4   The History of the Spiritual Community   41
  5   The Group and the Spiritual Community   51
  6   Authority   63
  7   The Positive Group and the New Society   71
  8   The Path of Dissatisfaction   79

Part 2 The True Individual
    Introduction   87
  9   The Evolution of the Individual   95
  10   The Integrated Individual   107
  11   Overcoming the Self   115
  12   The Artist as the True Individual   127

Part 3 The Network of Personal Relationships
        Introduction 143
  13 Being a Buddhist Parent 153
  14 Is a Guru Necessary? 167
  15 Fidelity 185
  16 The Meaning of Friendship 197
  17 Buddhism and Business Relationships 205
  18 Non-exploitation 213
  19 Gratitude 219

Conclusions Can the Spiritual Community Save the World?
  20 A Buddhist View of Current World Problems 235
  21 Buddhism and Western Society 243
      Notes and References 249
      Further Reading 257
      Index 259

ABOUT THE AUTHOR

Sangharakshita was born Dennis Lingwood in South London, in 1925. Largely self-educated, he developed an interest in the cultures and philosophies of the East early on, and realized that he was a Buddhist at the age of sixteen.

The Second World War took him, as a conscript, to India, where he stayed on to become the Buddhist monk Sangharakshita. After studying for some years under leading teachers from the major Buddhist traditions, he went on to teach and write extensively. He also played a key part in the revival of Buddhism in India, particularly through his work among followers of Dr B.R. Ambedkar.

After twenty years in India, he returned to England to establish the Friends of the Western Buddhist Order (FWBO) in 1967, and the Western Buddhist Order (called Trailokya Bauddha Mahasangha in India) in 1968. A translator between East and West, between the traditional world and the modern, between principles and practices, Sangharakshita's depth of experience and clear thinking have been appreciated throughout the world. He has always particularly emphasized the decisive significance of commitment in the spiritual life, the paramount value of spiritual friendship and community, the link between religion and art, and the need for a 'new society' supportive of spiritual aspirations and ideals.

The FWBO is now an international Buddhist movement with over sixty centres on five continents. In recent years Sangharakshita has been handing on most of his responsibilities to his senior disciples in the Order. From his base in Birmingham, he is now focusing on personal contact with people, and on his writing.

EDITOR'S PREFACE

During his long teaching career, Sangharakshita has spoken millions of words in the context of lectures and seminars, and these have all been carefully recorded, on tape and in transcript, until such time as they could appear in book form. In these 'spoken word' books, we aim to capture the spontaneity and accessibility that is characteristic of Sangharakshita's teaching style, while also translating from spoken to written word in a way that does justice to the author's own feeling for literary standards – although the prose we end up with is different in many ways from his own writing style.

Over the last ten years we have published a number of commentaries on Buddhist texts, as well as books introducing various aspects of Buddhist life and practice. There is a great deal of material to choose from, and our reasons for deciding to work on a particular text at a particular time are diverse. As I remember it, Jinananda and I came up with the idea for the first in the present series, *Who is the Buddha?*, in a café in West London over a plate of chips. We had just heard that Bertolucci was making a film about the Buddha, and it occurred to us that it would be timely to put together a book about the Buddha's life based on Sangharakshita's lectures. We sketched out an idea on the traditional napkin, and the book became reality in time for the release of the film.

The next book in the series is also associated in my mind with a particular place. This time, Jinananda and I were out for a walk during a Windhorse Publications team retreat in Norfolk. For quite some time we had been wrestling (I think that's the right word) with a book on the Abhidharma (now published as *Know Your Mind*), and we were discussing what to do next. I don't know why it hadn't been obvious to us before, but the notion that we could put together a book called *What is the Dharma?* suddenly dawned on us as we strode through the Norfolk fields.

From that moment, the creation of the present volume was, of course, inevitable – but what its content should be was not. Obviously a book about the Buddha will be about the Buddha's life and qualities, and a book about his teaching, the Dharma, will be about doctrines, principles, and practices. But what should a book about the Sangha contain? Indeed, what is the Sangha?

The terms Buddha and Dharma are well established in the West in a way that Sangha so far is not – a fact that is quite significant. It is perhaps fair to say that many Western Buddhists have tended to regard their Buddhist practice either as a personal and private affair, or as something between themselves and their spiritual teacher. In many Buddhist circles the term 'sangha' is used primarily to refer to the Buddhist monastic community, as distinct from the laity, and it is defined in these terms in the most recent Oxford dictionary. It is my impression that Western Buddhists are only just beginning to conceive of Sangha, spiritual community, as an ideal for all Buddhists, whatever our lifestyle.

But the Sangha has been regarded by Buddhists since the Buddha first taught the Dharma as an ideal to be honoured and aspired to, just as the Buddha and Dharma have always been. A book intended to introduce the Sangha to a modern Western readership would have to explain why that should be.

The most obvious answers to the question 'What is the Sangha?' are historical and geographical. One might write a history of the development of the Buddhist spiritual community, or describe the many and varied cultural conditions in which Buddhism has become established over the centuries. But such an approach, while it might be of great interest, would not get at the heart of the question. Why is it that the Sangha is to be regarded by the Dharma practitioner as an ideal of the same order as the Buddha and the Dharma?

I find it pleasing that although I can remember the initial discussion we had about this book, I can't remember when or where it took place. That seems congruent with the nature of the book itself, which is likewise tied neither to a geographical nor to a historical perspective. It does include these perspectives, but its fundamental concerns are more essential. It centres around themes to which Sangharakshita has given much consideration, and to which he gave expression in many of the talks on which this book is based.

It is not surprising that he has considered this question, 'What is the Sangha?', so fully. There are no doubt personal reasons: an understanding of the term 'sangha' is essential to an understanding of the name he was given at his ordination, and thus to an understanding of who he is – although his receiving that name was apparently a matter of chance. As Sangharakshita recounts in the first volume of his memoirs, *The Rainbow Road*, his preceptor, U Chandramani, at first gave him the name 'Dharmarakshita'. It quickly emerged, however, that there was already a monk of that name:

If there were two Dharmarakshitas, he protested, there would be endless confusion. People would not know which of us was which. My letters would be delivered to him. What was worse, his letters would be delivered to me. Neither of us would ever know where we were. 'Oh well,' said our preceptor, dismissing all this fuss and bother about names with a gesture of good-humoured impatience, 'Let him be Sangharakshita!' In this unceremonious manner was I placed under the special protection of the Sangha, or Spiritual Community, rather than under that of the Dharma, or Teaching.

This chance occurrence seems especially meaningful in view of the fact that, as Sangharakshita explains in his introduction to the present work, for the first few years of his Buddhist life he had almost no contact with any other Buddhist, and thus almost no experience of Sangha in the broadest sense. One of the themes of his memoirs is his search for and eventual satisfying discovery of kindred spirits in the spiritual life.

Furthermore, many years after his ordination, Sangharakshita himself founded a new Buddhist order, and thus made it possible for thousands of other people also to experience the 'protection of the Sangha'. While, as he says, there was no blueprint, no plan, for the development of this new movement, Sangharakshita did give very careful thought to the essential nature of Sangha. In particular, he was concerned to define a number of terms. For example, he drew a careful distinction between 'the group' and 'the spiritual community'. Human beings have always formed groups – family groups, tribes, nations, companies, clubs – and we all belong to a great number of them. But a spiritual community is different, in that it is made up of individuals, or at least aspiring individuals. But what is an individual? Clearly, the term is being used in a special sense: by Sangharakshita's definition, it signifies not the person who is an individual in a merely statistical sense, but the man or woman who has become, or is in the process of becoming, a 'true individual': a state of being which, as defined here, is associated with many highly positive and mature human qualities.

The first two parts of this book explore these terms, and the relationship between individuality and affiliation with others who are leading, or attempting to lead, a Buddhist life – a relationship that lies at the heart of the question 'What is the Sangha?' How are we to sustain, indeed develop, our individuality, and at the same time live in cooperation and harmony with others? These are questions that Buddhists everywhere, East and West, will need to consider.

In the third part of the book, the relationship of the individual to others is considered in terms of six kinds of relationship concerning which the Buddha himself gave guidelines: the relationships of parents and children, friends, spouses, employers and employees, monastics and lay people, and teachers and disciples. Each of us is involved in most, if not all, of these relationships, and it is therefore part of our spiritual practice to find positive and creative ways of handling them – this too is what the ideal of Sangha is about. I should note here that although it seems appropriate to retain the title 'Is a Guru Necessary?' for the chapter on spiritual teachers, Sangharakshita has observed that we should be careful not to misunderstand the term 'guru'. Indeed, so much has the term been debased in popular usage that perhaps, Sangharakshita has suggested, we should stop using it altogether, and instead be content with the traditional Buddhist term *kalyāṇa mitra*, 'spiritual friend' – or even just friend.

Discussion of the role of the Sangha in Buddhism very often goes into questions about the validity or desirability of monastic ordination, the presence or absence of misogyny, whether the Buddhist community is for or against the family, and so on. All of these are important questions, and they rightly receive a great deal of attention. But underlying all these issues is something still more important. How can Buddhists best help each other – and how can they help the world –

towards a more enlightened way of living, of being? How can we be good friends to one another in this sense? It is Sangharakshita's sense of the importance of these questions, and the importance of friendship, that has shaped this book.

The final chapters of the book consider the role of gratitude in the life of the Buddhist, and also the ways in which the Buddhist Sangha might have a positive influence on the wider world – and these themes are very much in my mind as I write this preface. For Buddhist publishers, the publication of a book is itself an exercise in the practice of Sangha, and quite a number of people have been involved in the production of this one. Like the Sangha as a whole, this book also has its historical and geographical aspects. The talks on which it is based were delivered over many years to many audiences in many places. This, of course, has shaped the teachings themselves. For example, the chapter entitled 'Being a Buddhist parent' is based on a talk given to Buddhist parents, and some of the other chapters have their origin in talks given on the occasions of Buddhist festivals, while yet others are based on public lectures intended for those with little or no knowledge of Buddhist practice. However, our aim has been to present all the material here in a way that is accessible to everyone.

The talks were given in a variety of settings, and work on the book has taken place in many locations too. The talks were transcribed under the direction of Silabhadra, from his home on the south coast of England – a great labour of love, this. It is to Jinananda that all the credit must go for the feat of making the transcripts into a book, and this was done in the midst of his childcare responsibilities in London. When I took up the editorial baton, I was *en route* to a retreat in Montana, and Sangharakshita read the first draft while on retreat in Spain. Varaprabha produced the array of original, appropriate, and exquisite illustrations at Street Farm, in the depths of the Norfolk countryside, and the whole thing was brought together, under the expert guidance of Padmavajri, at Windhorse Publications' offices in Birmingham, where as usual Shantavira did us proud with his copy-editing skills, Padmavajri created the index, Dhivati did the proof-reading, and – from afar – Vincent Stokes designed the lovely cover.

Speaking personally, I have much appreciated Jnanasiddhi's company in the editorial office. Editing is generally a solitary process, but we have had a most convivial time, swapping linguistic conundrums as we worked on our respective projects. And by the time you read this, the rest of our right livelihood team at Windhorse will have been involved too – Vidyasuri, David Tunnell, Keith Bellmore, and Stuart Wallis – and above all Dharmashura, whose direction makes Windhorse possible.

Now this network of people extends to you, the reader. May you benefit from the book, just as we have. Of course, all the benefit comes from the teacher, Sangharakshita, and he has been intimately involved with the publication of this book. He is himself an expert editor, and has given a great deal of time to working on this book – as well as having given the teachings in the first place. For all this, many thanks are due. Of course, he would say that he is simply passing on his understanding and experience of the Buddhist tradition, as members of the Sangha have done since the time of the Buddha. No Sangha, no transmission of the Dharma. Our gratitude must therefore extend back in time, to all those who have made it possible for us to contact this teaching, back indeed to the Buddha himself. And – as we learn in Chapter 19 of this book – the Buddha too was full of gratitude to everyone and everything that had made it possible for him to gain Enlightenment. It is gratitude, above all, one might say, that characterizes the Buddhist spiritual community, the Sangha. I am personally very grateful to have been involved in this project.

Vidyadevi
Birmingham
October 2000

PART 1

The Group and the Spiritual Community

INTRODUCTION

I FIRST CAME TO KNOW about Buddhism in the 1930s, when I was ten or eleven.[1] What I learned – from a series of articles in an encyclopaedia – did not affect me very deeply at the time. However, when I was sixteen I read two Buddhist texts called the *Diamond Sūtra* and the *Sūtra of Wei Lang*, and these made a very deep impression on me indeed. In fact, I can go so far as to say that through them I had my first glimpse of what is known in the Buddhist tradition as perfect vision, my first direct insight into the true nature of reality. From that time onwards I considered myself a Buddhist, but it was fully two years before I came into direct contact with other Buddhists. For two years I was on my own – reading, learning, trying to understand, and even eventually writing about Buddhism. I read everything I could lay my hands on that might throw light on it, including material from many other spiritual traditions.

Buddhism in the West has moved on a lot since then. For one thing, never before in the history of the world has it been possible to have translations of the great spiritual classics of East and West, all in cheap editions on one's own shelf, to read at one's leisure. All these spiritual traditions and teachings have suddenly found themselves in the melting pot together, all acting upon and influencing one another. And –

although there are many more Buddhist organizations these days – it seems that many people's first contact with the Buddha's teaching still comes about through reading; personal contact with Buddhists tends to come rather later. Those who live in big cities may be able to find Buddhist groups fairly easily, but beyond the main conurbations many people have to get on with their practice as best they can on their own, perhaps for many years. I have met individuals who have read about Buddhism, and even tried to practise meditation, for ten or fifteen years, without meeting a single Buddhist during that time.

We are conditioned by our experience, especially our early experience – everything that happens to us leaves some mark or other – and this is true even of our experience of Buddhism. If you have become accustomed to studying alone, meditating alone, thinking your own thoughts without testing them against the thoughts of others, or having any real communication with like-minded people, you may well question the necessity of joining a group at all, even a Buddhist group. You may feel that you're not the kind of person who joins groups.

But, as I discovered myself when I did finally meet other practising Buddhists, contact with other people who are following the Buddhist path makes a world of difference to one's own ability to do so. Indeed, the Sangha, the spiritual community, has from the very beginning of the Buddhist tradition been given an equal place with the two other great ideals of Buddhism: the Buddha, who represents the ideal of Enlightenment, and the Dharma, the way or teaching that leads to Enlightenment.

So how does joining a group relate to the ideal of spiritual community? It is this ground that we will be exploring in this book. In its most specific sense, the term 'sangha' refers to the men and women who, throughout Buddhist history, have gained Enlightenment through following the Buddha's teaching. The word 'sangha' is also used in some Buddhist traditions to refer to the monastic community, as distinct from the laity; and it is perhaps most commonly used simply to signify the Buddhist community as a whole. But in considering the question 'What is the Sangha?' we will be contemplating the essential nature of sangha – that is, the nature of the relationship between the individual Buddhist and the wider collectivity of Buddhist practitioners. As we will see, the sangha ideally consists of developing individuals, and its purpose is not to become a powerful organization, a group, but to further the development of the individual towards the ultimate goal of liberation for the sake of all beings.

To explore the nature of the sangha in these terms, we will need to examine some basic questions. For example, what is the difference between a group and a spiritual community? And what is it to be an individual? The first part of this book will be dedicated to drawing the distinction between the group and the spiritual community, and will include a brief history of spiritual communities, both Buddhist and non-Buddhist, as well as the beginnings of a definition of individuality. The second part will focus on the true individual – that is, what it is to be truly human – in the context of the evolution of consciousness, and will explore in various ways the qualities associated with individuality.

In its broadest sense, as we shall see, sangha can be said to be about communication, about relationships. The third and final part of this book will therefore look, or at least glance (this is a big subject), at the ethical implications of the individual Buddhist's relationship to others: friends, spouses, family, fellow workers, and spiritual teachers. And finally, in our concluding chapters, we will consider briefly the relationship of the individual Buddhist and the spiritual community to the world as a whole, and at least open up the possibility that the Buddhist sangha may play a part in improving the situation in which, globally speaking, we find ourselves.

1

THE SANGHA JEWEL

THE THREE MOST PRECIOUS THINGS

Every religion or spiritual tradition has certain concepts, symbols, credal forms, and ideals that enshrine its highest values. The sangha is one of the three ideals that lie at the heart of Buddhism, and I want to begin by considering it in this context.

The first of these ideals is the ideal of Enlightenment, a state of wisdom that is one with compassion, and compassion that is one with wisdom: an intuitive understanding of ultimate reality in its absolute depth and in all its manifestations. This ideal is represented not by any kind of divinity – not by 'God' or a prophet or incarnation or son of God – nor simply by a wise and compassionate human being, but by a man who became what has come to be called a Buddha. The historical Buddha was an ordinary human being who, through his own efforts, transcended his human limitations, to become for Buddhists the symbol of reality itself. To accept the Buddha Jewel as an ideal is to acknowledge that it is relevant to us personally, and that we ourselves can aim to become Enlightened. The Buddha, in short, shows us what we can become.

The second great Buddhist ideal is that of the Dharma. The word itself has a bewildering number of meanings, including attribute, law, principle, custom, practice, tradition, duty, and ultimate element of existence.[2] But here it means the path to Enlightenment – the sum total of all those practices, procedures, methods, and exercises that help us towards the realization of Enlightenment.

This way of defining the Buddha's teaching is central to any clear understanding of Buddhism. It is very easy as a Buddhist to fall into a doctrinaire attitude and start saying 'Such and such a way of doing things *is* Buddhism.' But someone from a different school of Buddhism might say just the opposite. For example, some Buddhists will tell you 'It all depends on your own effort'; others will say 'Any effort you make simply builds up the strength of your delusion – you just have to realize that there is no self to make an effort.' So how do we work our way through such conflicting messages? How do we get to what the Buddha truly meant to communicate?

Fortunately for us, this question occurred to one of the Buddha's original disciples, his old foster-mother and aunt, Mahāprajāpati – because differences of opinion as to what the Buddha actually taught existed even then. She, of course, was able to go straight to the source of all these different ways of understanding the Dharma. She asked the Buddha himself, 'How do we judge what is the Dharma and what isn't?' And he said, 'It's very simple. Those teachings which when put into practice (not speculated about, but *put into practice*) lead to such things as detachment, decrease of worldly gains, frugality, content, patience, energy, and delight in good – these, you may be sure, are my Dharma. And the opposites of these things are not my Dharma.'[3]

The Buddha here sets out the goals of the spiritual life in precise terms – this is not some woolly, subjective fantasy – and the means to those ends have to be equally precise. They also have to be functional; by definition, Buddhist practice has to work. This is why the Buddha described the Dharma on another occasion as being like a raft;[4] without it there is no means of getting across the raging torrent of craving, hatred, and delusion, but still it is only the means – it is not an end in itself. Once it has carried you over to Enlightenment, so to speak, it can be discarded; it is no further use to you personally.

The Mahāyānists took the Buddha's advice to Mahāprajāpati to a significant conclusion. Taking one of the rock edicts of the great Indian emperor Aśoka, which reads 'Whatever the Buddha has said is well said,' they reversed it. 'Whatever is well said (*suvacana*)', says the Mahāyāna – 'that is the word of the Buddha (*buddhavacana*).'[5] This means, of course, that we have to be very careful about what we take to be 'well said'. The care with which the Dharma should be interpreted can be expressed by translating the term as 'the real truth'. An authentic expression of the Dharma will always express the real truth about human existence. This is the second great Buddhist ideal – the Dharma.

Now we can focus on our main theme, the third great ideal of the Buddhist life, the Sangha. The word *sangha* means 'association' or 'society'. It is not an exclusively Buddhist term, being common to many ancient and modern Indian languages. In the context of Buddhism, however, the sangha in its broadest sense is the ideal of spiritual community, the fellowship of those who follow basically the same path towards ultimately the same goal. It may come as a surprise that the spiritual community should be regarded as being so very important – as important, indeed, as the ideal of Buddhahood itself, and as the Buddha's teaching. But from the very beginning the Buddha clearly regarded the sangha as being of supreme importance. He set great store by his disciples, especially his Enlightened disciples, insisting that any honour he received should be shared with them. On one occasion, someone wanted to offer him some rather valuable robes, and he said 'No, don't offer them to me; offer them to the sangha – the merit of such an offering will be the greater.'[6] The true significance of this is not that it indicates that members of the sangha are to be treated as VIPs. Rather, it points to the great value the Buddha placed on spiritual community, and specifically on spiritual friendship. As we shall see – and, I hope, come to feel – spiritual friendship is, as the Buddha said, the whole of the spiritual life.

The ideals of the Buddha, Dharma, and Sangha are known in Sanskrit as *triratna*, the Three Jewels or (as the Chinese translators put it) the three most precious things. They are called this because as far as the Buddhist tradition is concerned they embody the highest values of existence – or three aspects of the one ultimate value. Relating to them makes everything else worth while. Everything else exists for the sake of the essence, the reality, they represent. Every Buddhist subject or practice you could possibly think of is connected with one or more of these Three Jewels.

They come in a definite order. The Buddha Jewel came into existence first, when Siddhārtha Gautama gained Enlightenment under the bodhi tree. Then, two months later, when he delivered his first discourse to five old friends, the five ascetics, in the Deer Park at Sarnath, near Benares, the second Jewel, the Dharma, appeared.[7] And the

Sangha Jewel arrived last of all, when those five ascetics, one by one, bowed to him and said, 'Accept me as your follower.'

This pattern tends to be repeated in the way Buddhism is introduced into a new part of the world. In Europe, for example, it was at the end of the eighteenth century that the Buddha became generally (though imperfectly) known.[8] Gradually it was realized that the Buddha was an Indian teacher and that, for instance, the Buddha revered in Sri Lanka was the same as the figure known in China as Foh. But his teaching – the Dharma – was not studied until the middle of the nineteenth century. And it still took quite some time for the people who had become interested in that teaching to begin to form Buddhist societies, which constituted the rudimentary beginnings of a sangha. The Buddhist Society in Eccleston Square, London, founded in 1924, is probably the oldest of these. Even in the West today there is still some way to go in the formation of an effective Buddhist sangha. Indeed, not all Western Buddhists recognize the importance of sangha as providing the conditions necessary to support an effective Buddhist life.

WHAT IS THE BUDDHIST LIFE?

The question 'What is the Buddhist life?' can be answered in one word. It is a *committed* life. A Buddhist is not someone who has merely been born into a Buddhist family, or who has made an academic study of Buddhism and knows a great deal about its history and doctrines. Nor is a Buddhist someone who dabbles in Buddhism, who has a smattering of knowledge about it and airs their views on the subject, who mixes up Buddhism with Christianity, or Vedanta, or New Age ideas of one kind or another. A Buddhist is someone who is committed to the Three Jewels, who 'goes for refuge' to them (in the traditional phrase) and who, as an expression of that Going for Refuge, seeks to observe the ethical precepts of Buddhism. This is the heart of the matter.

Going for Refuge to the Buddha means accepting the Buddha and no other as one's ultimate spiritual guide and exemplar. Going for Refuge to the Dharma means doing one's utmost to understand, practise, and realize the fundamental import of the Buddha's teaching. And Going for Refuge to the Sangha means looking for inspiration and guidance to those followers of the Buddha, both past and present, who are spiritually more advanced than oneself.

Another term for the Three Jewels is the 'Three Refuges' (*triśaraṇa* in Sanskrit).[9] Referring to the Buddha, Dharma, and Sangha as jewels reflects how precious they are. But if you have really recognized their preciousness, you just have to take up a certain attitude in accordance with that recognition. If you truly regard something as valuable, you act as though it really is so. If you are convinced that the Three Jewels represent the three highest values of existence, you will act upon that conviction. This process of acting upon that conviction is what is known as Going for Refuge. It is equivalent to what in other religious systems is known as 'conversion'.[10]

The word 'refuge', which is the literal translation of the original Sanskrit term *śaraṇa*, does not have connotations of running away, of seeking escape from the harsh realities of life through losing oneself in pseudo-spiritual fantasies. Rather, it represents two great shifts in one's being. These are, firstly, the recognition of the fact that permanence, identity, unalloyed bliss, and pure beauty are to be found nowhere in mundane existence but only in the transcendental nirvāṇic realm; and secondly, the wholehearted resolve to make the great transition from the one to the other, from the mundane to the transcendental.

In many traditionally Buddhist countries this profound change of heart is institutionalized in the form of a ceremony called 'taking the Refuges'. In this form it inevitably tends to get trivialized. Any public meeting, even a political meeting, it is sad to say, will start with everyone 'taking' the Refuges and precepts – that is, reciting them – just to show that they are all good Buddhists. Another way that Going for Refuge gets cheapened is when it is taken as something you do once and for all, like baptism in Christianity, so that it is assumed that when you have 'taken the Refuges' from a monk, you are safely a Buddhist.

As a committed Buddhist one goes for Refuge – or tries to – all the time. As one's appreciation of the Three Jewels grows, one's Going for Refuge becomes correspondingly more profound. And this can sometimes have surprising results. It may mean that what brings you to Buddhism in the first place becomes, as you progress in your practice, not more but less important, as your deepening understanding comes to displace the comparatively superficial appreciation of Buddhism that was sufficient to get you going in the first place.

For instance, one may have heard it said that whereas Christianity is a religion of faith, Buddhism is a religion of reason, and one may be drawn to Buddhism on that basis.[11] But then as one goes more deeply into it, one finds that it isn't quite like that. One finds that while reason is given a definite and honoured place in Buddhism, it is by no means enthroned as its governing principle. But one remains a Buddhist because one has gone deep enough not only to be able to put reason in its proper place, but also to find other aspects of Buddhist practice profoundly meaningful.

Thus Going for Refuge is an experience – a spiritual experience – that is deepening and growing more multidimensional all the time. One accepts the ideal of Enlightened humanity, exemplified by the historical Buddha, as being more and more relevant to oneself personally; one takes that ideal as one's personal goal in life more and more to heart; and one tries to practise the Dharma in such a way as to realize that ideal more and more effectively.

A famous south Indian teacher called Swami Ramdas who died in the early sixties was once asked, 'Why is it that so many people who take up the spiritual life don't make any real progress? Though they go on with it year after year, they just seem to be standing still. Why?' His answer was simple and uncompromising. 'There are two reasons,' he said, 'In the first place, they have no clearly defined ultimate objective towards which they want to work. Secondly, they have no clearly defined way of getting there.'

So far as Buddhism is concerned, that goal is Buddhahood, and the way of getting there is the Dharma. These are the two necessary ingredients of one's spiritual life as a Buddhist. They may even appear to be sufficient. Why, then, should one have to go for Refuge to the Sangha as well? How does Going for Refuge to a spiritual community help us?

WHY GO FOR REFUGE TO THE SANGHA?

It has been said that the history of Buddhist philosophy can be summed up as the struggle between Buddhism and the abstract noun. So – to guard against the ubiquitous enemy, abstraction – we should be clear that when we speak of the spiritual community, we are not referring to some ethereal entity apart from the people who comprise it. Membership of a community means relationship with people within that community. We can now put our question another way: how is it that entering into relationship with other people who hold a common ideal and follow a common path should help us in our spiritual life?

In a sense, it comes down to the simple saying: 'Birds of a feather flock together.' That is how they survive. There was an occasion when the Buddha addressed the Vajjians, a tribe from the Vaiśālī area who had come under some threat. Among other things, he told them that they would prosper as long as they continued to meet regularly, in full and frequent assemblies, conducting their business in harmony and dispersing in harmony. Afterwards he went on to apply the same criteria to the spiritual survival of the sangha.[12]

The heart of the sangha is *kalyāṇa mitratā*, a very beautiful phrase; in fact, it is less a philosophical term than a poetic one. *Kalyāṇa* means beautiful, charming, auspicious, helpful, morally good. Thus the connotations are aesthetic, moral, and religious. The term covers much the same ground as the Greek expression *kalon kai agathos*, which means 'good and beautiful'. *Mitratā* means simply friendship or companionship. *Kalyāṇa mitratā* therefore means something like 'beautiful friendship', or 'morally good companionship', or – as I have translated it – 'spiritual friendship'. There is a well-known exchange between the Buddha and his disciple Ānanda which spells out its importance in the Buddha's eyes. Ānanda was the Buddha's cousin and became his attendant for the last twenty years of the Buddha's life. He accompanied the Buddha wherever he went, and they had an understanding that if by any chance Ānanda was not present when the Buddha delivered a discourse, or discussed the Dharma with anyone, when they were alone together the Buddha would repeat to Ānanda everything he had said. Ānanda had an astonishingly retentive memory; he was apparently the human equivalent of a tape-recorder. Indeed, it is said that we owe our knowledge of the Buddha's teachings to him. Because he made a point of listening to everything the Buddha said, storing it away in his memory so that he could repeat it later on for the benefit of others, his testimony was used to authenticate the teachings that were preserved after the Buddha's death.

But on this particular occasion the Buddha and Ānanda were on their own, just sitting quietly together, when Ānanda suddenly came out with something to which he had obviously given a bit of thought. He said, 'Lord, I think that kalyāṇa mitratā is half the spiritual life.' And then one presumes that he sat back and waited for some kind of appreciative affirmation from the Buddha. It seemed to Ānanda that what he had said was incontrovertible: having like-minded people around you who are also trying to grow and develop must be half the battle won. But the Buddha said, 'Ānanda, you're wrong. Kalyāṇa mitratā is not half the spiritual life; it's the whole of it.'[13]

Why is this? Of course we learn from those we associate with, especially those who are more mature than we are, and learning will clearly be important if we are to make progress in the spiritual life. But in what does 'progress in the spiritual life' really consist? What are we *really* learning? The knowledge we need, in the end, is self-knowledge. And the real significance of the deep individual-to-individual contact that Going for Refuge to the Sangha involves lies in a simple psychological fact: we get to know ourselves best in relation to other people. If you spent your whole life alone on a desert island, in a sense you would never really know yourself. As it is, though, we have all had the experience of clarifying our ideas through discussion – and even of discovering that we knew more than we thought we did – simply through trying to communicate with another person. It is as though trying to communicate activates an understanding that is already there but has never manifested until now, and even brings forth new aspects of oneself – aspects which one only ever discovers as a result of contact with another person. Through meeting the challenge of real communication, one comes to know oneself better.

It is not only a matter of activating one's understanding. Meeting certain people can disturb aspects of ourselves which had been rather deeply buried. We say that a particular kind of person 'brings out the worst in us'. Perhaps nothing is said, but they somehow touch a raw nerve. It can be a shock to realize what that individual has evoked in us, to find ourselves behaving in a way that we like to think is uncharacteristic of us, even expressing hatred or contempt towards the person who has triggered off this uncharacteristic behaviour. Of course, that unpleasant side of us was always there, but it needed that person to bring it to the surface. In this apparently negative – but highly spiritually beneficial – way too, other people can introduce us to ourselves. We cannot transform ourselves unless we have a full sense of what lies within us.

Conversely, certain people seem to 'bring out the best in us'. Again, nothing necessarily needs to be said, but just being with them makes us feel lighter, more cheerful, more energetic, more positive. Other people can also sometimes activate resources of kindness and decency that we didn't know we had in us. And in a specifically Buddhist context, there will be certain people who activate a quality of faith in us simply through contact with their own faith. Something that was not active before is stirred up.

The sangha is necessary, in short, because personal relationships are necessary for human development. This applies at all levels – cultural, psychological, and spiritual. The vast majority of people undoubtedly develop most rapidly, and even most easily, in the company of others

– or at least in contact with others. Not that it is impossible to develop entirely on one's own; indeed, there is a Buddhist term for those who do so: *pratyekabuddhas*, private or solitary Buddhas.[14] However, although there are a number of canonical references to them, it is significant that all these solitary Buddhas are located in the remote and legendary past. There appear to be no historical examples.

We generally need the stimulation, reassurance, and enthusiasm of others who are going in the same direction as we are. We are naturally stimulated by someone who shares our special interest in something. Even though we still have to put in the effort ourselves, at least we see the point of it more clearly – we are less undermined by doubts. Membership of the sangha also gives us the opportunity to serve others, to express our generosity and helpfulness. Even in such a simple activity as providing tea and biscuits at a Buddhist festival, we can discover in ourselves the capacity for generosity, altruism, and general positivity.

Thus the sangha is there to help us know ourselves and express ourselves better. It is able to do this because everyone who participates in it is committed to the Buddha as the ideal of self-knowledge in the highest and deepest sense, and to the Dharma, the various principles and practices by which that self-knowledge may be achieved. A common allegiance to the first two Refuges constitutes the bond of unity between the members of the spiritual community. We are all following – albeit at different stages – the same path to the same ultimate goal.

By the same token, if one is not really aiming for Enlightenment, and not really trying to practise the Dharma, then one may say that one is committed to these ideals, but whatever one may say, one is no more a member of the sangha than a donkey following a herd of cows can be a member of that herd. This is the image used by the Buddha in the *Saṁyutta-Nikāya*: as he puts it, 'The donkey may say, "I am a cow too, I am a cow too" … but neither in his horns nor in his hoofs is he anything like a cow, whatever he may say.' Likewise, simply reciting the Refuges does not make one a member of the sangha. The bond is inner and spiritual.[15]

At a certain point in our development, however much we may meditate and read books about spiritual practice, we have to recognize that these are not enough. There is no doubt that we can learn a lot on our own. But if we are to grow spiritually in a fully rounded way, we eventually have to experience the vital part that communication has to play in our spiritual life. The following verse comes from the

Dhammapada, a very early collection of the Buddha's teachings, here quoted in the original Pāli:

> *Sukho buddhānamuppādo,*
> *sukhā saddhammadesanā.*
> *Sukhā saṅghassa sāmaggī,*
> *samaggānaṁ tapo sukho.*[16]

The first line means 'happy – or blissful, or blessed (*sukho*) – is the arising of the Buddhas'. When someone becomes a Buddha, this is a happy thing for all humanity. The second line may be translated 'Happy is the preaching of the true doctrine.' The teaching of the Dharma is a blessing for the whole world. The third line is 'Happy is the spiritual community in following a common path'. In the fourth line *tapo* means 'heat' and refers to spiritual practices which are like a fire burning up all impurities. The line therefore runs, 'The blaze of spiritual practice of those on the same path is happy or blessed.'

It is not enough to have a distant *idea* of Enlightenment, the *theory* of the Buddha's teaching, or a Buddhist *organization*. There is no future for Buddhism without a truly united and committed spiritual community, dedicated to practising together. And when Buddhists do come together in the true spirit of the sangha, there is then the possibility of inhabiting, for a while at least, the *dharmadhātu*, the realm of the Dharma. In this realm, all we do is practise the Dharma, all we talk about is the Dharma, and when we are still and silent, we enjoy the Dharma in stillness and silence together. The clouds of stress and anxiety that so often hang over mundane life are dispersed, and the fountains of inspiration within our hearts are renewed.

2

THE TRADITIONAL SANGHA

CELEBRATING THE SANGHA REFUGE

It is easy enough to make a decision to commit oneself to the Three Jewels. However, it is by no means so easy to sustain that commitment. If we are not careful, the vision fades, we lose momentum, we become distracted and restless, or we get comfortable and settle down, and our commitment is lost. It is therefore absolutely essential that we should set up our lives to include regular reminders of our original commitment. There are many ways of doing this – in fact, one might argue that Buddhist practice in all its aspects is designed to do it – but one traditional reminder is the celebration of Buddhist festivals.

The Buddha's Enlightenment is commemorated on the full moon day of the Indian month Visākha (Wesak in Sinhalese) which occurs in April or May. This anniversary, otherwise known as Buddha Jayanti, is when we remind ourselves of what a human being is capable of attaining, and thus what we ourselves can aspire to. The Buddha's teaching, the Dharma, is celebrated on the full-moon day of the Indian month Asala, in June or July, and this too is an anniversary, commemorating the Buddha's first discourse, his first explicit teaching to humanity. As for the Sangha, its festival, which reminds us of all those who have followed the path to Enlightenment before us, and celebrates the very existence of the spiritual community, comes on the full-moon day of Kārttika (October-November). Sangha Day is different from the other two major festivals in that it does not commemorate a specific event in the life of the Buddha. Instead, it recalls an annual event in the life of the early sangha.

If we go back in imagination to the first spiritual community that gathered around the Buddha, we find that it was composed of what I shall call part-timers and full-timers. It is very much a feature of modern Buddhist life that one tries to find ways of being a full-time practitioner whatever one's lifestyle. But lifestyle does make a difference. In the Buddha's time there were many people who aspired to follow the Dharma but – by choice or through circumstance – remained at home. They married, brought up families, worked, and had civic and political responsibilities, and they meditated and practised the Dharma as best they could in those circumstances. They could therefore be described as part-timers (they were later known as lay-disciples). Other factors being equal, they did not tend to develop spiritually as rapidly as the full-timers, but they did make some progress, and in some cases considerable progress – even more than many of the full-timers.

By contrast, full-timers, who became what we now know as monks and nuns, cut off all connection with home, left family and secular employment, renounced all civic and political duties, and signalled their lifestyle by staining their clothes saffron with an earth dye called *geruamati*, so that people could recognize them for what they were when they came round with their begging-bowls. These full-timers were entirely devoted to the practice of the Dharma. They studied together, they meditated, and they took upon themselves the task of preserving the teachings of the Buddha by memorizing them. Study did not of course involve reading, because there were no books to read. The only way to study the Dharma was to hear it from someone who could recite it to you – or at least parts of it – so that you could discuss it and eventually memorize it yourself. In the end you would become a sort of living, walking book.

At this time one of the most significant characteristics of these full-timers was that they were peripatetic, wandering from place to place rather than settling down where they found friendly and congenial lay-supporters. This way of life was recommended by the Buddha in a particularly pithy little verse (here translated from the Pāli):

The water is pure that flows;
The monk is pure who goes.

However, there was a problem with always being on the move: the weather. The rainy season in India arrives punctually, almost to the day, in July, and it rains solidly, torrential rain drumming down for day after day, month after month, until October. It was not a time to be out of doors, unless you had rice to plant, and that would be the case only at the very beginning of the season. Obliged to take shelter like everyone else, the full-timers would stay in one spot during this period, usually in small groups. Thus an annual pattern developed of continuous wandering for eight or nine months, followed by three or four months in a cave, or some kind of shelter made of broad tropical leaves, or a bamboo and thatch cottage in someone's garden. In this way there arose the venerable institution of the rainy-season retreat, the *varṣāvāsa*.

In the course of time quite a number of full-timers would gather together for this retreat – scores or even hundreds of them – all studying and meditating in one place. They would be joined from time to time by local part-timers, for whom the monsoon was also a period of enforced inactivity, and who therefore had more time on their hands than usual. Normally, part-timers were too busy to give very much attention to the Dharma; the instruction they received from wanderers passing through was brief and probably soon forgotten amidst the chores and pleasures of the daily round. The rainy season was therefore a golden opportunity for them to go more deeply into their practice under the spiritual direction of the full-timers.

At the end of the rainy season retreat there would be a great celebration, in two parts. First, the *pravāraṇā* was observed, a ceremony in which everyone begged everybody else's pardon. After three or four months cooped up together, there were inevitably some unresolved tensions and misunderstandings that needed to be cleared up. So the seniormost full-timer would begin the process, saying, 'Venerable sirs, if I have committed any mistake, or offended anybody, or said anything I should not have said in the course of the last three months, please accept my apologies.' Everyone else would then follow his example one by one down to the most junior person present.

The second ceremony of the day was the *kaṭhinacīvaradāna*. *Kaṭhina* means 'difficult', *cīvara* means 'dress' or 'robe', and *dāna* means 'giving' – hence this is the ceremony of 'the difficult giving of robes'. We say 'robes', but in fact everyone wore 'robes' at this time, so the full-timers did not wear some special ecclesiastical garment of the kind that the term 'robe' brings to mind nowadays. The part-timers would make themselves responsible for providing the full-timers with new clothes. This was considered an especially meritorious offering at this particular time, after the rainy season. It was called a 'difficult' offering because you had this one opportunity in the year to make it, to send the monks off looking spick and span.

There is to this day a traditional procedure in Burma which makes the offering truly difficult. Every year the lay people – or rather the laywomen – set themselves the task of making the robes from scratch, all in the space of the day of the ceremony. They sit up all night spinning cotton into thread; then they weave the cloth from the thread, cut the cloth into strips and sew these together, and finally dye the finished robes ready for the ceremony – all within twenty-four hours. This feat is performed as a mark of their devotion to the sangha of full-timers.

Eventually, for one reason or another, the rainy season retreat began to extend beyond the rainy season itself. The full-timers would sometimes stay on for a while after the rain had stopped, perhaps to pursue some particularly challenging discussion of the Dharma to a conclusion. Then, perhaps, they would want to follow this up with a period of intensive meditation together.... In the end they would linger on so long that the next rainy season would almost be upon them, and they would decide there was little to be gained from going off just for a month or two of wandering. Gradually, their accommodation became less improvised, as temporary thatched huts or leaf shelters were replaced by more substantial dwellings. In this way monasteries came into being, and the full-timers became monks.

Although the full-timers began effectively to be on continuous retreat, the tradition of the rainy-season retreat continued to be observed even – as the Buddhist world expanded – in the desert regions of Mongolia, Tibet, and northern China, where there was very little rain, let alone a whole season of it. But whether it was called a rainy season retreat or a summer retreat, it would be a time of intensified effort. It became the custom in some countries to give ordinations at the end of the retreat, and the conclusion would invariably consist in the celebration of the *kārttikapūrṇimā*, the full-moon day of Kārttika, or Sangha Day.

THE TRADITIONAL CATEGORIES OF THE SANGHA

The fact of the existence of monks and lay people, full-timers and part-timers, shows that the sangha is not a single, homogeneous body. Indeed, by its very nature it comprises individuals at varying levels of commitment and spiritual attainment. It is possible to distinguish, for example, a social level, an ecclesiastical level, and a spiritual level.

The Mahā-sangha
At the social level, there is the *mahā-sangha*, the great assembly, so called because it is great in size. It consists of all those who, with whatever degree of sincerity, go for Refuge to the Three Jewels, and who observe a greater or lesser number of ethical precepts. It is the collectivity of those accepting the spiritual principles or truths of Buddhism, regardless of lifestyle, whether they are monastic or lay, whether they have left the world or remain very much in the world, even, in many cases, very much *of* the world. Thus the *mahā-sangha* consists of both full-timers and part-timers, and even people who are no more than nominal Buddhists. This is the broadest level of sangha.

The Bhikṣu-Bhikṣuṇī Sangha
Then, at the ecclesiastical level, there is the bhikṣu-bhikṣuṇī sangha. The term 'sangha' is sometimes understood as referring specifically to the community of full-timers, usually thought of as the community of monks or the community of nuns. These terms monk and nun will certainly do for many full-timers throughout Buddhist history. It is difficult for us to imagine how many of these there were in the ancient Buddhist monasteries. Until very recently in Tibet a monastery of five hundred monks would have been considered to be a small monastery. Hence a great many bhikṣus would have lived in monasteries. However, the bhikṣu sangha has never been a purely monastic order. If we are going to use the term 'monk' in a Buddhist context we need to remember that it carries a broader meaning than it usually does in English.

Today there are two main branches of the monastic order: the Theravāda branch in Sri Lanka, Burma, Thailand, Cambodia, and Laos, and the Sarvāstivāda in Tibet, China, Vietnam, and Korea. There is little difference between the way of life and the rules observed by the monks of these two great traditions. However, it should be noted that Tibetan lamas are not to be confused with bhikṣus. 'Lama' simply means spiritual teacher; a lama may sometimes be a monk but not always, especially in the Nyingma and Kagyu Schools. Japan is rather a special case because although the bhikṣu ordination was introduced there, it died out and was replaced by the Bodhisattva ordination.

There is also an order of nuns, *bhikṣuṇīs*. This died out in many parts of the Buddhist world even before it could be introduced into Tibet, so that neither Theravāda Buddhism nor Tibetan Buddhism currently has any bhikṣuṇī tradition. But the bhikṣuṇī ordination does survive in Vietnam, China, and Taiwan. (There is much discussion today about the desirability of reinstating the bhikṣuṇī ordination more widely, the controversy turning in part on the traditional subordination of nuns to monks.) Nuns observe roughly the same number of rules as monks, and are shown – at least they should be shown, according to Buddhist tradition – the same kind of respect as monks.

Whether one is living in a monastery, or as a wanderer or hermit, or as a kind of local priest, being a bhikṣu or bhikṣuṇī does not in itself signify a particular depth of Going for Refuge. What such members of the monastic sangha have in common is their particular set of ethical precepts. This is the sangha in an ecclesiastical sense: a group of people set apart, as it were, from the world and united as a religious order by a common way of life, especially by a common rule.

Novice monks observe just ten precepts, or thirty-two in some traditions, but when they receive *upasampadā*, full acceptance into the order, they have to follow 150 rules – and in some parts of the Buddhist world all 150 are indeed observed.[17] Many of these rules are no longer relevant, having been devised in the specific conditions of life as a wanderer in northern India two-and-a-half thousand years ago, and they have been tacitly dropped in modern times.

The four most important rules are the *pārājikas*. *Pārājika* means 'defeat'. If one breaks one of these rules, one is permanently excluded from the order and will have to wait till another lifetime to rejoin it. The first *pārājika* is that one must not intentionally take the life of another human being. The second is that one must not take what is not given – that is, anything of such value that taking it could bring one before a court of law. The third is that one must abstain from any form of sexual intercourse.

These three *pārājikas* are straightforward enough, but the fourth requires a little more explanation. This is that one must not lay false claim to any spiritual attainments. Westerners seem to think nothing of asking people if they are Enlightened, or if they experience *samādhi*.

But in the East it is considered spiritual bad manners to talk about one's personal attainments at all, except perhaps with one's closest friends and one's teachers.

The reason for this is illustrated by an episode from the Pāli Canon, in which the Buddha's great disciple Sāriputta has apparently spent the whole afternoon in the forest meditating. When he emerges in the evening, he meets Ānanda, who remarks, 'Your face is wonderfully bright today; what have you been doing?' Sāriputta replies, 'I have been meditating in the forest; but while I was meditating, there did not come to me the thought "I am meditating."'[18] The point he is making is that as long as this thought is there, you are not really meditating, because you haven't progressed beyond the level of the personal 'I', the subjective self. In a sense you are only meditating when there is no one doing it, when it just – as it were – happens.

Moggallana comments on this by way of a little pun. 'This is how true people speak,' he says, 'They tell the essence – or gist – of the matter (*attha* in Pāli) but they don't bring in the self (*attā*).' With most of us, by contrast, whenever we meditate a bit, or muster a bit of generosity, the self always wriggles in somehow. A momentary inflation takes place as we think '*I* did that' or '*I* had that experience.'

The rest of the rules are secondary to these four basic ones, in the sense that if one breaks them one can make reparation by confessing one's breaches of them to one's fellow monks. Even if one is a hermit, therefore, one should not completely lose touch with the larger sangha. One will want to report in at regular intervals, to feel a fatherly eye upon one.

Buddhist monks and nuns have various duties. Their first duty is to study the Dharma and practise it; they are especially enjoined to practise meditation. Secondly, they are meant to set a good example to the laity. Thirdly, they should preach and teach. Fourthly, they have the responsibility of protecting the local community from unwholesome psychic influences. In cultures where it is taken for granted that we are surrounded by occult forces, it is traditionally believed that while some of these forces are beneficial, others are malign, and that, by their austerities, meditations, and blessings, monks are able to ward off these malign forces and keep them from harming ordinary people. There isn't much call for this service in the West, but it is a very important monastic function in the East.

Finally, monks are supposed to give worldly advice. In the East, whenever things go wrong – your children get into trouble, or you have cash-flow problems, or drink problems or neighbour problems, or husband–wife problems – it is customary to take your problem to the monks and ask their advice. By virtue of the fact that they don't have these problems themselves, being without wives or children or money, the monks can perhaps be expected to take a more objective view of the situation, just as a spectator has a better view of a football match from the stands than any of the players do on the pitch.

The scholar Edward Conze once said that without a monastic order Buddhism has no backbone. What we can certainly say is that without full-timers, men and women who are fully committed to Buddhist practice, there will be nothing to build a sangha around. In Britain, the first monks appeared before Buddhist groups had been formed. The pioneer of the English monastic sangha was Allan Bennett, who was ordained as Ananda Maitreya in Burma in 1902 and returned to England in 1908.[19] But in the West, since then, the hard and fast categorization of monks as full-timers and laity as part-timers has largely broken down. And there is a further focus on the sangha that transcends any distinction of lifestyle whatsoever. This is the *spiritual* community proper: the *ārya-sangha*.

The Ārya-sangha
Ārya was originally a term used to refer to a certain group of tribes who invaded India from the north-west. Owing to the high status of the conquering tribes, *ārya* came to mean 'noble' in a more general sense, and then gradually acquired a spiritual significance and thus came to mean 'holy' as well. The *ārya-sangha* is therefore the community of the noble or holy ones, those who are in contact with the transcendental, those who have a knowledge of the ultimate reality of things.

As it includes lay people as well as monks, the ārya-sangha may be said to constitute the spiritual as distinct from the merely ecclesiastical hierarchy of Buddhism. It cannot be categorized in terms of any formal scheme or public, organizational set-up, but represents an intermediate hierarchy between Buddhahood and unenlightened humanity. Its members may not be in physical contact – they may live not only in different places, but even at different times – but the transcendental experiences or attainments they share unite them beyond space and time. The ārya-sangha is the Sangha in the purely spiritual or, better, transcendental sense. That is, it is characterized essentially by the quality of wisdom or insight.

The Buddhist path is often divided into three basic elements: ethics, meditation, and wisdom.[20] All three are to be cultivated together, but they culminate in wisdom, as ethics and meditation may be cultivated without wisdom, whereas wisdom cannot be cultivated except on the basis of ethics and meditation. And in its turn, the cultivation of wisdom (*prajñā*) is also divided into three constituents.[21] The first level is that which comes by hearing: *śruta-mayī-prajñā*. The term originally referred to oral learning, characteristic of a preliterate society, but it can be taken to include any kind of knowledge and understanding picked up from books as well as from conversation and lectures. One learns *about* the nature of reality, and even about the nature of insight into the nature of reality. At this level, the aim is to get a clear conceptual idea of how things really are.

The second level of wisdom is wisdom which is acquired through one's own thought and reflection: *cintā-mayī-prajñā*. Having heard or read something about the true nature of things, you turn over in your mind what you have heard, and in doing so you start thinking seriously about it and – in time – develop your own insights. And thus you gain a deeper understanding.

The third level of wisdom is that which comes through meditation: *bhāvanā-mayī-prajñā*. This is wisdom above and beyond any purely intellectual insight. It is not thought out; it is not conceptual at all. In fact, it is only when the mind is completely still that true wisdom can begin to arise in the form of flashes of direct insight: intuitive, non-conceptual understanding. In the concentrated mental state which arises through meditation, truth or reality can flash upon the mind directly, unmediated by ideas, thoughts, or even feelings about that reality or truth.

The ārya-sangha consists only of those who have experienced this third level of insight. However, nothing in the spiritual life comes all at once. Any mastery, whether of ethics, meditation, or wisdom, comes by degrees. Whatever bumps and jolts we may experience in our spiritual life at times, real progress is steady and systematic. So it is with the experience of insight, and thus with one's progress as a member of the ārya-sangha – for there are levels of attainment even within this exalted company. You may experience no more than a feeble flash of insight if your meditation is too weak to sustain anything stronger. But if your concentration in meditation is more powerful, the flash of insight you experience when it comes may be brilliant enough to illumine the depths of reality. It is according to this varying degree of intensity of insight that the different kinds of *ārya pudgala* (noble or holy person) are distinguished.

But how can different degrees of insight be measured? Traditionally, there are two ways: a subjective way and an objective way. Subjectively, insight is measured according to the number of 'fetters' that it breaks. We will examine this approach at the beginning of the next chapter. Objectively, it is measured according to the number of rebirths remaining to be lived through once that level of insight has been attained. This is the measurement we find used to define the Sangha in the 'Tiratana Vandanā', the salutation to the Three Jewels chanted by Buddhists all over the world. In the third section of this the Sangha is characterized as 'happily proceeding ... uprightly proceeding ... methodically proceeding ... correctly proceeding'.[22] And it is further declared that the Sangha comprises persons at four distinct levels of spiritual development. Each of these levels has its own title:

1. A stream-entrant or *śrotapanna* is someone who no longer has to struggle against the current, so to speak. He or she cannot fall back from the course of spiritual progress, and it is said that he or she will gain full Enlightenment within, at the most, seven more rebirths.

2. A once-returner or *sakṛdāgāmin* is someone who will attain Liberation in one more lifetime.

3. A non-returner or *anāgāmin* is someone who will not have to come back to the human plane at all, but will be reborn in the so-called 'pure abodes' (*śuddhāvāsa*) at the peak of the realm of pure form, the *rūpa-dhātu*. He or she attains nirvāṇa from there.

4. An arhant (which means simply 'one worthy of worship') is one who has already reached the goal.

These purely spiritual categories comprise the ārya-sangha. But the Buddha also described the ārya-sangha in more colourful terms. Comparing the order of monks to a great ocean, he said that just as the great ocean contained all kinds of monsters, so the Sangha likewise contained spiritual leviathans of its own.[23] These monsters of the deep, so to speak, make up the ārya-sangha.

Clearly it is good for the larger sangha to have regular contact with these leviathans, and this must be one of the advantages envisaged by the Buddha when he directed the sangha to make a point of gathering together in large numbers and on regular occasions. If you are used to living and working in the context of a small local Buddhist community, it is good from time to time to get a sense of the scope of the sangha as a whole, and see your own life and work within a much bigger context. It is salutary, if you are used to being a big fish in a small pond, to experience occasionally being a sprat in a great ocean. You may sometimes even get a glimpse of what seems to be a real monster – although, of course, who within the sangha is a tiddler and who is a whale is not always easy to tell.

THE BODHISATTVA HIERARCHY

The spiritual hierarchy of the ārya-sangha is outlined in the Pāli Canon, the collection of the records of the Buddha's teachings.[24] The Pāli Canon is accepted by all schools, and in the Theravāda schools of Sri Lanka, Burma, and Thailand, it is understood as constituting the full extent of Buddhist canonical literature. All other Buddhist scriptures come under the broad heading of Mahāyāna Buddhism – sometimes called 'developed' Buddhism – as found in Tibet, China, Japan, Korea, Vietnam, and a number of other Eastern countries – and Western ones too, these days. The term Mahāyaṇa means 'great way', and those schools that did not accept the Mahāyāna scriptures were termed – though not by themselves, naturally – the Hīnayāna or 'little way'.

The concept of the ārya-sangha belongs to the substratum of belief and doctrine common to all the different schools. But the Mahāyāna adds to this basic classification a further hierarchy. This is the hierarchy of Bodhisattvas, those who are aiming not for their own individual emancipation from suffering but for the Bodhisattva ideal: Enlightenment not just for one's own sake, but for the sake of all living beings.[25]

As with the ārya-sangha, there are four grades of Bodhisattva, according to the number of stages in their development (known as *bhūmis*) that they have traversed.

1. The novice Bodhisattva, or *ādikārmika-bodhisattva*, has accepted the Bodhisattva ideal in all sincerity, but has yet to achieve the first stage of the path, or any degree of transcendental insight.

2. Bodhisattvas 'of the Path' are those who are progressing between *bhūmis* one to six.

3. 'Irreversible' Bodhisattvas are those who have attained the seventh *bhūmi* (out of ten). Just as the Stream-entrant cannot fall back into the lower realms of existence, the irreversible Bodhisattva cannot fall back into seeking the goal of individual Enlightenment – a lesser achievement, from the Mahāyāna point of view – but is sure to sustain momentum towards Enlightenment for the sake of all beings.

4. Bodhisattvas 'of the *dharmakāya*'. This is a somewhat abstruse conception, referring to what may be described as personalized aspects of Buddhahood itself. Just as white light may be broken up into the seven colours of the spectrum as seen in a rainbow, the pure white light of Enlightenment may be broken up – as it were – into its own different colours, that is, into the different aspects of the Enlightened mind: love, wisdom, peace, freedom, knowledge, and so on. If the Buddha is a personification of Enlightenment itself, Bodhisattvas of the *dharmakāya* represent personifications of individual aspects of that Enlightenment.

The two hierarchies – the ārya-sangha and the four levels of the Bodhisattva path – clearly overlap to some extent; some Mahāyāna texts refer to Stream-entrants as 'Hīnayāna Bodhisattvas'.

Thus the sangha is a spiritual community existing at various levels, from the social and ecclesiastical level right up to the highest spiritual level. And you go for Refuge to the Sangha by joining it at whatever level you can. Firstly, you can join it at the level of the *mahā-sangha* just by being a member of the Buddhist community in a purely formal, external sense. Secondly, you can join it in an ecclesiastical, and more definitely committed, sense by receiving ordination. In the Theravādin tradition ordination means becoming a monk, but in the Mahāyāna, the Bodhisattva ordination is in principle for monk and laity alike, although in practice one finds that the term 'sangha' is often used with reference to monks alone. In the order I founded there is only one ordination, whatever one's lifestyle or gender. And thirdly, you can join the sangha at the level of the ārya-sangha or Bodhisattva sangha by virtue of your spiritual attainments. Let us go on to see what such attainment really entails.

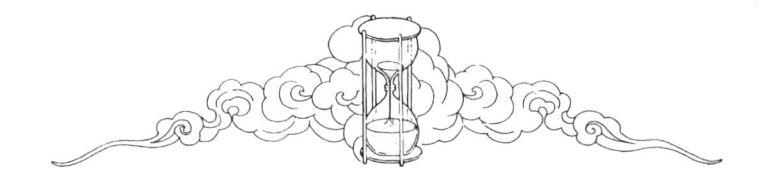

3

INDIVIDUALITY: THE ESSENCE OF SANGHA

SO FAR, I have spoken of the general principles of the sangha in traditional and historical terms, describing how its basic institutions and concepts have emerged. I now want to look behind those formal institutions and concepts and try to define the deeper principles of spiritual community, independent of any traditional Buddhist context.

The term ārya-sangha is usually translated as 'Sangha of noble – or superior – ones', but the word I prefer to use to render the Sanskrit term *ārya* is 'individual'. The four kinds of individuals to which the 'Tiratana Vandanā' refers are called just that – individuals. The expression used is *purisapuggala* – 'persons who are individuals'. A spiritual community consists, in essence, of individuals. And where non-individuals organize themselves together, there can never be a spiritual community, but only a group.

I have presented this idea that some people are radically more developed than others in rather stark terms, but it is absolutely fundamental to Buddhist thinking. It is vital that we appreciate how significant this distinction between the individual and the non-individual is. The development of true individuality is, comparatively, a very recent development in terms of world history, and we certainly cannot take it for granted.

But what is an individual? The second part of this book will explore various ways of answering this question. But let's begin with the traditional Buddhist answer, which is usually put in terms of the ten fetters you need to break in order to gain ultimate freedom.[26] Of these, the most significant from our point of view are the first three. If you can break these, your continuous development towards Enlightenment is assured, and you become a Stream-entrant, a member (albeit at the humblest level) of the spiritual community in the highest sense. You become, in short, a true individual. It should be emphasized that this is a goal within the reach of any seriously practising Buddhist.

The first fetter is *satkāya-dṛṣṭi*. *Sat* means real or true, *kāya*, body, and *dṛṣṭi* is view; the term as a whole is usually translated 'personality-belief'. This is the belief that one's present personality, one's self as it is here and now, is fixed, final, unchanging: an absolute fact. This belief is the first fetter that hampers one's growth as an individual.

Satkāya-dṛṣṭi is often explained, particularly in the West, in purely philosophical terms, as though it consisted in adherence to a particular school of thought with regard to the nature of the self, but it isn't really that at all. This fetter consists in holding one of two opposing extreme views. One of these is the belief that the self continues to exist after death as an essential entity, a sort of spiritual billiard ball ricocheting around the universe, regardless of whether you believe that it goes to heaven or reincarnates. The other is the belief that the self disappears altogether with the death of the physical body. The Buddhist view of the self, in contrast to both of these, is that the various psychological and spiritual processes which in all their complexity constitute one's personality continue after death, but that there is no unchanging essence underlying this stream of psychical events.

However, this fetter is more like a deeply-rooted attitude than an intellectual viewpoint. It can be rationalized in philosophical terms, but it is essentially a largely unconscious attitude – one that says, in effect, 'I am what I am and there's nothing to be done about it.' If I have a bad temper, well, that's the way it is; it can't be helped – it's a basic fact of my nature. I was born that way and I must just live with it. And yes, I suppose others are going to have to live with it too. This is the way God made me. Who are we to play around with God's handiwork? You'll just have to take me as you find me, warts and all.

Even if we do admit the need for change in ourselves, we can conceive only of one that is superficial. If we try to imagine ourselves radically changed and then look carefully at this imagined self, we will find that it bears a striking, fundamental, and detailed resemblance to the way we are now. Really to imagine the possibility of radically changing would involve letting go of whatever idea we have of ourselves as we are now.

The true individual knows that progress of any kind involves change, and that change means that something must go, something must die – *you* must die. To produce a new self, there has to be a death of the old self. It is the only way. An individual happily accepts this death as a necessary condition of growth.

The second fetter is *vicikitsā*, usually translated 'doubt', 'perplexity', 'uncertainty', or 'scepticism'. Again, we are not concerned here with an intellectual position. *Vicikitsā* is much more volitional than intellectual. It is less an intellectual uncertainty than an emotional inability to commit oneself, an unwillingness to make up one's mind, to think things through to a conclusion. It is a reluctance to put one's heart into what one does. It is not that honest doubt of which Tennyson speaks:

There lives more faith in honest doubt,
Believe me, than in half the creeds.[27]

Vicikitsā is lack of integration. One is literally not an individual but a loose congeries of selves. Out of this association of selves, one self will emerge to commit the whole 'person' to a decision; the next day another self, thinking better of it, will reverse that decision. One self gets enthusiastic about something, only to be replaced by another self that wonders what all the fuss was about. Thus one self follows another, like waves breaking on the shore of one's present state of mind. Everyone is familiar with this state of affairs, but it is particularly obvious to people who meditate. One self wants to meditate, another doesn't. One self gets going with its meditation dragging all the other selves protesting in its wake; but gradually it weakens and goes under, submerged in a welter of other selves (technically called 'distractions') which, if they can, will bring the meditation to an end altogether. In this way we drift through our meditation. And in this way we drift through life, borne this way and that, pulled in one direction and then another. As Shakespeare's Richard II comes to realize, wasting time is how we disintegrate:

I wasted time, and now doth time waste me.[28]

Only an individual, one who is integrated, a unified personality, can commit himself or herself in such a way as actually to make spiritual progress.

The third fetter is *śīlavrata-parāmarśa* – literally 'grasping (*parāmarśa*) moral rules (*śīla*) and religious vows (*vrata*)'. This does not mean 'attachment to religious rites and ceremonies', which is how the expression was first translated into English towards the end of the nineteenth century. This was in the days of the great ritualist controversy: adherents of the Oxford Movement had tried to bring the old Catholic rituals back into the Church of England, and they were vigorously opposed by the more Protestant wing of the church. It seems that the early translators of the Pāli Canon could not help taking this fetter as some sort of anti-ritualist statement, and thinking of the Buddha as a proto-Protestant or even an early rationalist, opposed to the more colourful side of religion – a view of the Buddha which flies in the face of all the evidence. In fact, the fetter is dependence on ethical rules and religious observances *as ends in themselves*.

Even when we have translated the Pāli term correctly, it is still open to misinterpretation. Ethical and religious observances in no way constitute a fetter in themselves. What holds us back is our depending on them, treating them as ends in themselves rather than as means to Enlightenment. We are held back, in other words, by conventional morality and conventional religion. The idea that this should be a fetter is often thought of as a specifically Zen attitude, but it is basic Buddhism – and even basic Christianity: 'The Sabbath,' as Jesus says, 'was made for man, not man for the Sabbath.'[29] Likewise, ethics and practices are there to be useful, not to use us.

Why do we always miss this point (as to some extent we must if we are not Stream-entrants)? Yet again, we are concerned here not with a consciously maintained viewpoint but with an unconscious emotional attitude. It is to do with the fact that we tend to want to get something from our spiritual practice that has nothing to do with its true purpose. Often we derive from our practice some kind of status within the group, a measure of acceptance by other people, respectability, security, a sense of belonging. This is a well-known phenomenon of whatever spiritual tradition is dominant within a culture. In the West, it used to be virtually obligatory to go to church, and your church-going established your reputation in the community. Indeed, this was usually what people went to church for – not to worship God, but to create a good impression.

But even if you simply attend a small Buddhist group, which may do nothing at all for your conventional social standing, after a while you may find yourself going along mainly for the positive, friendly atmosphere. Despite your best intentions you will go through the motions of meditation, devotion, study, spiritual friendship, and so on, in order to get the kind of self-affirmation which, deep down, is what you really want from the group meeting. In order to break this fetter one needs to treat all these practices and activities – crucial as they all are – as means to a specific end, which is one's own development as an individual.

So much for the first three fetters.[30] Beyond this point, the Once-returner has weakened the fourth and fifth fetters, while the Non-returner is released from any further human rebirth by breaking them altogether. (An arhant breaks the last five as well, but we need not go into these, as they are of little immediate relevance to where most of us actually are.)

The fourth and fifth fetters are *kāma-rāga*, desire for sensuous experience, and *vyāpāda*, anger or animosity. These two are much heavier fetters than the first three, more deeply set. In fact, they bind us very tightly indeed, and it is sobering to reflect that even one so spiritually advanced as a Stream-entrant is still bound by them, at least in subtle forms. A little imagination shows us how it is that even a 'Once-returner' has only weakened – not broken – these fetters. In the case of the fourth fetter, one has only to imagine what it would be like to go suddenly blind, say – not to see the light, and all the myriad details of the visual world around us that we take for granted – to realize with what inexpressible longing one would desire that visual world. Or suppose you suddenly went deaf, and were plunged into a totally silent world, with no voices, no music, none of the constant background of sound reminding you that you share the world with other living beings. You would long to have that sort of contact again, long for the beauty of the most simple music, more than anything else in the world. The same goes for the world of touch, and even taste.

The longing that would arise on being deprived of all our sense experience is almost literally unimaginable. But at the time of death this is what happens. The mind is torn from these things, suspended in a void that is truly dreadful for those who still want to be in contact with the external world through the five senses. *Kāma-rāga* is therefore what causes one's consciousness to seek expression in the form of another sense-based existence, and it follows that on the breaking of this fetter one becomes a Non-returner.

As for the fetter of anger or animosity, it is more or less impossible to imagine being without some element of discontent, irritation, resentment, impatience, or ill-humour; these states almost constantly hover somewhere in the background of our experience. And this is not even to mention our more noticeable outbursts of anger, which draw on the apparently bottomless wellspring of animosity within us.

But even if we cannot as yet break these fetters, we can be aware of them, and of the need to weaken them through the practice of meditation, in which we attempt to withdraw from sense experience at least temporarily, and to let go of our animosity as well – this latter being the particular object of the *mettā bhāvanā* practice, the development of universal loving kindness.[31]

We now have the traditional answer to the question of what makes one an *ārya* – that is, what makes one an individual. If you are an individual you are prepared to change, to let go of any fixed idea of yourself, even to die. You are integrated enough to be able to commit yourself wholly, and you do not confuse means with ends. These are the attitudes that we need to nurture if we are to break the first three fetters and achieve Stream Entry. Further to this, an individual is aware of the influence that our sense experience has upon our minds, and of the need to reduce that influence through the practice of simplicity, contentment, and meditation. And an individual tries to be aware of negative emotion, not expressing it in harmful ways, and trying hard to cultivate positive emotion.

This is one way of defining an individual, and it is enough to give us a provisional understanding of the way I want to use the term. We shall be exploring other ways of seeing the individual, and other aspects of individuality, in the second part of this book. For now, we will focus on the relationship between the individual and the spiritual community, a relationship that began with the emergence of the individual comparatively recently in our human history. Let us go on to look at the development of the individual – and the spiritual community – from a historical perspective.

4

THE HISTORY OF THE SPIRITUAL COMMUNITY

HISTORY IS A PERILOUS undertaking, an attempt to be objective about what happened in the past that has no real hope of success. Straightforward facts are hard to come by. Did King Alfred really burn those cakes? Nobody knows. Did King John really lose his jewels in the Wash? Nobody knows. Did King Richard III really do away with those two little princes in the Tower? Again, nobody knows. Historians are still discussing all these things. Even when the facts are agreed upon, further pitfalls await the unwary historian. Schoolchildren no longer imagine that 'Geography is about maps; history is about chaps.' History is no longer simply 'the lengthened shadow of a man'. There are all sorts of alternative perspectives to take. One may make broad sweeping generalizations, or undertake narrow, highly focused surveys of data. One may take a social view, a cultural view, an economic view, a feminist view ... and there are radically different and even contradictory angles that one may take within each of these and other areas of study.

But having proffered this reminder that in speaking of history we have to be circumspect, I am going to throw caution to the winds and embrace a vision of history as a whole. I use the word vision deliberately because I want to convey in a few crude brush-strokes a vivid general impression. Of course, such large-scale overviews of history tend to come and go just like anything else. Hegel saw history as the progressive manifestation of Spirit, and as a process, moreover, that moved from East to West, from ancient China to modern America.[32] Following on from Hegel, Karl Marx presented history in terms of economics and class conflict, and as passing through four great stages – theocracy, feudalism, capitalism, and communism – in accordance with who controls the means of production.

Then came Toynbee's vision of the rise and fall of civilizations, which enumerated more than two dozen distinct civilizations, some of which survive only in the form of their monuments, as in Egypt, while others, like Hinduism, are still thriving, and some, as in Tibet before the Chinese invasion, exist only in what Toynbee calls a fossilized form (though most Buddhists would disagree with this particular assessment).[33] None of these visions of history has survived the twentieth century in very good condition; and Francis Fukuyama's recent attempt to predict the end of history already looks somewhat premature.[34]

However, the existentialist philosopher Karl Jaspers (1883–1969), in his conception of the Axial Age, affords us an insight into the historical emergence of widely scattered examples of a radically individualized consciousness that cannot be ignored in any discussion of the human ideal of individuality.[35] From this starting point we shall go on to a brief historical survey of spiritual communities – that is, individuals organizing themselves on a collective basis.

The history of mankind as a species covers hundreds of thousands, even millions of years. Much of this time is usually referred to simply as the prehistoric era. The emergence of specifically human consciousness produced for the first time a species that could not be defined in purely biological terms. Gathering roots, fruits, and seeds, and later hunting game, scattered family groups or tribes roamed through a world which was very much smaller than our own. Their views of the past and the future were narrow, and their view of the world around them was restricted to their immediate locality. What they were conscious of was immediate experience, here and now. What they knew, they knew directly and intimately. They were ignorant of more or less everything except how to survive, though this they knew very well indeed. At the same time, because their numbers were so few, the natural world through which they roamed must have seemed to them terrifying in its vastness.

They wandered through forest or savannah, lodging in caves, or holes in the ground, or among the roots of trees. They had the use of nothing inherited from the past – no houses, villages, bridges, roads, or even huts or paths. There were no laws, nor was there any authority beyond that of the head of the family. There was no mechanical sense of the flow of time against which to measure your experience: you simply saw the sun rise and set, and watched the procession of the seasons. The bare trees budded and opened their fresh leaves to the light, and then you would see the same leaves turning yellow and fluttering to the ground. These changes went with changes of temperature, and changes in the way you went about getting food. But you knew nothing of the past, nothing of history. You knew your parents and grandparents, your children and grandchildren, but beyond that there was just a mist. You knew nothing about other human beings, living in other times or other places. There was no 'knowledge' in our sense of the term at all. Primitive man was ignorant and, as far as we know, happily ignorant. We can hardly imagine such a state of affairs; to us this age can only seem very remote.

However, in a sense it is not remote at all. The period of prehistory is virtually conterminous with the history of humankind itself. The ten to twenty thousand years of modern or historical humanity is no more than a full stop to the long, meandering palaeolithic and neolithic periods of our development. In fact, we are still living on the fringes of the Stone Age. Almost everything we value – higher culture, civilization, literature, science and technology, work, and leisure – has been completely unknown to our species for virtually its entire history. Our roots go very deep indeed. For almost our entire existence as a species we have been primitive and ignorant; and, under the surface, very largely we still are. Indeed, a great deal of our unconscious conditioning derives from the exigencies of primitive life.

These almost unimaginably vast and almost completely blank wastes of prehistory are sometimes termed, more poetically, the age of Prometheus, after the demigod who, according to Greek myth, stole fire from heaven for the use of humankind. As well as making use of fire, primitive human beings made stone tools and developed the beginnings of language and religion. The great cosmic or nature myths originated towards the end of this period, and along with religion came art, which until very recent times was not separate from religion.

Then suddenly – and it was, comparatively speaking, quite sudden – around twenty thousand years ago this erstwhile hunter-gatherer species started to till the ground, to sow seeds and reap crops. With the development of agriculture, nomadic life gave way in some places to village settlements, and eventually towns and even cities, especially in the great river valleys of Asia and North Africa: the Nile, Tigris, and Euphrates, the Indus and Ganges, the Huang Ho and Yangtze Kiang. Agriculture promoted the development of forethought; tilling the ground for the sake of a future harvest was a considered activity, not a spontaneous impulse, and it was thus the first step towards civilization.

The rate of development increased exponentially, and the Stone Age was followed in quick succession by the Bronze and Iron ages. Alphabets were invented; literature and history of a kind began to be written; basic geometry and astronomy were mastered; government, administration, and law took shape; and commerce, war, and conquest spread these developments further afield. Fertility myths replaced the old cosmic or nature myths. This whole period is known as the Age of Agriculture, the River Valley Age, or the Age of Divine Kingship.

Then, about 2,500 years ago, there was another major shift in consciousness, termed by Karl Jaspers the Axial Age, when the great religions came into being, together with a succession of great empires. We may identify a further revolution commencing around five hundred years ago: the Age of Science and Technology, or the Age of Anxiety. But the crucial moment in the development of human beings, the moment at which the species fully realized its unique potential for the first time, was the Axial Age.

The term coined by Jaspers derives from Hegel, who speaks in his *Philosophy of History* of the axis of history, the point upon which the whole of human history turns.[36] For him, this point was the appearance of Christ, but, as Jaspers points out, such an interpretation can have meaning only for the believing Christian. If there is indeed an axis in history, it will be found to be a set of circumstances which has significance for everyone. In order to carry conviction as a historical frame of reference common to all, such an axial point must do without the support of any particular religion.

Jaspers finds this decisive turning point in a spiritual upheaval that he identifies as having taken place between 800 and 200 BCE. All over the world – or at least the more developed parts of the world – humanity seems suddenly to have awakened from the sleep of ages. At this time, individuals were born whose achievements and ways of looking at the world have profoundly influenced, directly or indirectly, almost the entire human race. Even after 2,500 years, many of these individuals are still revered household names, and their work is still appreciated, consulted, and discussed.

The *Analects* of Confucius (551–479 BCE) are probably still the greatest single influence on the Chinese character, while the *Tao-te Ching*, composed by the altogether more mysterious figure of Lao-tzu (?604–?531), is a perennial worldwide best-seller. These two are only the best known of a host of Chinese sages, including Mencius (372–289 BCE) and Chuang Tzu (c.350–275 BCE). India can boast a galaxy of sages responsible for the wisdom teachings of the Upanishads, as well as the founder of Jainism, Mahāvīra, and of course Gautama the Buddha. More or less contemporaneously, Persia was graced by the figure of Zoroaster or Zarathustra (?628–?551), whom we know as the founder or refounder of Zoroastrianism, the faith of the Parsees. This was the religion of the Persian Empire, and it heavily influenced all the Semitic monotheistic religions: Judaism, Christianity, and Islam.

The tiny country of Palestine produced the great Jewish prophets: Amos and Isaiah, Jeremiah, the Second Isaiah, and a number of others, whose sublime moral insights were much later developed by Jesus of Nazareth, and indeed still resound throughout the Western world today.

Finally, in Greece there was an outburst of philosophical, spiritual, and artistic creativity unequalled anywhere else, before or since. A.N. Whitehead remarked famously, if a little boldly, that Western philosophy is little more than a series of footnotes to Plato.[37] Plato was the pupil of Socrates and the teacher of Aristotle, whose works dominated medieval Muslim and Christian thought. But these three represent only the highest point of a complex philosophical tradition.

The epic poetry of Homer, the lyric poetry of Pindar, the fables of Aesop, the poetic drama of Sophocles, Euripides, and Aeschylus, the comedies of Aristophanes, and the sculptures of Phidias and Praxiteles, represent the most sublime works of art still extant from within a culture of unimaginable richness, which also produced the first modern historians, Herodotus and Thucydides, and the physician Hippocrates, whose oath of medical ethics still has relevance for doctors of medicine in the West today. Finally, Thales, Anaximander, Pythagoras, Archimedes, and Euclid were just a few of the Greek thinkers who between them established the principles of mathematics and scientific method that two thousand years later would set off another intellectual explosion, giving us the modern world as we know it.

Simply reciting such a litany of names makes it clear that, as Jaspers observes, 'In this age were born the fundamental categories within which we still think today, and the beginnings of the world religions, by which human beings still live, were created.' Jaspers goes on: 'Myths were remoulded, were understood at a new depth during this transition, which was myth-creating after a new fashion, at the very moment when the myth as a whole was destroyed.... Man is no longer enclosed within himself. He becomes uncertain of himself and thereby open to new and boundless possibilities.... For the first time *philosophers* appeared. Human beings dared to rely on themselves as individuals.'[38]

When we ask what such a diverse array of individuals have in common, this is the obvious answer. It is not simply that they were seminal figures – founders of religions or of schools of thought or of forms of artistic expression. They certainly did not think of themselves in such terms, even though, when we look back on what happened as a result of their lives, we can see that many of them did become founders in one way or another. No – what they all have in common is that they are all true individuals. They stand out from the mass of humanity, not because of whom they dominated, ruled over, or conquered, but because of who they were in themselves. Even across the gulf of millennia we recognize them as sharply defined individuals, and thus we can, in a way, enter into a personal relationship with them. They represent a new strain of human being that was simply not evident before this period. They thought independently. They were not psychologically dependent on the group. They were able to stand, if necessary, alone.

THE HISTORICAL DEVELOPMENT OF SPIRITUAL COMMUNITIES

As a result of this new mutation (so to speak) we find, from a spiritual point of view, two forces henceforth working in opposition to each other throughout history: the group and the individual. To these, a third force should be added: spiritual communities. Because it is generally characteristic of the individual to enter into relationship with other individuals or proto-individuals, we usually find them working in the context of spiritual communities.

Thus in ancient Greece there appeared a number of schools of philosophy – the Milesian school, the Platonic school, the Neoplatonic, the Stoic, the Epicurean. These should not be thought of as academic schools of thought in the modern sense. They were founded as spiritual communities – at least in certain respects – of masters and disciples, searching for the truth together. Indeed, the school of one of the most influential of Greek thinkers, Pythagoras, was known explicitly as a mystical society. Such spiritual communities occurred throughout the Graeco-Roman world.

In Palestine at the same time communities such as the Essenes provided the soil in which Jesus of Nazareth planted the seed of his teachings, and subsequently, Christian communities spread rapidly all round the Mediterranean. Meanwhile, around the third century CE, communities of Manicheans – followers of the prophet Mani – were to be found in what is now Iraq and Iran, and a little later, in the same area and beyond it, arose various Sufi communities. Throughout this period in India the Buddhist sangha was spreading, and to a lesser extent the Jain sangha as well. One might expect to find spiritual communities in China also, but until Buddhist sanghas were formed there in the second century CE one can point only to a literary élite as fulfilling such a role.

Three traditions of spiritual communities were, and still are, of particular importance on account of the number of individuals involved in them, the length of time they thrived, and their influence on the world. These are the Buddhist, Sufi, and Christian communities. Of these, the Buddhist sangha is the longest-lived. It is not often realized that the Buddhist sangha is, so to speak, the classic form of the spiritual community. Buddhists formed a spiritual community from the beginning, not as a sort of afterthought. Indeed, it could be said that Buddhism *is* essentially a spiritual community. The sangha is an integral part of the Three Jewels at every level. And it exists in two great forms, as we have seen – the Hīnayāna (or, better, the Theravāda) and the Mahāyāna. In the Theravāda the spiritual community tends to be identified with the monastic community, but in the Mahāyāna countries, where the great unifying factor, historically speaking, is not so much the Three Refuges as the Bodhisattva ideal, it is identified with monastic and lay people alike.

The Sufi family of spiritual communities or brotherhoods, while scattered all over the Muslim world, have at best an ambiguous relationship with orthodox Islam. Al-Ghazālī is probably the most distinguished and best known of all Sufi mystics. Sufi ideas derive from Neoplatonism, Manicheism, and even Hinduism and Buddhism, and therefore, from an orthodox Islamic viewpoint, Sufis are often heretical, and some have been executed for their heretical pronouncements. However, Sufi communities have continued to nourish the Islamic world to the present day.

The beginnings of the Christian family of spiritual communities – the Christian churches – are shrouded in obscurity and controversy, but in the fourth century, Christianity became the official religion of the whole Roman Empire, and thus virtually ceased to be a spiritual community. It became an aspect of 'the group', the ecclesiastical wing of the state. Eventually it became a political power in its own right, claiming its own authority, with its own sphere of influence and control. Through the centuries it became, especially in the form of the Roman Catholic Church, increasingly authoritarian, intolerant, coercive, and persecuting.

It has to be said that the seeds of this degeneration were present in Christianity from the beginning – as they are, perhaps, in all forms of monotheism. However, within this official Christianity – and to some extent in protest against it – spiritual communities continued to arise in the form of monastic communities, where the real Christians, the real individuals, were to be found. The monasteries were islands of civilization and culture throughout the Dark Ages from the collapse of the Roman Empire in the fifth century until the reign of Charlemagne in the eighth, preserving much of the Latin and even some Greek literature.

In this connection the Benedictine order – founded by St Benedict in the sixth century in Italy – is of particular importance. In fact, it was less an order than a loose association of autonomous monasteries, each under its own abbot. In the course of time, some of these became economically and politically powerful and, as the original Christian church had succumbed in earlier times to the pressure this inevitably produced, by the eleventh century the monasteries had ceased to be spiritual communities and had become 'groups' – part of the church in the narrow, socio-political, ecclesiastical sense.

Once again, a need for reform arose, and this need was met initially by the Cistercian monastic movement and the Carmelites or White Friars in the twelfth century, followed in the thirteenth century by the Franciscans, the Dominicans, the Poor Clares, and the Austin Friars. These movements were the orthodox aspects of a spiritual ferment that gripped Europe during the Middle Ages, throwing up all kinds of more or less heretical movements – the Lollards, the Brethren of the Free Spirit, the Taborites, and others – who were ruthlessly persecuted by the church and in many cases eventually stamped out.

But in the sixteenth century, Lutheranism arose. This was a heresy that could not be stamped out, but sparked off an explosion of heresies throughout central, western, and northern Europe which came to be called the Reformation. All kinds of spiritual movements emerged, large and small, all more or less Christian. Some of these lasted only a few months, some lasted for years, and a very few lasted for centuries. Of the movements that emerged out of the seventeenth-century Puritan revolution in England, for example, the Diggers lasted only for a few years in the late 1640s, while the Quakers have flourished to this day.

Thus, it is clear that spiritual communities have played a more significant part in European history than is generally acknowledged. Indeed, one can say that for two thousand years in the West, a great battle has been fought between official religion, more or less tied in with the 'powers that be', and the spiritual community in a multiplicity of changing forms. It is a battle between power and love (or *mettā*, to use the Buddhist term), authority and spiritual freedom, stagnation and growth, reactivity and creativity. This battle is continuously being won and lost again, and there is no guarantee that any one spiritual community will survive for very long, nor any certainty that the spiritual family of which communities are a part will survive.

Manicheism is just one example of a spiritual tradition that lost the battle. Manicheism was a pacific, tolerant, almost eclectic teaching. Philosophically, it was a form of dualism – that is, it proposed the existence of two ultimate principles, light and darkness, neither of which could be said to originate from the other. The Manicheans believed that however far you went back, you would always find these two principles, independent of and sometimes in conflict with each other. The task of human beings, according to Mani, is to liberate the light within us from the darkness in or around us.

According to some scholars, Mani may have been influenced by Buddhism – he certainly refers to the Buddha's teachings in some places in his own writings – and Manichean spiritual communities appear to have been similar to Buddhist ones in many respects. There is even some evidence to suggest that central Asian Manicheism in turn influenced the later development of Mahāyāna and Vajrayāna Buddhism. For example, it is possible to detect touches of Manicheism in the life of Padmasambhava, one of the founders of Tibetan Buddhism. One of the most striking features of Manicheism was its stress on the importance of beauty in the spiritual life. According to tradition, Mani was himself a painter – it seems that even now the word *mani* means painter in modern Arabic – and he encouraged the visual arts, including calligraphy.

Manicheism spread phenomenally quickly, from Iraq and Iran through the whole of the late Roman Empire, all over central Asia, to penetrate India, China, and even Japan. However, this popular, tolerant, and peaceful religion attracted a commensurate degree of vilification, intolerance, and persecution. In the West, it was mercilessly crushed throughout the Roman Empire by the orthodox Christian church. In the Middle East it was exterminated by fanatical renascent Zoroastrianism, and Mani himself was martyred by the Zoroastrians. Even in China Manicheans were persecuted, by Taoists and Confucians alike. The very literature of this worldwide spiritual community was destroyed so systematically that only fragments remain. Scholars have been able to reconstruct their history and teachings only from scraps and fragments, from scrolls discovered in the desert, and from the occasional dismissive or hostile reference in the literature of the Manicheans' enemies.

So here is an important lesson from history. A spiritual community can be as hugely successful as Manicheism was, and still disappear almost as if it had never existed. This is just one historical example of something that is an ever-present danger. Just as the world has seen the emergence of spiritual communities of various kinds, it has also seen the emergence of 'the group', by which I mean the various collectivities into which humanity has organized itself. If you are a member of a spiritual community it is important to remember that you are engaged in a constant battle with the group. So far as the spiritual community is concerned it is a non-violent battle; but the enemy will not be quite so particular, if the past is anything to go by. It is the distinction – and the relationship – between the spiritual community and the group that we must now go on to consider.

And that relationship, I should add, need not necessarily be such as to crush the possibility of the spiritual community out of existence. If it has been possible for the Axial Age to occur, then a still greater change may take place. If individuals and spiritual communities can emerge from time to time out of the group, then we must also believe in the possibility, however remote, that the spiritual community may one day outweigh the group, that light may overcome darkness. Also, there is such a thing as what I would call a 'positive group'. We need to define our terms. Let us go on to look in more detail at the group and the spiritual community.

5

THE GROUP AND THE SPIRITUAL COMMUNITY

AS DEFINED IN TERMS such as those outlined in the last chapter, individuals are clearly in short supply. Spiritual communities are no less rare – because it is individuals who form them. Individuals sometimes exist in comparative isolation; more often, it seems, they are found together, though in very small numbers. When they come together, they make up between them a spiritual community. When non-individuals get together, though, what you have is a group. It is the distinction between the group and the spiritual community that we will be exploring here.

A group is basically a collection of people who are not individuals. There is no term in English for such people, interestingly enough, but the traditional Buddhist term is *pṛthagjanas* – 'ordinary folk' – and they are clearly distinguished from *āryas*. According to Buddhist tradition, most members of the human race fall within this category; most of us are individuals only in a statistical sense. We are separate from one another, one could say, in every way except the one that really matters. We have separate bodies, and separate votes if we are lucky, but we can hardly say that we have separate minds. If we look carefully at where our opinions and decisions come from, we will see that only too often we don't have minds of our own at all. What we think and feel is determined by our conditioning, by the particular circumstances of our own particular existence. If we are self-conscious at all, it is in only the most vague and intermittent way; we tend to think and feel and act according to how others are thinking, feeling, and acting, and we will almost always accept, very often implicitly, the norms and values of the various groups to which we belong. At those times when we fail to act like individuals, our minds, such as they are, have been effectively submerged in a kind of collective, group mind.

THE CHARACTERISTICS OF THE GROUP

In axiomatic – if extreme – terms, we might say that, set against the individual, the group is always wrong. Why? In principle, a group comprises a number (and the nature of the group usually makes this a very large number) of 'statistical individuals' or 'social units'. That is, it consists of people who possess no true individuality, people with a comparatively low level of consciousness and self-awareness. Their emotions will tend to be crude and reactive, they will not like to be alone, they will need the support of others for their views and feelings, they will like to be part of a crowd or gang, and so on.

This is not to say that such people are of no account. Quite the opposite: they are of infinite – though as yet unrealized – account. It is precisely because all human beings are capable of becoming individuals that we need to be able to distinguish between those who are aiming to realize their potential and those who are not. (Not as yet, anyway.) We shall then have some idea of where we are going and where we are choosing not to go. The fact that the vast majority of people are not interested in developing as individuals, and in this life are unlikely ever to be so, does not mean that they do not have the capacity to become individuals.

The bonds that hold us as statistical individuals together in groups are usually more or less material (without necessarily attaching any deprecatory meaning to that word). People are united by ties of blood with their family or their tribe. They are united by ties of soil with those who live and work on the same land, through their common allegiance to the land that they and their ancestors have occupied for so long. They are united, especially in the case of larger groups, by ties of economic interest. And they are united by fear, by the need to defend themselves against larger, more powerful, more aggressive groups.

Since the Axial Age, individuals and spiritual communities have continued to emerge at irregular intervals and in different places. Much more marked, however, has been the development of the group. Starting with the family group, the tribe, the state, and the empire, we have inherited over the centuries a vast and complex web of groups to which we may be affiliated: schools, businesses and multi-national corporations, football clubs and Rotary clubs, councils, churches, committees and societies, pubs, interest groups, political parties, and so on. We also belong to a social group or class, an economic group, a religious group, a cultural group, a linguistic group, a racial group. We are born into some groups, but we have to join others by conscious choice, by paying a subscription, being initiated, joining the colours, or whatever it may be. These two categories overlap to some extent but, by and large, the groups into which one is born tend to be more group-like than those which one joins voluntarily.

Many of these groups are associated with their own distinctive symbols, so that to see the symbol is immediately to be reminded of the group it symbolizes. Totem poles, national flags, national anthems, and national dress all serve this function. There is also the old school tie, the fraternity pin, the union card, the party badge. With these symbols go slogans and sayings expressive of group loyalties: 'God's own country', 'Home sweet home', 'Land of hope and glory', 'Land of the free', 'Land of my fathers', 'The bulldog breed', 'Maybe it's because I'm a Londoner', 'The old firm', 'Don't let the side down', 'Workers of the world unite'....

Group feelings of loyalty go very deep indeed. That loyalty may not always be expressed, or even conscious, but it is there, deep down, and if someone's group loyalties are offended they can swiftly turn a mild-mannered model citizen into a fanatical partisan, ready to tear limb from limb anyone who challenges their group, or questions their group loyalty.

At a football match or a rally, or when you are conscripted into the army, you find that the collective spirit of the group you have joined seems to take over and you become submerged in it. There's a sort of group mind or soul which you obey almost despite yourself – it seems to control you. This is not just occult mythology, but a widely-reported phenomenon.

So strong are the feelings involved, so ubiquitous, so invariable, so universally distributed amongst human beings, that some anthropologists and psychologists even go so far as to speak of a group instinct, no less compelling than the reproductive instinct. The group instinct quite simply impels us, they say, to get together with other people. Whether we can really speak of a group instinct is questionable – some psychologists say that the word 'instinct' is a red herring dragged across the path of psychological theory, and doesn't correspond to anything at all. However, what we can say is that the group consists of statistical individuals – that is, individuals whose consciousness is an aspect of the group consciousness and whose thoughts, feelings, and behaviour conform to group patterns and norms.

Among animals, of course, groups fulfil a definite biological function. If it is bitterly cold, and you are in danger of being frozen to death, with no fire, artificial shelter, or clothes to supplement your fur, hair, or wool, you will huddle together with others to keep warm. As well as warmth, the group also provides safety; its fit and strong members will often protect those who are younger and weaker. Even a lion will only prey on the weaker animals if they are allowed to lag behind. In this way the group on the animal level facilitates the survival of the species concerned.

Wanting to belong to a group is in our bones, in our blood. We have a long history of gathering together in groups. If we include our primate ancestors, we have about twenty million years of group conditioning, as ape-man, man-ape, and human. To begin with we used to live in something like an extended family group or small tribe of perhaps fifty individuals, with just occasional encounters with other small tribes. With the development of language we have been able to accommodate a somewhat larger tribal grouping than this. But almost all our relationships would have been within this home group, and in some ways this is the sort of group that we would all naturally like to get back to.

It is only within the last few thousand years (which is really no time at all by comparison) that we have developed all sorts of much more complicated social groupings. Today we find ourselves struggling to get what we need from ever more distorted, even aberrant social institutions. It is more and more difficult to find groups of the right scale. On the one hand we have the isolated nuclear family, which can be so cramping as to be – as some psychologists say – a breeding ground for neurosis; and on the other, we belong to a group – the nation state – which is so big as to be meaningless on a personal level. Between these two institutions we establish, in a partial and intermittent fashion, membership of or loyalty to all sorts of other groups. But none of these seem to satisfy our ancient need to belong to a small tribe of between thirty and sixty people, a group in which we can live and work, in genuine and continuous personal relationship with all its members.

We have all been born into groups, and we are all therefore subject to the conditioning arising from those affiliations. Our ideas, our views, our feelings, the way we react to people and situations, our convictions – all these will tend to be determined by group conditioning of one kind or another, except in so far as we become conscious of such conditioning and distance ourselves from its influence. The groups themselves often overlap or even cohere. And all these overlapping groups together make up 'the world'.

Groups fear individuality and all its manifestations, and always tend to discourage it. The group requires conformity. This is because it is based on power, which whether physical, intellectual, or economic is always the power of the strong over the weak, the power of those who have the resources, the cunning, or the knowledge to be able to impose their will on others, deploying brute force or subtle manipulation in order to exploit others for their own, usually selfish, purposes. The group consists of those who wield that power, as well as of those who give it to them. Such power is exercised within any group, whether political, cultural, tribal, familial, or even religious.

THE SPIRITUAL COMMUNITY

The purposes of a community of individuals – or spiritual community – are utterly different from those of the group. They are twofold: firstly, its members help one another to develop spiritually; secondly, in whatever way they can, they help others outside the community to develop their individuality. In essence, a spiritual community is a free association of individuals. To form one, therefore, the first requirement is a number of individuals. You can no more have a spiritual community without individuals than you can have an omelette without eggs. A spiritual community is not created by getting yourself a building, an exotic form of dress, and a long list of rules. You don't need a building, you don't need an 'authentic tradition', you don't even need a religion. What you need are individuals; that is the basic ingredient. In other words, you need a number of people who are relatively emancipated from the group, relatively integrated and aware, and with an inner direction and positive purpose to their lives. Where there are no individuals, there will be no spiritual community, call it by whatever name you please. If you want to create a spiritual community, first catch your individual.

Next, there should be regular personal contact between these individuals. This is not simply polite social interchange. Nor does it involve herding together in a group for psychological warmth and comfort and support. The spiritual community consists of individuals who are in deep personal contact with one another. It will challenge you to be yourself, and demand that you take further steps towards being a true individual. People within the spiritual community will do what they can to spark off real communication, genuine spiritual exchanges. Within the Buddhist tradition, such communication is called kalyāṇa mitratā, 'lovely friendship'. Yes, you are all trying to develop, but you are also trying to develop *together*. Not only that, you are also *helping* one another to develop.

Clearly such emergent individuals are not going to agree on everything. However, it is important that the members of a particular spiritual community all share the same general outlook upon and approach to the spiritual life. There must be a common spiritual framework within which they are all trying to develop. This framework constitutes their medium of communication, without which they will find it difficult to help or even understand one another. It consists mainly of two things. Firstly, the spiritual community must have a common spiritual ideal, all of its members aiming ultimately for the same higher states of consciousness, the same realization. And secondly, they must have a common means of realizing that ideal, a common path or teaching, a common practice or method. They are walking the same way *in* the same way. As we have already seen, in Buddhism, these two things are known as the Buddha Jewel and the Dharma Jewel. The spiritual community itself of course is the Sangha, the third Jewel.

A spiritual community, or part of it at least, may well choose to live under the same roof. This will not only encourage closer personal contact, and thereby greater mutual helpfulness, between its members, but will also produce a more intensive situation than can otherwise be achieved. This is not to say that it is essential to be with one's spiritual friends all the time. Even after one has become a member of the spiritual community, it is good to be on one's own sometimes. Nevertheless, we definitely stand the best chance of developing spiritually if we have prolonged contact over a period of years with others who are progressing, and particularly with others who are more advanced than we are. The best kind of spiritual community will include at least one person who is more developed than the others, and who can provide some kind of direction for the rest of the community. Such a person is known traditionally as a kalyāṇa mitra, a spiritual friend, although on occasion all members of a spiritual community should be able to act as kalyāṇa mitras to one another.

Spiritual communities are by definition – and this is a sobering reflection – very small, and very few. You can't really have a worldwide spiritual community. It seems to be a law of human development that when a spiritual community reaches a certain size it starts to feel (so to speak) the gravitational pull of the group and tends to take on the characteristics of the group. As it does so, it degenerates. Most conventional, traditional, orthodox religious bodies were once genuine spiritual communities that expanded and were then absorbed back into the group in a form that was more acceptable to the group. However, although true spiritual communities may be insignificant in size, they exert a powerful leavening influence on the 'doughy mass' of the general population.

HOW THE GROUP AND THE SPIRITUAL COMMUNITY AFFECT EACH OTHER

The group and the spiritual community are trying to do two quite different – even opposite – things. The group is trying to produce good group members: good family men, good wives and mothers, dependable employees, loyal citizens, obedient soldiers, party members who can be relied upon to toe the line. The spiritual community, by contrast, is trying to produce individuals. The group insists on conformity, while the spiritual community encourages freedom of thought. But this is not all. The defining principle of the spiritual community, as opposed to the group's insistence on conformity, is more than simply freedom of thought, important as that freedom may be. It is freedom to grow.

Limited though it is in so many ways, the power of the group cannot be overestimated. It governs the lives of the vast majority of people, and most people are happy for it to do so. We therefore need to ask ourselves what we are really looking for, and also to be clear about the nature of the alternatives before us. Are we really looking for a spiritual community, or do we simply want a group? The spiritual community is not a collectivity of any kind – it is a community of individuals. It is not even a substitute for a group, which in a time of transition like the present is what many of us are looking for. Many old established institutions, customs, and traditions are breaking up. The old groups are breaking up – starting with the family. Family ties are not nearly so significant as they used to be. Nowadays, who bothers to keep up connections with their second and third cousins? Well, you hardly know who they are sometimes. But formerly people kept track of every single person even remotely related to them.

In the East, the family still does rule people's lives. When I lived in India, I would often be introduced to someone with such words as 'He's a close relation of mine – he's my brother.' I soon learned that this did not mean quite what it appeared to mean. 'Oh,' I'd say, 'Same mother, same father?' 'Oh no, he is my great grandfather's sister's daughter's husband's brother's grandson.' People used to keep in touch with every single relation they had, sometimes even a couple of hundred of them. But in the West today the family is in many respects a dead letter.

The nation state is another group that is breaking up. To leave the country of your birth used to be a rare event; even to leave your village was a mark of some enterprise. In times past it was held up as an ideal to live out your days hearing the sounds of the next village, without ever wanting to go there. Today, however, people are proud to have 'been places', as we say. To go to live and work or study in another country is no longer regarded as a sad exile, unless you are a refugee driven from your home by force, and even then you will generally be more than happy to be given asylum in a prosperous foreign country.

Class loyalties too are breaking down. In the old days, if you were born a serf, you died a serf. If you were born a nobleman, even if you died on the scaffold you had special privileges befitting your rank – such as that of having your head cut off rather than being hanged. Nowadays, everything is much more fluid. People identify themselves less by their class than by what they do, and as they rise in their profession, many leave behind the social milieu into which they were born and lose touch with old friends.

The result of all these shifts is that many people, having moved away from family and friends and even their own country, find themselves with no prescribed social set to fit neatly into. Naturally they feel lonely and isolated, and equally naturally, even unconsciously, they start looking round for a group to which they can belong. In this way they may come in contact with a spiritual community, formed by a number of individuals. Liking the positive atmosphere, the lonely person may want to join this community. But they are joining it not as a spiritual community, but as a group. They are not joining it in order to develop spiritually, but for the sake of warmth and companionship – perhaps because they just can't face the four walls of their cold apartment. In this way, the spiritual community becomes a substitute for the group. You haven't got a family? All right, join this spiritual community. You aren't a member of any club? Well, there's always that spiritual community down the road. You don't belong to a tribe, you haven't got a chief or a totem of your own? Don't worry, you'll find something that will do instead at your friendly neighbourhood spiritual community.

In this connection, certain developments in modern Japan are quite illuminating. Over the last hundred or more years, what with the Meiji restoration, and the modernization and industrialization that followed, the feudal structures that used to be the focus of loyalty in Japan were swept away. As a result, the average Japanese person was left dangling in mid-air, as it were, with nothing to belong to, nothing to be loyal to, nothing to commit hara-kiri for. The family was too small to satisfy the strongly felt need for a more clan-like structure, while the country as a whole – the Land of the Rising Sun – was too big.

Apparently, many modern Japanese have solved the problem by adopting the company they work for as their 'clan'. 'The lone peg gets hammered into the ground,' they say. In the West a young man or woman will often try all kinds of jobs, but that is not the way they do things in Japan. Quite simply, you never leave your job. You serve the firm unstintingly, and it takes care of every aspect of your life, from your mortgage to your marriage. You go on holidays organized by the firm, with fellow employees, and you look up to the chairman of the company with reverence, as a sort of clan chief, even to the extent of feeling you would give your life for him.

Religion has also been harnessed to the great Japanese need to belong. In the West you find well-meaning ecclesiastics calling for a renewal of faith to fill the spiritual void at the heart of our society – and few people listen. But in Japan, since the war, they have had a religious revival of epic proportions. New sects and even new religions have been mushrooming – there's a new one almost every week. The teaching of all these sects and religions is mainly Buddhist in origin, drawing on Mahāyāna Buddhism in general and Nichiren Buddhism in particular,[39] and most of all upon the *Lotus Sūtra*. But the teaching is apparently not really the point. What matters is the organization.

Each of these sects has a founder, who takes the title of Patriarch or Archbishop – as they are styled by everyone, including the press – of whatever the sect is called. The founder usually has a wife, and together these two lead the sect. In other words, they are the archetypal father and mother, and are sometimes even called father and mother by their devoted followers, who not unusually number hundreds of thousands, even millions. Some of these devoted followers occupy important government positions. Naturally, there is a complex hierarchy, consisting of perhaps a dozen different grades of membership, all with their distinctive, colourful robes and uniforms, badges, sashes, and headgear. They erect huge temples, and mansions for their leaders. Some of them have their own department stores, and even their own railway stations. They have the inevitable mass rallies in great stadiums, and semi-military parades through the streets, with banners and slogans, music and chanting, and nobody stepping out of line.

Whether it's the company or the new religion, it comes to much the same thing: both fulfil the need to belong to a group. Clearly we should not use the spiritual community as a substitute for a group in this way. The only real danger facing the spiritual community is that it can so easily become a group – any other danger is contained within that. Or rather, the danger is that the spiritual community is replaced by the group. The spiritual community as such cannot become a group; it can only wither away or disappear and be replaced by a group bearing the same name and having the same external appearance.

This happens on a grand scale when a universal religion degenerates into an ethnic religion. What I mean is that at a certain point a religion ceases to meet the spiritual needs of the individual, as all universal religions by their very nature profess to do, and starts providing for the collective needs of the group. Priests start guaranteeing fertility, blessing tanks, and so on. It is as if the group exerts a kind of gravitational pull on any spiritual community which is not vigilant.

The residential spiritual community is particularly vulnerable to this danger. When people are living together under one roof, the danger is that they will start to make themselves more and more comfortable, until the kitchen, rather than the shrine-room, becomes the focus of their life together. The fact is that prior to the attainment of Stream-entry, you can't stand still, you can't rest on your laurels. You can't ever feel, 'Well that's enough for this life, I'll put in some more work in my next life.' The minute you stop making an effort, you start slipping back.

All this may make it seem as if the group is the villain of the piece. It isn't really. We just need to be clear about what it is, and keep it in its rightful place. The desire to belong to a group is a basic human need which cannot simply be by-passed. We have to take account of it. Although the group and the spiritual community are trying to do two very different things, they are closely, even intimately, connected. There is a dialectical relationship between them, each exerting a strong influence on the other. The spiritual community has a refining and softening, even civilizing, influence on the group. By its very presence within the group, it helps the group to be open to higher values, to be what we may call a positive group, a group within which individual development is possible, even if not actively encouraged.

If the spiritual community can exert a positive influence on the group, however, the influence of the group on the spiritual community is more or less destructive. The group mentality always tries to turn the spiritual community into another group, and it always, eventually, succeeds. The spiritual community then has to be re-established by those individuals who realize what has happened. However, the spiritual community cannot cut itself off from the group entirely. Its commitment to higher values includes compassion – a commitment to working with the group mentality and developing individuality from it. Another way of putting this is to say that you cannot be born into a spiritual community. A hereditary spiritual community is a contradiction in terms. The lower evolution may be determined by the replication of particular genes, but the higher evolution is not a biological process at all. (We will be examining in some detail what I mean by 'higher evolution' in Part Two.) The spiritual community has to be recruited afresh in every generation. This is its weakness but it is also its strength.

Hence it is not enough simply to create a spiritual community of developing individuals; it is also necessary to establish healthy groups within which it is possible for healthy group members – and thus potential individuals – to arise. Such groups will be based less on authority and power than on friendliness and love. In the next two chapters we will consider first the relation of authority to the spiritual community, and then, by contrast, the development of what I call the positive group.

6

AUTHORITY

THE TERM 'AUTHORITY' is very ambiguous. In ordinary parlance, it means the power that is exercised by a person by virtue of their office, their legal, social, or political position. Someone has authority in this sense not by virtue of their qualities as an individual, but merely by virtue of their position. Authority in this sense is very different from true individuality. The ambiguity comes in when we speak, for instance, of moral authority. Here the word carries a different shade of meaning, one closer to its original meaning (as derived from 'author'). But nowadays authority is generally understood to mean power exercised by virtue of one's office or one's position, and it is in this sense that I want to discuss it here.

The precise nature of authority in this sense is similar in principle to the idea of representing something apart from oneself – as in the case, for example, of an ambassador, who represents the monarch, or a Member of Parliament or Senator, who represents a constituency or state, or a delegate, who represents a trade union, or even a salesman, who represents a business. In all these cases, someone is entrusted for certain purposes with the power of the group or organization to which he or she belongs. The group accepts or agrees to whatever he or she accepts or agrees to as that group's representative. The power that the representative exercises is not his or her own, but the power of some other person or persons – the power of the group.

It is much the same in the case of authority. Here also you exercise power not by virtue of what you are as an individual, but by virtue of the office or position you hold. Your qualities as an individual may of course fit you for that particular position, but the power you exercise in it derives from the position, not from your personal qualities. In other words, the power you exercise is not your own; it belongs to the particular group or organization that has created your office or position.

From all this there follows an important conclusion. When we deal with someone who is some kind of representative, or with someone occupying a position of authority, we are not dealing with them as an individual; nor are they functioning as an individual. And from this follows an even more important conclusion. As we have seen, we can deal with others within the spiritual community only as individuals; if we deal with them in any other way, the spiritual community ceases to exist. Within the context of the spiritual community, therefore, we cannot deal with others as representatives, or as occupying some kind of official position. Indeed, in the spiritual community there can be no representing, no official positions, and therefore no authority deriving therefrom.

If we deal with others as occupying positions of authority or as representatives, we are not dealing with them as individuals and therefore, *ipso facto*, we are functioning not within the spiritual community but within the group. Even within a Buddhist team-based right-livelihood situation there can be no authority. After all, who employs whom?

Sometimes people like to assume positions of authority; they like to speak for others. An individual will resist such roles as far as possible, although others may make this difficult. For example, I spent altogether nearly twenty years in India, and while there I had no other interest than to immerse myself in Buddhism. In pursuit of this sole interest I adopted the Indian way of life completely, to the extent of being sometimes mistaken for an Indian (sometimes, but not always, as we shall see). For years on end I never saw or spoke to any member of the European community. Nevertheless, some of the Indians with whom I came into contact persisted, notwithstanding my commitment to Buddhism and to the Indian way of life, in regarding me as British – and, moreover, as in some way representing Britain. In 1956 I was asked more than once, 'Why have you invaded Suez?'

People who asked that question did not see me, the individual, Sangharakshita, but only a representative of Britain, and they treated me as such.

The same sort of thing happened in reverse when I returned to England in 1964. Newspaper reporters used to come and see me – usually nice young ladies with notebooks and pencils and all sorts of weird ideas about Buddhism – and they would ask me in the nicest possible way, 'Why do you believe in self-mortification?' Once again, they didn't see me; there was no attempt to find out what I actually did believe. They saw me as a representative of what they understood Buddhism to be. There was no awareness of me as an individual at all.

What being a representative and holding authority have in common is of course power. You exercise power over others, or you have the power (sometimes thrust upon you) of speaking for others. This word, too, has an interesting ambiguity. Power can mean the ability – physical, mental, or moral – to act. It can also mean force or energy applied or applicable to work. But what we are concerned with here is power in the sense of the possession of a controlling influence over others, the capacity to coerce others, directly or indirectly, physically or psychologically.

Spiritual coercion is a contradiction in terms. Power in the sense of a capacity to coerce has no place in the spiritual community. Power has its place – it is in fact necessary – but it is necessary to the *group*, and that is its place. Indeed, the group is based on power, and cannot exist without it. Group issues are always political issues, and power is what politics is about; politics is essentially about who coerces whom. The spiritual community, on the other hand, cannot coexist with power. As soon as one exercises power, one ceases to treat others as true individuals. And when that happens the spiritual community ceases to exist.

The group consists of people who relate to one another in terms of power; power is the principle that governs their relationships. The spiritual community, on the other hand, is the embodiment of a very different principle, and it consists of individuals who relate to one another in terms of that principle. The obvious place to look for this principle is in a universal religion, which is ideally a spiritual community (by contrast with an ethnic religion, which by very definition is a group religion). There should, again ideally, be no place in a universal religion for authority and power. Unfortunately, this is not always the case with religions as historical phenomena. Power tends to creep in, and to the extent that this happens, the religion ceases to be a spiritual community, and becomes a group. This seems to have happened more with some religions than with others. The theistic religions, those based on belief in a personal God, a Supreme Being, the creator and ruler of the universe, tend to be corrupted by authority and power more markedly than are non-theistic religions, although the latter are not unmarked by such corruption.

The reason is quite simple. The definitive element of theistic religions – God – does not appear or speak for himself to ordinary people, so he needs a representative to tell people what he wants them to do. A prophet or messenger of God, sent to tell people what to do, is such a representative. The incarnate Son of God, appearing in human form to tell people what to do, how to live and so on, is another.

The representative not only tells us what God wants us to do; he has also been entrusted with God's power. He has the right to coerce us into doing what God wants us to do – if we are unwilling to do it of our own free will. So the crucial question is, exactly what manner of being is represented here? In most theistic religions the concept of God is ambiguous, ambivalent, even self-contradictory. The attempt is made to combine two different Gods – the God of Power and the God of Love, or the God of Nature and the God of Morality – into one. The consequences of this amalgamation can be distressing for the theist. If, for example, your nearest and dearest were to be struck dead by lightning, this would be an 'act of God' (and is still defined as such in English law) because lightning is a part of nature, and behind nature there is God. But this God of Nature is also the God of Love, so you have to interpret your dreadful loss as having been visited upon you and yours for your and their own good. The whole event has to be an expression of God's love in some way. You experience the effects of power, but you have to interpret them as acts of love; that is, you have to convince yourself that they are the actions of a loving God.

The question must arise: does God's representative represent both of these aspects of God? You can be entrusted with power and exercise it on behalf of a higher authority, but can you entrust your love to somebody? In popular parlance we say, 'Give so-and-so my love,' but can you really give love that is not your own? No, of course not. It is impossible to pass on one person's love to another person. In other words, whereas power can be delegated, love is a quality of the individual.

A representative of God cannot, therefore, represent the God of Love, but only the God of Power. To reinforce his authority and power, he may claim to represent the God of Love, but no amount of claiming will ever make such a thing possible. The representatives of theistic religions always exercise power because that is all they can exercise. In consequence, the theistic religions always are – or tend to become – group religions, power structures.

This is strikingly evident in the case of Christianity, especially the Roman Catholic Church. As we have already seen, Christians originally constituted, in the very early days, a kind of true spiritual community called the *ecclesia*, later known as the Church. It began as an underground movement – quite literally, because its members are said to have met in the Catacombs beneath the city. Gradually this spiritual community of early Christians came out into the open and Christianity spread into most parts of the Roman Empire until in the fourth century it became the official religion of the entire Empire. Other religions were prohibited, and various heresies were proscribed, although it was never easy to determine what was and what was not heretical. To do all these things the Church had to assume and exercise temporal power.

According to three out of the four Gospels, Christ himself rejected temporal power. Power was one of the three things with which the Devil tempted him in the wilderness, and he rejected it. But the Church was unable to follow his example. This was not just out of human weakness, but due to the self-contradictory nature of Christianity itself. The Old Testament teaches a God of power, a God of battles, a God who encourages his worshippers (in this case the children of Israel) to slaughter their enemies. But the New Testament teaches a God of Love; it teaches his worshippers to forgive their enemies. It is obviously impossible to follow both these directions at the same time. So which do you choose?

The Church was bound to follow the God of Power, to employ coercion in propagating its faith, and thus to turn from a spiritual community into a group, for two connected reasons. Firstly, as we have seen, a God needs a representative to interpret him, and you cannot represent love. Sometimes the Pope has been criticized for not representing the God of Love. For example, a play called *The Representative* written in 1963 by the German playwright Rolf Hochhuth attacked Pope Pius XII, who refused to condemn Hitler's massacre of the Jews, for just this reason. But such a criticism is beside the point, because a representative cannot represent the God of Love. He can only represent the God of Power.

Secondly, the Church started exercising temporal power, and it was only natural that it should come to represent a God in heaven that matched its own role in the world. This applies especially in the case of the Roman Catholic Church, which regarded itself as inheriting the political power of the Western Roman Empire. The head of the Roman Catholic Church, the Pope, was originally just Bishop of Rome, but eventually – after a few centuries – he came to be known as the Vicar of Christ (vicar meaning 'representative'). Thus, from the Middle Ages right down to the nineteenth century, the Popes have claimed to be vicegerents of God, with the literally God-given right to exercise complete control over kings and princes. At times they have actually raised armies, fought battles, and even led their troops into battle in person. They launched a number of crusades against the Muslims, and even against the unfortunate Albigenses of southern France. Worst of all, they founded the Inquisition, through which they tried to enforce uniformity of belief.

Recently the Pope made a generalized apology for the crimes and abuses committed in the name of the Church, but one has to see this as being largely a political gesture. On the five-hundredth anniversary of the founding of the Spanish Inquisition, the Spanish bishops were asked to express their regret for the excesses of that body, but they refused, for the same political reasons.

In the course of centuries, many thousands of people were cruelly tortured and slaughtered by the Inquisition and other agencies of the Roman Catholic Church. During the Middle Ages and even afterwards the Church behaved in every way like a power structure of the worst type, and virtually the only trace of Christianity as a spiritual community was to be found in the monasteries. Even there, it rarely lasted long. Thus the Roman Catholic Church provides us with the most prominent example of power creeping into and more or less taking over a spiritual community. But it has happened in the case of other religions too, including Buddhism, albeit in far subtler ways.

Within the spiritual community, however, some people may be more individual than others, but they use their experience, and even their natural authority, not to dominate other people, nor even to impose their own vision on others, but to help them develop as individuals. But if the spiritual community is not a power structure, what is it built around? Clearly, if the principle that governs the group is power, the principle embodied by the spiritual community is love. However, the English word 'love' is a treacherously ambiguous word, because what is called love is all too often only a form of power. The appropriate word in Pāli is *mettā* (*maitrī* in Sanskrit). This is usually translated 'friendliness', but it is friendliness raised to the highest conceivable pitch of intensity, a sort of supercharged friendliness. Such friendliness is practised and experienced only by true individuals, only by members of the spiritual community. When we feel mettā towards others we see them as individuals, and we treat them as individuals. The importance of mettā is reflected in the fact that most Buddhists regularly and systematically cultivate it in the form of a meditation practice, the *mettā bhāvanā*.

Mettā is not expressed with violence, through coercion, or by authority. Such use of power may well be necessary in all sorts of situations, but these situations by their very nature will not occur within the spiritual community. If mettā is present, force is unnecessary. Each individual sees for himself or herself what needs to be done in any given situation – or they see it as soon as it is pointed out to them in a friendly manner – and seeing it, they are happy to do it.

One could go further and say simply that positive emotion in general is at the heart of the spiritual community: not only *mettā*, but also *karuṇā* (compassion), *muditā* (joy in the virtues and happiness of others), and *upeksa* (peace or equanimity), as well as *śraddhā* (faith and devotion). The spiritual community embodies all these sublime, uplifting, animating emotions.

But even then there is something missing. There is a metaphysical or transcendental dimension which must also be present if the spiritual community is to be sustained. The ultimate principles governing the spiritual community are *mahāmaitrī*, the *great* friendliness, and *mahākaruṇā*, the *great* compassion: that is to say, friendliness or compassion conjoined with *prajñā*, transcendental wisdom. In other words, the principle governing the spiritual community is nothing less than what we call the *bodhicitta*, the cosmic Will to Enlightenment,[40] as reflected in the hearts and minds of all the individuals who make up the spiritual community.

7

THE POSITIVE GROUP AND THE NEW SOCIETY

IT IS DIFFICULT to imagine a community dominated by – or rather imbued with – wisdom and compassion. But as potential individuals we do have experience of such a community from time to time, and to a limited extent; and there is no excuse for our not attempting to live by such light as we may have. Most of us, most of the time, are functioning as members of a group, and we are therefore accustomed to relating to one another in terms of power – not just direct, naked power, but also power in the form of fraud, exploitation, and manipulation. In our better moments we must want to change all that. We must want to learn to relate in terms of friendliness and compassion – want to relate to one another as individuals, that is, in terms of that transcendental compassion-cum-wisdom.

Another way of putting this is that we must want to relate on the basis of the *bodhicitta*. This is a term from Mahāyāna Buddhism, and it refers to the Will to Enlightenment that is immanent in each and every individual. When the *bodhicitta* (the word literally means 'Enlightenment-heart') has arisen in us, we are strongly motivated to gain Enlightenment, and that motivation has a definitely altruistic orientation; that is, we seek to gain Enlightenment not just for the sake of our own liberation and happiness, but for the benefit of others – indeed, as the traditional phrase has it, for the benefit of all sentient beings.

When we go for Refuge to the Buddha, Dharma, and Sangha, we go from the group to the spiritual community, from being governed by the power principle to being inspired by the principle of the *bodhicitta*, from the old society to a completely new, different kind of society. Buddhists speak in terms of moving from the world, *saṁsāra*, to Sukhāvati, the Pure Land, a world in which conditions are entirely conducive to the practice of the Dharma. All of us surely, at least sometimes, feel dissatisfied with the world as it is, and would like to live in a better, more beautiful world than the one we at present experience, a world which supports and encourages what is best in us – our generosity, our kindness, and our awareness – instead of conspiring to undermine those qualities.

Many people throughout history have felt this same desire, of course, in the East as well as in the West. We can be sure that people felt it in the Buddha's own day, because we have, for instance, the story of Vaidehī, the wife of King Bimbisāra, who was the ruler of the north Indian kingdom of Magadha. Vaidehī's story is related in the *Amitāyur-Dhyāna Sūtra*, the sūtra on the meditation of the Buddha Amitāyus, the Buddha of Eternal Life.[41] (This is one of a group of three sūtras dealing with Sukhāvati, the Happy Land, and its Buddha Amitābha or Amitāyus, the other two being the larger and the smaller *Sukhāvati Vyūha Sūtras*.)

The story begins with Prince Ajātasatru seizing the throne of Magadha and imprisoning his own father, the righteous old King Bimbisāra, whom he intends to starve to death. But Vaidehī, the king's chief consort (and the mother, as it happens, of Ajātasatru) manages to smuggle food to her husband and thus keep him alive. When Ajātasatru finds out what she has been doing, he threatens to kill her, but in the end is satisfied with imprisoning her.

So there is Vaidehī, alone in prison, hated by her son and unable to supply food to her husband. Understandably, she is thoroughly miserable. But she does not just abandon herself to her misery. Completely disillusioned with being queen, and with worldly life in general, she gives up all thought of her fine palaces, considers her family as lost to her, and concentrates her mind on the Buddha, who is, as it happens, only a few miles away, on the Vulture's Peak. She even contrives to prostrate herself in his direction. And thereupon, the Buddha appears before her. Whether he appears quite literally in his physical form or in some sort of vision we are not told, but when the queen raises her head after paying homage to him, there he is. It is the world-honoured one Śākyamuni, his body glowing purple gold (according to the text), sitting on a lotus flower consisting of a hundred jewels, with Mahāmaudgalyāyana on his left and Ānanda on his right. Above him Vaidehī sees the gods who protect the world showering down heavenly flowers, making offerings to him.

At this sight Vaidehī again prostrates herself on the ground, sobbing, 'Oh world-honoured one, what former sin of mine has produced such a wicked son?' But she is not just concerned with her own misfortune. She goes on, 'Oh exalted one, what cause and circumstance has connected your life with that of Devadatta, your wicked cousin and once your disciple? My only prayer,' she says, 'is this. Oh world-honoured one, please preach to me in detail of all the places where there is no sorrow or trouble, where I should go to be reborn. I am not satisfied with this world of depravities, with Jambudvīpa (that is, India) which is full of hells, of hungry ghosts and brutish life. In this world of depravities there assembles many a multitude of the wicked. May I not hear again the voice of the wicked. I pray that I may never again see a wicked person. Now I throw my entire body and limbs to the ground before you and seek mercy by confessing my sins. I pray for this only, that the sun-like Buddha may instruct me how to meditate on a world wherein all actions are pure.'

By his magical power, the Buddha shows Vaidehī a number of different Pure Lands where there is no suffering, where there is heard no voice of lamentation or even the echo of it. She sees them all in an extended vision, and she chooses to be reborn in Sukhāvati, the Pure Land of Amitābha or Amitāyus, the land of bliss in the west. Then the Buddha proceeds to instruct her in what she must do to achieve this. She must go for Refuge, she must observe the ten precepts – in short, she must follow faithfully all the fundamental teachings of the Dharma. On top of this she should meditate on Amitāyus, the Buddha of Eternal Life, and his Pure Land, Sukhāvati. She should visualize them, see them – at least in her meditation – in this very life, and the Buddha teaches her how to do this by way of a series of sixteen meditations.

The first meditation consists of concentrating on an image of the deep red disc of the setting sun. Then one visualizes a ground, foundation, or base of lapis lazuli, deep blue in colour, extending to infinity in all directions, criss-crossed with a network of golden cords. Next, from amidst the golden cords there spring up trees made of jewels, lakes made of jewels, lotuses made of jewels. And eventually, after a whole series of meditations, in the midst of all these brilliant forms of deep colour and dazzling light, one sees Amitābha himself, the Buddha of Infinite Light, attended by his two great Bodhisattvas, Avalokiteśvara and Mañjuśrī, embodying his compassion and his wisdom.

The Buddha tells Vaidehī that having meditated in this way, when she comes to die she will be reborn in this higher realm upon which she has been so intensely focused. She will find herself sitting in the calyx of a beautiful lotus flower, the petals will open, and she will see Amitābha seated before her. She will hear his teaching from his own lips, face to face. And she will have nothing to do but practise it and meditate upon it.

Thus conditions in the Pure Land are archetypally ideal. Discourses on the Dharma are heard in the form of the music of the wind blowing through the jewelled trees, and the cries and calls of curlews and waterfowl and birds of paradise. Literally everything speaks to you of the Dharma, and all the conditions of life conduce to the attainment of Enlightenment. Even under these perfect circumstances it is not easy to attain Enlightenment, but at least nothing in your environment holds you back.

This picture, painted for the benefit of Vaidehī in her prison cell, is beautiful, but it may seem a little alien, so remote is it from the world we ordinarily inhabit. But Sukhāvati is not just another world; our task is to create it, as best we can, on this earth. We have to improve things here, make the situation in which we live more and more conducive to the flowering of the spiritual life and the attainment of Enlightenment.

That is why, in 1967, I founded a new Buddhist movement, and why in the following year I ordained the first members of the Western Buddhist Order, as the spiritual community at the heart of the positive group. The idea was to create – and enable others to continue to create – our own Sukhāvati, here in our own world, on howsoever small a scale. Over the years I have seen this movement grow slowly but steadily. Every year sees a new Buddhist centre, a new retreat community, or a new right-livelihood business being created somewhere around the world, and I am always delighted to visit them, and attend their inaugurations when I can.

One of the most significant of these ceremonies was the opening of the London Buddhist Centre in Bethnal Green, East London, in 1978. On that occasion we conducted ten days of celebration and appreciation, culminating in the dedication of two shrine-rooms. In the larger of these, the focus of the ceremony was a more than life-size image of Amitābha, the Buddha of the West, the Buddha of Infinite Light, who – just as Śākyamuni told Vaidehī – presides over the Pure Land called Sukhāvati, 'the happy land' or 'the place of bliss' or simply 'abounding in bliss'. Sukhāvati is the name given to the whole complex (community space and public centre) in Bethnal Green.

But what is Sukhāvati, really? What were we really celebrating at the opening of the centre? Were we congratulating one another on our having built a place where people can come along once a week to discuss Buddhism and listen to lectures given by someone who has read a great many more books on the subject than they have? Did we work so hard so that we could do a little therapeutic meditation and take a medicinal dose of Buddhism once in a while just so that we could keep going with our normal life in the same old way? ('Don't let them meditate for more than five minutes,' I was once told by a prominent English Buddhist. 'More than that is dangerous for Westerners.')

The name Sukhāvati was chosen to signal an aspiration that this centre should serve a more noble, radical, even revolutionary function than simply giving people their spiritual vitamins to help them stagger along on the path of worldliness for another few days. Any centre associated with the movement I founded is intended to be nothing less than the nucleus of a new society.

'A new society'? The expression is not new – it was even the name of a weekly magazine – but under the slogan is a simple but profound, sublime, and radical human aspiration. The new society is designed to allow people to develop as human beings. It will not try to do for people what they can only do for themselves; but it provides facilities, opportunities, and an environment of encouragement, as well as a social and spiritual context of human fellowship, which makes it easier for people to develop as human beings.

To speak of trying to create a new society within the old one is to acknowledge that the old society cannot function in this way, because most of its members are not interested in human development. Far from helping the spiritual aspirant, society at large makes it difficult for us to develop even if we want to, and much of the energy which should be going into the work of spiritual transformation gets frittered away in simply trying to resist society's counter-evolutionary forces, its oppressive, coercive, spirit-crushing influence. In an ideal society we would not have to be on the defensive all the time in order to preserve a little space within which we could grow. Our energies would be liberated for the purpose of our own spiritual development in free association with other like-minded people.

But how can a Buddhist movement function as a new society in miniature? What is its structure? How does it work? It is essentially a fellowship of people who are trying to develop as individuals. At least, a few of its members are doing so, keeping in more or less regular contact with one another and trying to develop together and help each other to develop. These individuals constitute the spiritual community within our movement; and they constitute also the heart of the movement. But we cannot expect that everybody connected with the movement will be making that kind of effort.

The movement therefore has two parts, two levels: a spiritual community proper, and what could be described as a healthy or positive group. First, there is the order, a spiritual community which is open to anyone who is sufficiently integrated as an individual as to be able to make a valid commitment to the path to Enlightenment, and who can thus seriously undertake the primary act of all Buddhists everywhere – Going for Refuge to the Three Jewels. The heart of the movement, therefore, consists of individuals. And the positive group is open to anybody who wishes to take part in its activities. These are the two distinct but overlapping – even interfusing – levels within the movement as a whole. Together they comprise what one could call a Buddhist group, although I prefer to use the expression 'movement' because this suggests that it is in its essence a dynamic process.

All the activities of this movement have one purpose, and one purpose only: to help people grow and develop as individuals. It has never been our aim to build up an organization in the ordinary sense, like that of some modern Japanese Buddhist sects. Our aim is not to march with banners through the streets of London and take over the Albert Hall, or to end up with just a self-serving institution. Indeed, the presence of the spiritual community in the midst of the positive group is intended to ensure that this does not happen.

When I say that members of the order are members of the spiritual community, I mean that they belong to the real, living, joyful spiritual fellowship of those practising the Teaching and following the Way. When I say that they are those who go for Refuge, I am not speaking simply of repeating the Refuge formula two or three times a year on the occasion of some Buddhist festival, as happens in so many parts of the Buddhist world, and even in some Buddhist groups in the West.

By Going for Refuge I mean actually committing oneself to the realization of the ideal of human Enlightenment in this very life, and being prepared to give up whatever stands in the way of that commitment.

This spiritual community is just a part of the wider positive group, and this in turn is a part of what is traditionally called the sangha, the spiritual community of the four directions – north, south, east, and west – and the three periods of time: past, present, and future.

Howsoever embryonic its development, we are forming the nucleus of a new society. We have initiated a society in which the idea that someone can represent the position or views of someone else, or claim special authority on account of their position, or seek to exert pressure upon or power over someone else, is absurd. In this society there can be room only for individuals living in free association with one another, inspired by the principles of great compassion and transcendental wisdom, and above all by the *bodhicitta*, the Will to Enlightenment for the sake of all beings.

8

THE PATH OF DISSATISFACTION

SO HOW DO YOU JOIN a spiritual community? Obviously, you can't do it just by paying a subscription. You can't even do it by kneeling in the snow outside closed monastery gates, Japanese Zen-style. In themselves, these formal procedures do not introduce you to the spiritual community. Firstly and essentially it is a question of trying to become an individual, trying to develop spiritually. Then it consists in making contact with other individuals who are also trying to develop, and engaging in spiritual practice with them within a common spiritual framework. This is what joining the spiritual community really means.

To put it the other way round, one joins the spiritual community by leaving the group. One ceases to identify oneself with the group; one ceases to feel that one belongs to any kind of group. Nowadays, the pressure of our responsibilities may make it very difficult to do this literally; we cannot simply leave our responsibility for our dependants to be picked up by someone else. But this is no excuse for avoiding any kind of tangible renunciation of the group. There is, I'm afraid, always the possibility of self-deception. You may say, 'I can get on perfectly well without my home and family – I'm not emotionally dependent on them,' but there is no way of knowing this except by trying out how life feels without them. You may say, 'I'm not particularly attached to living in my native country – I'd be able to manage quite happily anywhere in the world,' but until you have tried coping with totally unfamiliar surroundings, weather, institutions, and customs, and speaking a foreign language for months at a time, you will never be sure. It is easy enough to feel that one is dissociating oneself from group attitudes, but as one's emotional dependence on the group tends to be somewhat unconscious, one will have difficulty proving this to oneself.

The Buddha himself effectively joined the spiritual community by leaving the group in the form of his family home. In the traditional accounts of the Buddha's life, this event is often related dramatically and beautifully. We are told how, one moonlit night, the Buddha, having made his fateful decision to leave everything in the world that he loved, set out alone for the first time in his life.[42] Before he left, he went into the inner apartment of the palace and saw his young wife asleep, with their child lying by her side. Tempted to wake them for a last farewell, he thought better of it – it would be so painful for his wife, and perhaps she would even try to prevent him from going. Standing in the doorway, he just looked at them for a few moments, then turned swiftly away. As well as his wife and child, he also left his father, who, as chief of the clan, was in a position to give him the best start in life, his foster-mother, who looked after him when he was a baby, and his friends. He became, for a number of years, a mendicant, known in those days as a *parivrājaka*, which means 'one who has gone forth' – gone forth, that is to say, from the household life into a life of homelessness, or even, one might say, grouplessness.

In the Buddha's day there were many men, and even a few women, wandering about as parivrājakas – rootless, homeless, groupless – all over northern India. They subsisted on alms, going early in the morning from door to door with an alms bowl, taking whatever food people cared to give them. These parivrājakas were the spiritual ancestors of the modern Indian sadhus, whom one can still see going from village to village on foot, sitting on the steps of temples and at the feet of great spreading banyan trees.

Going forth as the Buddha did, you cease to belong to the group and become a sort of lone wolf, an individual on your own. So far as the group is concerned, you no longer exist. In orthodox Hinduism this renunciation is marked in dramatic, even terrifying fashion by a special ritual in the course of which you officially become a wanderer. You kindle a sacred fire and pour libations into it while chanting mantras, and then you place on the fire certain personal possessions, finishing with two highly symbolic articles. The first of these is your *tiki*, a tuft of hair which every orthodox Hindu layman has growing on the crown of his head. You snip it off and place it in the fire. Then you take the sacred thread which, if you are a caste Hindu, you wear around your body, and put it on the fire as well. This is a tremendous thing to do because Hindu social life is pervaded by caste through and through – your caste is the most significant aspect of your identity. But you haven't come to the end of the ritual yet, by any means. You conclude by performing your own funeral ceremony. You act as the priest at your own cremation. Whoever you were before, that person is now dead. According to Hindu tradition (although not in modern India) you are officially dead. In terms of the group you don't exist; you have no legal or civil rights. This is the length to which Hindus traditionally used to go – and to some extent still do go – in order to sever at the root their connection with the group.

For the Buddha, complete physical dissociation from the world, and the renunciation of one's social identity, was an accepted practice in a way that it is not for us in the West. But we can try to emulate the Buddha's great renunciation as far as we can by going forth – to use the traditional Buddhist term – from as many groups as possible: from home and family, from social position, from national identity, and so on. Such a renunciation is all the greater in a society like ours which makes no allowance for it as a lifestyle choice. By doing so you have embarked on the transition from being a group member to being a true individual.

The Buddha only became the Buddha – 'the one who knows' – after six years of desperate struggle and unceasing search as a parivrājaka. When he began to make known what he had discovered, most of his disciples were recruited from the parivrājaka class (which was the classless class, you might say, as its members had all renounced their class along with all their other affiliations). In most cases they had been wanderers for many years before they came in contact with the Buddha, embraced his teaching, and were accepted by him – or by other disciples on his behalf – into the spiritual community.

Hence we can distinguish two separate phases of entry into the sangha. First, there is a phase of going forth from home, giving up the group, and wandering, without identifying oneself with any particular collection of people. The second phase consists in joining the spiritual community. These two, one might say, are the negative and positive aspects of one and the same process. Moreover, these two phases are reflected in the Buddhist ordination procedure even today. When you are ordained as what in the West we call a Buddhist monk (though 'monk' isn't an entirely appropriate term) there are two ordinations: the so-called lower ordination, the *pabbajjā* or going forth, and the higher ordination, the *upasampadā*. The going forth symbolizes breaking free of the group, cutting off biological ties, social ties, group loyalties, and political connections of every kind – being simply an individual, on one's own, even isolated; and the higher ordination represents the acceptance of that individual into the spiritual community. The individual is accepted on the basis of having been tried and tested, as it were, in the fires of solitude. He or she has not run back to the group, and can therefore be accepted not as someone taking refuge in a snug little religious coterie, but as an individual accepted by other individuals as a responsible member of the spiritual community.

But how, today, do we begin to make this transition from the old society to the new? One can of course approach any one of a number of traditional Buddhist organizations which more or less resolutely follow the mode of life of Eastern Buddhism in modern Western society. But assuming at least the nucleus of the new society to be already in existence, in the form in which I have described it, one can also make that all-important transition via a Buddhist centre. This is the bridge, the common ground, where these two worlds meet and overlap.

What one brings to the Buddhist centre, at least initially, is a sense of dissatisfaction. This might seem an unlikely attitude for Buddhists to encourage – we are all surely familiar enough with dissatisfaction. Anyone who has ever picked up a mail order catalogue, pored over its glossy pages, found something depicted therein that is too tempting to resist, and filled in a form and sent it off, waiting for that winter coat or that electric drill with its guarantee of full and complete satisfaction, will know the meaning of dissatisfaction. When it finally arrives and you unwrap it somehow it seems less glamorous, less luxurious, flimsier, smaller, than in the photograph. Sometimes it is even the wrong colour, or there's a part missing. Our disappointment may be such that we have no hesitation in sending the offending article, unsatisfactory as it is, back for a refund, perhaps accompanied by a strongly-worded note.

But we have all taken delivery of one article which, when we compare it with the design specifications, is clearly incomplete or botched, and yet we seem more than satisfied with it. That article is, of course, ourselves. We want everything else in our lives to be properly made, polished and shiny, but we cherish ourselves in our imperfect state. So how can we become dissatisfied? Quite simply, we become dissatisfied when we compare ourselves as we are here and now with how we could be in the future. We become dissatisfied when we get a glimpse of a potential which is without any limit and see that by comparison we are at present distinctly unsatisfactory and limited. When we espouse that vision we are in a sense taking the first steps towards sending ourselves back in disgust and demanding a properly functioning human individuality.

Dissatisfaction – if it is not just disgruntlement but a genuine and creative mood of inner revolt – is a positive and powerful impulse. Indeed, such a mood is the starting point. You are dissatisfied, perhaps, with the quality of your relationships, with your work, with your leisure activities – and perhaps, more often than not, you are pretty fed up with yourself as well. You start looking around for a new direction, and you hear, perhaps, about Buddhism, and then about the Buddhist centre, about meditation classes, and you start going along to those classes, and to listen to talks. You may even go on a weekend retreat. And as a result of all this, you start to change.

Such change is quite noticeable. I have seen it taking place many times. One sees people visibly changing almost before one's eyes – and this, one might say, is a miracle: that people can change, not just piecemeal, but from top to bottom. Indeed, the Buddha himself referred to this as the greatest of all miracles.[43] In general he condemned the display of so-called miracles or supernormal powers. The ancient Indians were very interested in these things, and even now people tend to perk up and take notice as soon as the subject comes up. The Buddha was often asked to demonstrate miraculous powers, and sometimes he did, if he saw good reason to do so. But for him they were entirely insignificant, and if he thought that they were being taken too seriously, he refused to have anything to do with them. He even went so far as to say 'I condemn and abhor them, I look down upon them.' 'These,' he went on to say, 'are not real miracles. The real miracle is when someone who was following the dark path changes and starts following the bright path, the path of skilful activities, the path of the spiritual life: that is the real miracle.'

It is a miracle which continues to occur – often, it seems, against all the odds. People come along quite literally off the street, looking hopeless and dejected, as if they carried all the cares of the world on their shoulders. They start meditating, they become more aware, and in the course of a few weeks, sometimes in the course of a weekend retreat away in the country, you see them beginning to look bright and cheerful. They begin to see something of the Buddha's vision of existence, and they change. One might think that when someone has travelled along the same old rut for decades, it is too late. But that is a great mistake. If you find the right sort of encouragement and the right sort of conditions, you can change at any time of your life.

After this initial positive change takes place, you will perhaps be visited with a deeper dissatisfaction. You may start feeling that you cannot go on living in the same old way. You begin to find your old relationships and old work very restricting. You experience, in short, something of what the Buddha himself experienced when he made the decision to go forth. At that point you might decide to take some action: to move into a residential community for a couple of weeks to see what it's like, for example, or to work in a Buddhist right-livelihood project for a trial period.

The whole process – from initial dissatisfaction to going forth – may only take two or three months, but it is more likely to take several years. It varies a great deal from one person to another. But when the transition from the old society to the new is finally made, you are henceforth part of the new society, and your strength as an individual strengthens that new society. From then on you live in a situation which is conducive to your development as a human being, one in which the possibility of growth is infinite. And that is a very rare opportunity indeed. As I know from my own experience, one seldom encounters such an opportunity in the Buddhist East, and one has had little hope at all of ever coming across it in the West until recent times, with the establishing of a number of effective spiritual communities. Having found such a context, one is well on the way to becoming a true individual. It is the nature of true individuality that we will now go on to consider.

PART 2

The True Individual

INTRODUCTION

AM I AN INDIVIDUAL, or just a social unit? This is, at bottom, the central question of our personal lives, and it is one we need to keep asking ourselves, and keep trying to penetrate more deeply. It is also, as we have seen, the key to the development of a sangha, a spiritual community. No individuals, no sangha. Any consideration of what the sangha is must therefore include as full an understanding as possible of the nature of individuality. So – what is an individual? We have seen already that the true individual can be defined in traditional Buddhist terms as someone who has broken through the first three fetters and has thus gained Stream-entry. We have also witnessed the emergence of the individual in the context of human history. In the following chapters we will be considering individuality from various other points of view.

First, we will take a brief look at the qualities typical of an individual. Then, in Chapter 9, we will broaden our scope to consider the development of individuality not just in terms of relatively recent history, but in the context of the evolution of consciousness as a whole. But then, having expanded our vision to take in such a broad and lofty perspective, we will narrow our focus to address a question that may already have occurred to you. Is it really legitimate, in terms of Buddhist doctrine, to speak of the 'individual'? Isn't Buddhism famous for its 'no-self' doctrine? It is worth taking some time to clarify the ways in which it is – and is not – appropriate to think of the spiritual life in terms of the development of individuality; this we will do in Chapter 10, 'The Integrated Individual'. And in Chapters 11 and 12 we will relate our developing conception of individuality to two other fields of thought and experience: Western philosophy, in the form of the thought of Friedrich Nietzsche, and the arts, in which context we will consider whether or not it is appropriate to think of the artist as a true individual.

But to begin with, what – in general – are the characteristics of the true individual? I should say straightaway that there are, of course, all sorts of qualities that the individual will tend to develop, and no account of them will ever encompass the full range of possibilities. Individuality cannot be measured or weighed or estimated in terms of any number of qualities or characteristics. It is unfathomable and inexhaustible, and the same can be said for its qualities and characteristics. There are, however, certain qualities of the individual that seem especially relevant to many people's experience and behaviour. To be an individual, before anything else perhaps, you need objectivity, clarity, and intelligence in the broad sense. You need to be aware that actions have consequences, that you are responsible for your actions and therefore responsible for their consequences too. This is a *sine qua non*, without which one cannot proceed further. You also need to be receptive – otherwise, again, you are stuck. But beyond these fundamentals, the following positive characteristics may be said to constitute together the nature of the individual.

Firstly, as an individual you are free – or at least comparatively free – from group conditioning, and you constantly try to see beyond your own conditioning. You are aware of the world, of the shaping of the world, of how it comes to be the way it is, of history. One way in which this kind of awareness can be developed is, of course, through travelling. As many people have discovered, the process of moving away from the familiar supports to one's views and experiencing the very different group conditioning that obtains somewhere else can be enough to make one question the absolute validity of the way one is accustomed to look at the world.

Secondly, you have developed self-consciousness – not in the adolescent sense of agonizing over the notion that everyone is looking at you, but in the sense of being aware of what you are doing and why.

I use the word 'developed' here deliberately; it takes discipline and effort to develop self-consciousness, and indeed many of the traditional Buddhist practices are designed precisely to develop it. Primitive man was conscious but not self-conscious, not aware, and all too often the same goes for modern, 'civilized' man. But as an individual you are aware.

Broadly speaking, this awareness has four dimensions: awareness of self, of nature, of other people, and of reality.[44] The first of these dimensions, awareness of self, includes many things. To begin with, you are aware of your physical body – its position, its movements. You are also aware of your emotions, whether positive or negative, and of your thoughts – of ideas, concepts, reflections, reasoning. You are aware of your conditioning too – your upbringing, your environment, your early experiences, your associations, your skills and tendencies, likes and dislikes. You are aware of your own basic motivations – you are able to be reasonably objective about yourself, to weigh yourself up fairly accurately.

Essentially, you are aware of your own uniqueness, aware that 'universal consciousness' has focused itself in you, and that as one of an infinite number of foci of that consciousness, you are irreplaceable. You are intensely, luminously aware. You feel the very vibration of your own individual existence. You are aware of yourself as sharply distinguished, differentiated, from the whole of the rest of nature. You are aware of your absolute unrepeatability – of how in the course of ages, through hundreds and millions of years, there will never be anybody else like you.

The second dimension of awareness is awareness of nature. You are aware of nature as something completely other, something which is not yourself, even though you have emerged from it, grown out of it. You are aware of your physical surroundings, the environment. With the third dimension of awareness you are aware of other people, particularly others who are also self-aware. You are aware of what is happening between you and others – that is, you are aware of the nature and quality of your relationships.

Finally, and above all, you cultivate the fourth dimension of awareness: awareness of reality. You are aware of the mysterious, elusive thread of unity that runs through the whole of the vast fabric of things. That is, you are aware – or seek to become aware – of absolute reality, of what is sometimes called the transcendental. You have a direct, personal relationship with the deeper reality of things. We can go so far as to say – somewhat poetically, perhaps – that the individual is one through whom the deeper reality of things, the truth behind appearances, functions or is present in the world. Through the individual is seen the universal: in fact, the individual and the universal coincide.

If you are an individual, you know what you are doing. You are not reactive, or mechanical, or impelled; you are not driven, or dragged along by blind instinct. You are not the victim of your own unconscious urges. You are spontaneous and free.

Thirdly, and following on from this self-awareness, you are, if you are an individual, set apart from the mass of humanity. You are no longer submerged in the species, in the group. You are yourself. We may even say that each individual constitutes a distinct species. The Tibetan text called *The Precepts of the Gurus* lists 'ten signs of the superior man'; the ninth is as follows:

> *To differ from the multitude in every thought and action is the sign of a superior man.*[45]

This is not to say that you go out of your way to be different. An individual is not necessarily an eccentric. Nor is an individual to be confused with an individualist, or with someone with an inflated ego which they like to inflict on others. It is simply that you think for yourself and therefore, inevitably, that you think rather differently from others. You may respect the thoughts of others, and even make use of them, but you will yourself give careful thought to the actual validity of other people's thinking.

It doesn't occur to you to desire to be different from others – it isn't that you want to 'stand out from the herd'. Nor do you set yourself 'above the herd'. An individual is certainly not someone who simply gets to the top of the social group, like kings, ministers, millionaires, film stars, and so on. An individual is different in kind, different in quality from others. You differ from others simply by being yourself.

Fourthly, you are not psychologically dependent on others. You do not require the approval of the group for your own peace of mind. You don't mind differing from other people, you don't mind entertaining ideas that nobody else would dream of adopting. The disapproval of the group will not pressure you into conformity. If need be, you are prepared to go it alone. This doesn't mean going it alone as a matter of principle – on the contrary, the need to appear independent of others is just another form of dependency. Nor do you have to eschew help from others in order to be independent: elderly people who refuse to accept their own objective limitations, saying 'I've always been independent' do not thereby display real independence. Real independence is independence of mind: you are autonomous, you make your own choices.

With this freedom and self-determination goes creativity. One way to put this is to say that primitive humanity is reproductive, modern humanity is productive (i.e. producing material things – food, housing, clothing, artefacts), but the individual is creative. That is to say, what you create as an individual, even though it may be material in form, has a spiritual significance. Whether you are creating music, literature, philosophy, religion, or whatever, you are really creating yourself. The individual is his or her own greatest work of art. This is obvious in the case of men like the Buddha, Confucius, or Socrates. But in much later times we see it, perhaps on a diminished scale, in the case of, for example, Goethe. He is the greatest poet of the German language, but we may say, nevertheless, that his greatest poem is his life. This commitment to his own development as an individual comes out very well in his *Conversation with Eckermann*: he worked on his own character, his own personality, his own life, quite consciously, in the same spirit in which he created his literary works.

The French theatre director Antonin Artaud (1896–1948) expresses a similar commitment in very passionate terms in his 'Points':

> *I hate and renounce as a coward every being who consents to having been created and does not wish to have recreated himself, i.e. who agrees with the idea of a God as the origin of his being, as of the origin of his thought.*
>
> *I hate and renounce as a coward every being who agrees not to have been self-created and who consents to and recognizes the idea of a matrix nature of the world as his already created body.*
>
> *I do not consent to having not created my body myself and I hate and renounce as a coward every being who consents to live without first having recreated himself.*
>
> *I hate and renounce as a coward every being who does not recognize that life is given to him only to recreate and reconstitute his entire body and organism.*[46]

Fifthly, as an individual you may be, and you accept that you may be, unpopular. Unpopularity is not of course a characteristic as such of the true individual – it is just something that he or she often experiences. The Buddha himself (before he became the Buddha) had to be prepared to lose the friendship and respect of his five followers on the path of asceticism, when he decided that self-torture was useless and started taking proper food again.[47] Even after his Enlightenment he was not at all popular in some quarters, because he challenged the vested interests of an entrenched hereditary priesthood. Fortunately, the Indians on the whole are a rather tolerant people. Other great individuals have not been so fortunate. Socrates was condemned to death, Confucius was driven from state to state, and almost died of starvation in a ditch. The prophets of Israel were liable to be stoned. As for the creative artist of modern times, he or she can still arouse fury in the mob.

Sixthly, the individual will develop emotions that are positive and refined. Everyone is of course capable of positive emotion – even Stalin was a kindly fellow from time to time, apparently – but it is clear from this example alone that you cannot just rely on your natural human warmth to express itself as compassion, sensitivity, peace, and joy. Whether positive or negative, human emotion naturally tends to be crude, even violent. A positive, refined, focused emotional nature therefore needs to be consciously developed. You need to take full responsibility for your own mental states. You recognize that your emotional experience is self-created.

Seventhly, your energies flow freely and spontaneously, cleanly and harmoniously. There are no blockages, no inhibitions, no 'hang-ups'. All your energy is always available. You are therefore able to be creative in whatever you do.

Eighthly, you are alone. To be an individual in the midst of people who are not individuals is to be alone. To create in the midst of people who merely produce or reproduce is to be alone. As an individual you may feel this very intensely – and you may not know whether to be glad or sorry about it. You are glad because, having created yourself anew, you experience something you have not experienced before, but you are sorry because the greater your experience is, the harder it is for you to share it with others. The Buddha himself no doubt experienced aloneness, especially during the period between leaving home at the age of 29 and gaining Enlightenment six years later at the foot of the bodhi tree. Even after that, until he was able to share his experience of Enlightenment, he would have experienced his aloneness even more intensely. At one level or another, this is always the situation of the individual.

However, being alone is not your aim. The final characteristic of the individual I want to draw out here is that you encourage others to be individuals in their own way. You are willing to take responsibility in any situation in which you find yourself, to help make it a creative situation both for yourself and for others. This is, as we have seen, the basis upon which individuals create a spiritual community.

In all these ways you accept responsibility for yourself, for your own individual growth, for your own life, and for the effect that your life has on the life around you. And you act accordingly, because you see such growth as being the most important thing in life for each and every human being. You therefore commit yourself wholeheartedly to the process of individual development. In more traditional, more Buddhistic terms, as a true individual, you commit yourself to the Three Jewels.

9

THE EVOLUTION OF THE INDIVIDUAL

ON THE BASIS of the above description, who would not want to be a true individual? At the same time, we have already seen that individuals are extremely rare, which suggests that it is not easy to become one. So how do you become an individual? Indeed, how does *anyone* become an individual? What is the process? We have seen how individuals first began to emerge during what Jaspers called the Axial Age. But how did that happen? We can explore this in terms of a concept which is in many ways the most significant idea in the whole range of modern thought: evolution.

The *locus classicus* of evolution as a concept is of course Darwin's great theory of natural selection and the origin of species. However, evolution need not be restricted to a specifically scientific application. In general terms, it refers to the way in which all processes, however much they appear on the surface to be fixed in their forms and functions, are conditioned and impermanent adaptations or sets of circumstances that have grown out of earlier sets of circumstances or less highly organized adaptations. This is perhaps the most significant use of the term evolution from a Buddhist point of view.

As a general principle, evolution can be applied to almost anything. It enables us to understand the whole of existence – from the formation of planets, to the central Darwinian concept of biological evolution, all the way through to human institutions, and even ideas themselves – as being in the process of some kind of unfolding, some kind of growth. The universe, we can say, is one gigantic process of becoming. And we are part of that process.

The model of evolution we know best is that of a blind, accidental, and ruthless groping towards ever more successful adaptations to ever-changing environmental circumstances. If one species develops a new genetic configuration which gives it an edge over its environment, then other species have to develop adaptations of their own to meet that challenge. Even what we know as the self can be explained as a more or less successful way in which a certain group of organisms have adapted themselves to their environment. It is, one might say, a development driven from underneath.

This model is an essentially mechanistic one, and it leaves all sorts of important questions unanswered. Some would even say that it is wisest to leave them unanswered, arguing that no such explanation can begin to dispel the essential mystery of things, particularly the mystery of consciousness and the self. It is to engage with this mystery that another, quite different model is sometimes invoked. According to this way of thinking, evolution is not so much driven from underneath as drawn up from above. Of course, generally speaking such ideas are the province of religion, which usually has a vitalist or teleological perspective on the whole principle of evolution. The very fact of evolution beginning to reflect upon its own workings is seen as indicating that the process is also a progress, and that it must be in some sense directed from above or beyond itself. That is, if progress is observed occurring within the process of evolution, it is assumed that this progress happens in relation to some identifiable goal, value, or principle above or beyond that whole process.

Neither of these models works altogether satisfactorily on its own, but they do not have to be set in opposition to each other. If one is not rigidly literalistic about either model, they may each be said to be relevant to particular aspects of our situation. Thus, in the faltering, unforeseeable steps of Darwinian evolution we could also read the progressive manifestation through time of an absolute, transcendent reality whose very presence makes possible the emergence of one new quality and characteristic after another in that evolutionary process. There is not, obviously – from a Buddhist perspective, anyway – some preordained grand plan behind the whole process of evolution, but we can say perhaps that this absolute reality is a kind of reservoir on which evolution, especially human evolution, continually draws.

The purpose of bringing evolution into a discussion of Buddhism is not so much to explain evolution in spiritual terms as to use the idea of evolution to throw light on the spiritual development of the individual. It is not meant to suggest anything merely scientific, historical, or even religious. It is a way of describing a process within ourselves as individuals. It concerns ourselves as continually growing – *evolving* – beings, as beings who are capable, indeed, of infinite development.

First, we can look back at how we have evolved. We are the product of billions of years of cosmic evolution, about half a million years of human evolution, and ten thousand years of cultural evolution. Biologically speaking, we have evolved from lower, simpler forms of life, and anthropologically we have evolved from savagery and barbarism to civilization and culture, while psychologically we have evolved from unconsciousness to simple consciousness, and from simple consciousness to the rudiments of self-consciousness. Secondly, we can look forward to what we are developing into – not as a group, not as a species, but as individuals. The dividing line between these two kinds of development is represented by self-consciousness, or awareness.

So we stand at this watershed. Human beings at their best – aware, responsible, intelligent, sensitive – stand at this turning point where a higher evolution emerges from the 'lower' evolution. Unfortunately, we are capable of sinking well below this point as well as of rising far above it. We like to think of ourselves as leading fully human lives, but it has to be said that most of the time our ingrained animality – our group-consciousness – is only fitfully illuminated by individual self-awareness. Real humanity, in other words, is an achievement rather than something with which we are born.

This is in no way to deny our common humanity. It is to remind us of what being human is about, of what distinguishes us from the lower evolution. The higher evolution is the evolution of our humanity, which must always be an ongoing process. The freedom we gain by virtue of our self-awareness necessarily allows us the freedom to surrender that freedom. But we are also capable as individuals of building upon that basic level of humanity. We have the capacity to evolve beyond the point of self-consciousness towards another crucial point. This is where transcendental awareness – direct awareness of reality – emerges; and this awareness propels us even further, towards what Buddhists call Enlightenment. It is in this way that we can see

Buddhism not as a religion in the conventional and debased sense of the term, but as the path of the higher evolution, as the whole evolutionary process becomes self-conscious in human beings.

The Russian novelist Vladimir Nabokov, when asked what distinguishes us from the animals, answered as follows:

> *Being aware of being aware of being. In other words, if I not only know that I am but also know that I know it, then I belong to the human species. All the rest follows: the glory of thought, poetry, a vision of the universe. In that respect, the gap between ape and man is immeasurably greater than the one between amoeba and ape. The difference between an ape's memory and human memory is the difference between an ampersand and the British Museum library.*[48]

Though there is some continuity in the growth of the higher evolution from the lower evolution, there is one crucial discontinuity. The lower evolution is collective: a mutation must be shared amongst a whole group of organisms before it can be said that a new species has evolved. By contrast, the higher evolution is carried by the individual, because the growing point is the development of self-consciousness, awareness, mindfulness. To the extent that there is awareness, there is the higher evolution, and vice versa. Just as when you see a bud on the bare branch of a tree, you know that sooner or later there will be a leaf, and even a blossom, in the same way you know that if in anybody's life you see some glimmer of awareness, you may be certain that sooner or later they are going to develop beyond that level of awareness.

As a result of developing awareness, a single individual can ultimately develop qualities that are different from those found in the generality of people not just in degree, but in kind. He or she can become an entirely new kind of being – what the Buddhist tradition terms a Buddha, an Enlightened One. It is important to understand that the true purpose of any universal religion (as distinct from ethnic or tribal religions) is to produce such beings, and that they are not just the same old thing reissued in a new and improved edition, but an altogether new species of being, a fresh 'meta-biological' – so to speak – mutation.

The higher evolution being a matter for the individual, we have to think of it not in general, but in particular, even personal terms. Having looked at the vast processes of evolution as if through a telescope, we must take a microscope to the subject and examine how the individual evolves or develops. Under the microscope we shall be putting, in effect, ourselves.

Human beings consist, roughly speaking, of two broad divisions: the physical body and the mind or consciousness. The body belongs to the lower evolution. We have inherited this body, so wonderfully made, from a long series of animal ancestors, extending back into dim and distant ages. As for the mind – well, it would tie things up neatly if we could say that the human mind belongs essentially to the higher evolution. But we definitely cannot. Aristotle defines Man as a rational animal, but ordinary rational consciousness is not enough, in itself, to raise us above the lower evolution. Indeed, some of the higher mammals clearly possess rudimentary powers of reasoning of their own. All we can say is that the human mind has the *potential* to embark on the higher evolution. The development of both our powers, both the physical and the mental, is severely limited by our evolutionary genetic inheritance. But in the mind there lies the possibility of a continued development, of what I am calling a higher evolution. In a sense, we are mind rather than body, and if our future lies anywhere, it lies in the mind. In other words, the future evolution of humanity will be mainly, if not exclusively, psychological and spiritual.

Before we describe the stages of development through which consciousness passes, it would be appropriate to define what we mean by consciousness. Unfortunately, one has to confess at once that any definition would be tautological. Here is one dictionary's attempt at a definition of consciousness: 'A character belonging to certain processes or events in the living organism which must be regarded as unique and therefore as indefinable in terms of anything else, but which can perhaps be best described as a view of these processes or events as it were from the inside.' The individual is, as it were, inside what is happening – that is as near as we can get to, if not a definition, at least a description, of consciousness. Consciousness, therefore, is synonymous with awareness, whatever that may be.

The difficulty we are faced with is that of differentiating successive stages in the development of something which is unique and indefinable. If consciousness at one stage is unique and indefinable, it will be equally so at every other stage. How can one unique and indefinable thing be distinguished from another?

The difficulty is more apparent than real. Consciousness has been described as 'a view of certain processes or events in the living organism'. Where there is a view, there is obviously something viewed. The stages of development through which consciousness passes may therefore be distinguished on the basis of their respective objects. If we do this we can make out four degrees or levels of consciousness: simple consciousness, self-consciousness, transcendental consciousness, and absolute consciousness.[49] These terms are provisional – others might conceivably do just as well. Alternatively, for example, these levels could be called sense consciousness, subjective consciousness, objective consciousness, and universal consciousness.

The first level – simple consciousness – is synonymous with sense-based perception. It consists, that is to say, in awareness of sensations arising from contact between the sense organs and the external world. This is the level of consciousness we share with animals; it connects us with the vast process of biological evolution, a process of almost unimaginable extent, stretching from the simplest unicellular organism to the miraculous intricacies of our biological functions as primates.

The second level – self-consciousness – is not merely perceiving, or even conceiving (through the cognitive sense). You perceive that you perceive. You are aware that you are aware. Not only do you experience sensations, feelings, emotions, thoughts, and volitions, and so on; you experience yourself as experiencing them. Not only are you aware of what comes to you through your senses; you are able to stand aside, as it were, and be aware of yourself as being aware of the things you are sensing, rather than being, as it were, immersed in them, identified with them.

It is in this reflexive form of consciousness – consciousness bending back, as it were, on itself – that our humanity most characteristically resides. It connects us with the tens of thousands of years in which self-reflective consciousness has gradually allowed us to distinguish ourselves from the rest of the animal world. Here we find ourselves in the human realm proper, the realm explored in the cognitive and social sciences. This is the culmination of the lower evolution and the inauguration of the higher evolution. It stands as a watershed between the two, and is thus of crucial importance. However, this is not all we are capable of: we can go further still.

With the development of full self-consciousness we see ourselves as we truly are. With the development of the third level, transcendental consciousness, we see the world as it really is. This is where philosophy and religion come into their own. It is where we make some kind of connection with the nature of reality, culminating in an experience of transcendental awareness. This awareness is of the higher spiritual reality that embraces both oneself and all conditioned existence – the whole evolutionary process. It is described as transcendental because it transcends the distinction between subject and object.

At least, up to a point. At this stage an object is still perceived as an object, but it is as though the 'line' where subject and object meet and divide off from each other is replaced by a crack – which may widen into a clear gap – through which shines the light of absolute or universal consciousness. Starting off as a narrow flickering shaft of light, this is the flash of insight in the light of which we see the transcendental. And this light in which we see the transcendental is also the light in which the transcendental sees us. In other words, the awareness or consciousness by which we know the transcendental is identical with the awareness or consciousness by which the transcendental knows us.[50] Awareness is no longer wholly identified with the self and its subjective, psychological conditionings. It is for this reason that transcendental consciousness may also be spoken of as objective consciousness.

The fourth level, absolute or universal consciousness, is the gradual flowering of Buddhahood itself out of that experience of transcendental consciousness. It frees us from the whole cycle of human life and death, and may therefore be termed the supra-human level. The crack widens to become an aperture, and the aperture goes on opening out, expanding, as it were, to infinity. In this way consciousness becomes one with its object, which is infinite. Subject and object entirely disappear. Hence here there is nothing to be said.

The practical reality of how consciousness evolves – at least beyond the stages of the lower evolution – is obviously more various and uncertain than this account can suggest. There are all sorts of intermediate stages in the evolution of consciousness; I have delineated these four principal ones in order to give a clear, broad, and simple outline of the subject.

It has been suggested that the process of human gestation recapitulates in nine months the hundreds of millions of years of evolution that underlie the human species as a whole. The child also recapitulates in his or her early years the evolution of consciousness from simple consciousness to self-consciousness, from animal to primitive humanity. At the time of birth the child is an animal with merely animal needs; but within about three years he or she develops reason, memory, and language, and the rudimentary self-consciousness that these accomplishments reflect and nurture.

However, progress slows down dramatically during those first three years. From traversing the equivalent of hundreds of millions of years in the womb we go on to cover just a few million years of evolution during our first three years outside it. And after that point there is practically no development at all, in comparison with the staggering development that takes place in those early years. In the remaining years allotted to us, we learn to read and write, we acquire knowledge – even a great deal of it; we perhaps learn to paint or play the piano, and we almost certainly learn to drive a car. In other words we recapitulate, more or less sketchily, the history of civilization. But in terms of consciousness we remain throughout life more or less where we were at the age of three.

Why is this? Why do we stop at this point of rudimentary self-consciousness? The reason is to be found in the distinction between the lower evolution, which is a collective process, and the higher evolution, which is an individual achievement. The higher evolution cannot be recapitulated in the way the lower evolution is recapitulated in the development of the foetus. You can inherit simple consciousness from your parents, but not self-consciousness – much less transcendental consciousness. Even if you were lucky enough to have parents endowed with transcendental consciousness, you yourself would still have to start again from the beginning. The good news is that the path of the higher evolution can be traversed within the limits of a single human life.

The lower evolution carries us up to the point of rudimentary self-consciousness, and then it leaves us there. From then on, our progress depends on our own conscious effort. Without that, no further progress is possible. This predicament is somewhat reminiscent of another crucial episode in evolution, when life was leaving the sea in which it had been engendered and beginning to invade the dry land. The tide washes on to the shore sea-creatures that are developing a capacity to make some very limited use of conditions on land – perhaps to lay their eggs. Then, when the tide retreats, it leaves these creatures stranded on the shore, to make their own way. The sea cannot do any more for their development. Our predicament, we may say, is a little like theirs. Life has swept us on to the shores of self-consciousness and left us there to fend for ourselves. The general surge and flow of evolution can do no more for us. From here onwards it is all up to us individually.

We are therefore confronted with a choice – not a collective choice, not a choice facing us as a species, but an individual one. It confronts you and me. We – that is, you and I – can either stop where we now are, or continue the process of evolution. And if we do decide to continue, the evolution we embark on will mean one thing – the development of consciousness.

Moreover, if we continue the process of evolution, we can do so only by virtue of our individual determination and effort. Nature – Mother Nature, even – will not help us do it. A human existence is – and by definition must be – a struggle, even a fight. Life can seem just to drift along, and no doubt we can drift along with it. But if some aspects of life involve passively riding a prevailing current, the higher evolution is not one of them. Self-development – the development of consciousness to a higher level – is a struggle with some very recalcitrant material indeed.

This is because most of us, most of the time, think of self-development, if we think of it at all, in terms of physical or intellectual development. We may wake up in the morning and think 'I'm going to get fitter today' or 'I'm going to read something about Buddhism today.' But how often do our aspirations include the objective of developing our consciousness – self-development in the fully and distinctively human sense of the expression? If the answer is 'Not very often, if at all,' we have to face the fact that we are failing to lead truly human lives.

There is no compulsion to follow the path of the higher evolution. In fact, most people are not even aware of the possibility of doing so, and most of those who are don't bother to take advantage of that awareness. Even being prepared to entertain such a question therefore puts one in a small minority. Any minority finds itself in a difficult position, and the minority who set out on the path of the higher evolution have the particular difficulty that it is a path from which it is very easy to be diverted.

The higher evolution is traditionally the concern of the universal religions – that is, the religions of the individual, the religions that speak not just to one particular ethnic group but, in principle, to all people. But today there is little to be gained from going to ministers, priests, and mullahs for guidance in how to develop one's levels of consciousness. In most parts of the world – including Buddhist ones – the universal religions have become essentially ethnic in their concerns. They are part of the establishment, offering themselves as forms of community service and no more. There is probably more concern for the development of consciousness to be found within the sphere of the arts and some branches of psychology than in more conventional attempts to live a spiritual life.

There is a verse in the *Bhagavad Gītā*, the celebrated and popular Hindu text, in which Krishna (who, we may say, embodies absolute consciousness) is represented as saying that out of a thousand men, only one seeks him, and that out of a thousand who seek him, only one will find him.[51] So, according to Krishna, the goal will be attained by perhaps one person in a million – and this is probably rather a generous estimate.

The *Dhammapada* makes the same point from a less dramatic perspective. The Buddha says, 'It is difficult to attain the human state. It is difficult to hear the real truth. The arising of an Enlightened one is difficult.'[52] To paraphrase, we can say that it is difficult really to be a human being – it is easier to withdraw from that challenge into a more or less animalistic state. It is difficult to develop self-consciousness, and more difficult still to develop transcendental consciousness. It is difficult to be an individual, to go on making an effort to be aware.

The difficulty has to be emphasized, not to discourage us, but to give us some hope of success. So long as we realize that the process is difficult and take that difficulty seriously, we shall be able to overcome it. But if we don't allow ourselves to realize how difficult it is going to be, if we think it can't be as difficult as all that, then we won't be able to do so.

Although the odds are stacked against us, and the goal seems remote, our immediate task is clear. It is to develop our rudimentary self-consciousness into full self-consciousness, as well as to begin to develop the third level of consciousness, transcendental or objective consciousness. Though the third level cannot be perfected before the second is fully developed, the two are nonetheless developed together. The full development of self-consciousness perfects one's humanity; and with the full development of transcendental consciousness, this makes one a Stream-entrant, someone in whom the influence of the higher evolution outweighs that of the lower evolution.

The higher evolution is a formidable proposition and it will take all our energy. If we are going to concern ourselves with it, we will have to concern ourselves with it – with the development of consciousness – always and everywhere. We cannot dedicate half our time and energy to it. It is all or nothing. Whatever situation confronts us, whatever experience befalls us, whatever opportunity presents itself to us, we always have to ask ourselves: 'What bearing does this have

– directly or indirectly – on the higher purpose I have set myself?' We have to raise this question in relation to our work, our personal relationships, our social, cultural, and sporting activities, our interests – the books we read, the music we listen to, the films we watch. The question is always the same: what effect is this going to have on my development as a human being?

Making the living of a religious or even spiritual life in a conventional sense our main consideration will not necessarily have any kind of positive impact on our development. But if we make the development of consciousness the primary motivation in everything we do, we will make sure progress. And if we don't – well, we won't.

10

THE INTEGRATED INDIVIDUAL

INNATE WITHIN US is the desire to change, to grow, to evolve. That is what being human means. And yet, as we have seen, the evolution of consciousness is not an automatic process. As anyone who has ever aspired to change will know, it is hard to sustain the effort to do it. However inspired we sometimes are, we are only too likely to find it almost impossible to sustain that inspiration, or to translate it into consistent effort towards greater self-awareness.

Why is this? The reason is that we are not so much a self as a succession of selves, perhaps even a bundle of selves. We are not a unified, continually operative self, but a whole number of selves battling for supremacy, only one of which is in control at any one time. This explains why we so often fail to do what we have set out to do. For example, the assumption behind a decision to get up early in the morning is that the person who makes the decision and the person who will carry it out are one and the same. However, when we wake up we are apt to find that during the night another self has come on duty, a self who has no intention of getting up, but rather fancies a lie-in this morning. So we lie there, vaguely remembering the decision made the night before, and wondering what happened to it.

Becoming an individual, therefore, is a process of integration. Somehow we have to find a way of unifying the different selves that are within us, integrating our total being, conscious and unconscious, intellectual and emotional. As well as this integration, which we could call 'horizontal', there is also 'vertical' integration to achieve: an integration with our own unrealized higher potential, which is achieved through allowing ourselves to experience our heights – and our depths. Thinking of the Buddhist life in these terms, we can see that committing ourselves to the observance of ethical precepts helps us to live in such a way that we mean what we say, and do what we mean to do; in other words, we develop integrity. The traditional Buddhist practice of mindfulness in all its forms also nurtures the integration of our many 'selves', as we make the effort to maintain continuous awareness throughout the activities of daily life. And meditation can be described as a direct method of integrating ourselves. Firstly, it brings about 'horizontal' integration, as our scattered selves are gradually drawn together through our focus on the object of concentration. Then, on the basis of that horizontal integration, we can engage in meditation practices in the course of which we reflect on and progressively experience higher truth, in a process of 'vertical' integration. Devotional practices and Dharma studies also help us to move towards this kind of vertical integration.

But even once we have understood the need to develop awareness in all senses, and have perhaps made a start with trying to developing it through such methods, it is still not certain that we will develop it in the right way. There is a danger that we will develop instead what I think of as alienated awareness. In an age of transition, when there are no stable, universally accepted values upon which we can base our lives, many people lose any very solid sense of identity. Also, many people are conditioned to clamp down on their bodily sensations, especially those connected with sex, and to repress negative emotion, to feel what they are told they ought to feel rather than what they truly feel. So, for a variety of reasons, many of us find ourselves unable, or unwilling, to experience ourselves, especially our feelings and emotions. As a result, when we try to develop awareness, we may become aware of ourselves without actually experiencing ourselves. In a sense, we are aware of a non-experience of ourselves, of ourselves not being there.

This failure to experience ourselves is disastrous because it tends to create a split between the conscious and the unconscious, between that part of ourselves which we allow ourselves to experience continuously, and that part which we have made an unconscious decision not to experience and which we therefore experience only intermittently and partially, if at all.

But refusing to experience a certain part of oneself does not mean that the part in question has ceased to exist. Unacknowledged it may be, but it is still very much alive; and not only alive, but kicking. In one way or another, it will make its presence felt, typically in the guise of moods. Suddenly we feel depressed, or angry, or anxious; the mood seems to take possession of us, and we don't really know why. We sometimes even say, 'I didn't feel quite myself yesterday,' or, 'I don't know what's come over me today,' – almost as if we feel we are someone else for as long as that mood persists.

Unfortunately, the painful state of alienated awareness has in the past been aggravated by certain Eastern spiritual teachers who have made all sorts of statements that fail to take account of the differences between the modern Western mentality and the traditional Eastern way of seeing things. Buddhist teachers, for example, and many of their Western disciples, have been known to assert, on the authority of the Buddha's teaching of *anattā*, that we have no self, or that the self is an illusion. Hindu teachers, meanwhile, will tell you that you are not the body, you are not the mind, you are not your feelings or emotions or thoughts; you are, in fact, God.

True awareness, integrated awareness, is developed by learning to experience yourself more fully, to be more aware of what you experience in your physical body, and in your feelings and emotions, particularly those feelings that you like to think you don't experience. One of the basic but very important functions of the sangha is to provide a safe environment in which we may disclose ourselves to others and – in having our experience acknowledged by others – gradually learn to acknowledge more of it ourselves.

Another way the sangha plays a big part in all this is to help us to become aware of what is going on. It is obviously very difficult for us to tell whether there are aspects of our experience that we are not allowing ourselves to be aware of, as the problem is lack of awareness itself. But our spiritual friends may well be able to see what is going on better than we can ourselves, and will find ways – kind and sympathetic ways – to draw it to our attention. And, of course, we will be able to do the same for them.

In discussing all this, certain questions inevitably arise. If awareness is about experiencing oneself, what is to be understood by the term 'oneself'? Is the self identical with consciousness? What is the relation between the self and individuality? Are they two things or one and the same? Then again, what is personality – and where does the ego come in? A great deal has been said on all these subjects in the spiritual traditions of the world, and in the contexts of philosophy, both ancient and modern, and modern psychology. They are variants, in a sense, of that most basic question, 'Who am I?'

I do not propose to enter into a discussion in this context of the nature of the self, interesting and important though the subject certainly is. Here, I just want to make a simple point about terminology. All these terms – self, individual, personality, ego – tend to be used rather freely, but it actually matters a great deal what they mean. Questions such as 'What is the self?' are not just matters of semantics, not just quibbling over words. Or rather, they are indeed semantic questions, but semantics happen to be of the greatest practical importance, even in the spiritual life.

No less a figure than Confucius attests to the value of semantics. In the China of his day (more or less the time of the Buddha) there were hundreds, even thousands, of small states, each administered by a prince or duke, and some of course were better run than others, giving rise to a certain amount of speculation and consulting of sages on the part of the more philosophical rulers as to how best to reform one's state. Confucius was once asked, 'If you want to create the ideal state, what is the first thing you need to attend to?' (Of course, Western sages like Plato and Thomas More have applied themselves to this same question.) One can easily imagine the kind of issues most people would start thinking about: defence, revenue, agriculture, education, law – even, at a stretch, religion or culture. But Confucius replied, 'The rectification of terms.'[53] This must come first. You have to start by being precise about what you are saying, by defining your terms; if you do this, orders will be unambiguous, and actions decisive.

This advice is relevant not only to the reformation of the state, but also if we want to reform ourselves. And Confucius' advice is particularly pertinent to us in the West today. We have so much advice to choose from. There are so many spiritual teachers, and they all use the same sort of language – but they use it to give quite contrary guidance. One of them may tell you just to ask yourself, 'Who am I?' Nothing more than that. When you are speaking, ask yourself 'Who is speaking?' When you are listening, ask 'Who is listening?' When you are thinking, ask 'Who is thinking?' When you are experiencing anything, don't bother about the object, concern yourself only with the subject; ask yourself 'Who is experiencing this?' The idea is that you just keep turning these questions over and over in your mind.

But another, equally authoritative teacher may say, 'No, give up all thought of the self. It's pure illusion. It's when we ask ourselves "Who am I?" that all the trouble starts.' Then again, another authority will say 'Realize the great self, see that your true self is God, that you are this great self which is God.' And someone else will insist that you have to come down to earth and get on with your life, be yourself, cultivate your own personality, do your own thing, develop yourself from the roots up. But then someone else will say, 'No, you must tear up the ego by the roots, blow it up with dynamite if necessary.' One well-known British Buddhist once said in a lecture that you have to hack off great bleeding lumps of self to lighten your load for the spiritual ascent.

In this way we can become confused about what is a quite fundamental issue. We don't know who to believe, so we don't know what to do about the most central and at the same time most inchoate aspect of our experience. When we try to get to grips with it, we discover that we are just dimly aware that there is something around, and we call it 'I', we call it 'me'. We are pretty clear – at least most of the time – that there is something there, call it what you like; and it seems that this something we call 'I' or 'me' is the same something to which such terms as ego, self, and so on refer. But what is this something that all our experience dances around? And what should we do about it? We may find that there seems to be no clear consensus about this. But the experience of 'me', of 'I', is undoubtedly there, even if it ought not to be. Even if we tell ourselves that we only *think* it is there, that it doesn't really exist, still, the thought is there, deluded though it may be. If we want to get seriously confused we may even fall into thinking that we only think that we think it is there (i.e. that our thoughts are simply chasing their own tails).

Still the practical question remains: what do we do about the something we call 'I' (or about the thought of 'I', for it comes to the same thing either way)? Should we cultivate it, refine it, idealize it, or reject it? And if we are going to reject it, should we eradicate it, or ignore it, or undermine it? Or should we just look at it gently and steadily until we see that it isn't really there at all? Unless we settle this issue, our spiritual life is more or less at a standstill.

I venture to propose that Confucius' political solution – the rectification of terms – can be applied to clear this spiritual impasse. Terms such as self, person, individual, and ego all have somewhat ambivalent meanings. Each of them is either to be cultivated or eradicated, depending on the sense in which the word is used. Indeed, we can draw out these ambivalent meanings into separate terms, so that we can identify more clearly what is to be cultivated and what eradicated. Thus, we get true individuality and false individuality; the higher self and the lower self; the person and the personality; being ego-directed and being ego-centred.

But what is the basis of the distinction between the positive and negative interpretations of these terms? If we go back to the question of alienated awareness, we shall see that it arises due to one's failure to experience oneself, especially one's feelings and emotions, and perhaps most especially one's negative feelings and negative emotions.

Pragmatically speaking, we don't have to concern ourselves with the reality or otherwise of the self or the individual in any metaphysical sense. We are self-aware and there is no doubt that this is our experience. The task ahead is to clarify and intensify that experience of self-awareness, to cultivate the higher self, true individuality, and ego-directedness, and become an integrated person.

This, then, is the basis for the distinction between the negative and the positive usages of the terms self, individuality, person, and ego. It is to do with the degree of integration or unification they refer to. True individuality is integrated; false individuality is not. One is to be developed, the other got rid of. The same applies to higher self and lower self, person and personality, and ego-directedness and ego-centredness. The first of each of these terms refers to the experience we try to cultivate through spiritual practice: an integrated experience of 'I' or 'me'. Jung gives a good sense of this in the following definition of the self (as summarized by one of his disciples): 'The self by definition comprises the full scope of a personality from its most individual traits to its most generic attitudes and experiences, actual as well as potential. Hence it transcends the existing personality. The archetype of wholeness or of the self can therefore be regarded as the dominant of psychic growth.'[54] We achieve this experience by recovering and acknowledging whatever aspects of ourselves we may have tried to disown, and allowing ourselves to experience them again.

This is what it takes to become a true individual. But, one might ask, is becoming an individual such a good thing? How does this idea of the development of individuality fit in with the Buddha's famous *anattā* ('no self') doctrine,[55] or indeed with the general idea that a truly spiritual life entails becoming in some sense 'selfless'?

The Buddha's teaching of *anattā* is the apparently categorical denial that anything like a self exists. When I was studying Pāli, Abhidhamma, and Buddhist logic in Benares, my teacher used to be fond of pointing out that the word *anattā* (*anātman* in Sanskrit) is a compound expression, made up of the word *attā* (*ātman*) usually translated as 'self', prefixed by *an*, meaning 'no' or 'not'. He would go on to say that if one wanted to understand the meaning of the whole expression, one could do so only after having understood the meaning of *attā*. You can't realize the truth of non-self unless you first have some idea of what is being referred to by 'self'. This might seem obvious, but it apparently wasn't obvious to everybody. Some Theravādin monks were outraged at his point of view, which seemed to them utterly heretical.

But he was quite right. You cannot understand what is meant by non-self unless you know what particular conception of the self is being negated by that prefix. It is clear from the various contexts in which the word *anattā* occurs in the Buddhist scriptures that the Buddha was concerned to negate the brahminical idea (which was current at the time) of a permanent unchanging self. He did not teach that our experience of ourselves is a complete and utter delusion and that we are not in reality here at all. He taught that the empirical self, the psyche, is not a fixed entity, that it is constantly changing, and that it is because it is changing that it can evolve. All that we know and experience and name as the self is in a state of constant flux – this is what is meant by *anattā*. Thus the purpose of the teaching of *anattā* is entirely practical. It should be taken not as a metaphysical statement, but as a means of keeping the path to Enlightenment clear. Only if we understand, not just intellectually but deep in our hearts, that there is nothing fixed at the heart of our experience, can we evolve.

11

OVERCOMING THE SELF

MY PRINCIPAL AIM in bringing forward my own favourite modern Western philosopher in this context is to introduce a concept from his thinking that elucidates the defining characteristic of the Buddhist path. It seems to me, speaking from a Buddhist perspective, that Nietzsche's work constitutes the most important of all the lines of thought that the modern West has produced. I therefore propose to give a brief outline of the life and work of Nietzsche and then compare his central concept of the superman or overman – and allied ideas, especially that of a continuing process of evolution within the individual – with Buddhism as the embodiment or exemplification of that continuing evolutionary process.

I became acquainted with Nietzsche's writings at the age of about eighteen, during my early army days, when I was still in England. One glorious summer's day, taking advantage of a day off, I went to Box Hill, a famous beauty spot in Surrey, and lay on the grass in the brilliant sunshine, reading *Thus Spoke Zarathustra*. The combination of profound thought and beautiful poetry in this, Nietzsche's most famous and popular work, made such a tremendous impression that as I looked up it seemed almost as though its words were written across the blue sky in scarlet letters. I have had something of a taste for

Nietzsche ever since that day, and have continued to return to him every now and then.

Nietzsche was born in Germany in 1844, the son of a Lutheran pastor. (It was in fact Nietzsche who said that the Lutheran pastor was the father of German philosophy.) His father died in 1849, and Nietzsche spent the rest of his childhood surrounded by women – his mother, his sister, his grandmother, and two maiden aunts – until he was sent to boarding school. He went on to the universities of Bonn and Leipzig where he studied classical philology, and he was appointed to the Chair of Philology at Basle at the age of 24, before he had even graduated, on the recommendation of the eminent scholar and philologist Ritschl, who had been deeply impressed by Nietzsche's work as an undergraduate. At Basle Nietzsche took a particular interest in the philosophy of Schopenhauer and the music of Wagner, and in 1872 he published his first book, *The Birth of Tragedy*. Other works followed, but in 1879, when he was still only 35, he resigned his university post, terminating his academic career, and thereafter spent most of his active life in Switzerland and Italy.

It was a life of intense loneliness; indeed, no one who reads about the details of his isolated and pain-filled life can fail to be touched. He was almost completely on his own, understood by no one apart from one or two friends with whom he corresponded. He was also physically unwell, and sometimes in quite unbearable pain. He continued to write until 1888, and between 1883 and 1885 he produced *Thus Spoke Zarathustra*. But his work received hardly any recognition. When the fourth part of *Zarathustra* came out, only a few dozen copies were sold. Finally, in 1889, Nietzsche became insane and he died, still insane, in 1900, at the age of 55.

As far as Nietzsche's thinking is concerned, the term philosophy is a misnomer. Nietzsche fired off a number of illuminating ideas which certainly hang together – or at least the leading ideas among them do. However, he did not aim to come up with a logically consistent interpretation of all existence, or the whole of experience. His great predecessors – Kant, Hegel, Fichte, Schelling, Schopenhauer – had all attempted to build up a systematic philosophy, but Nietzsche was not a system builder. He did not aspire to erect a lone and gigantic edifice of thought within which everything could be accommodated. Indeed, he insisted on the iconoclastic paradox that 'the will to system is a will to lack of integrity'.[56]

Therefore, with the exception of *Thus Spoke Zarathustra*, all Nietzsche's later writings are simply strings of aphorisms. He is, one might say, the master of the aphorism. No one else seems to have been able to say so much in so few words. His only possible rival, as far as I can see, is William Blake, with 'The Proverbs of Hell' from *The Marriage of Heaven and Hell*, and here Blake is perhaps even more pithy than Nietzsche himself. But that was Blake's sole attempt at that particular form. He wrote 'The Proverbs of Hell' when he was quite young, and as he got older he became rather more prolix. Nietzsche, on the other hand, became increasingly aphoristic and brilliant, devastating and iconoclastic, as he got older, and his pronouncements became more and more like thunder-claps or hammer blows.

Nietzsche's aphoristic and unsystematic approach is not accidental. He is aphoristic because he chooses to be. Indeed, it is of the essence of his method. Some of his aphorisms have something of the spirit of the sayings of the Zen masters of China and Japan. Each of them penetrates deeply into the reality of existence from a particular point of view, and each stands on its own merits. The truth of one aphorism is not dependent on the truth of another; they are not logically connected in that way.

Coleridge once said of the great actor Charles Kean, 'To see him act is like reading Shakespeare by flashes of lightning.' Similarly, reading Nietzsche is like trying to make out a landscape – the landscape of human existence, if you like – by the fitful but brilliant illumination of flashes of lightning. For an instant, just in a few words, it is as though everything is flooded with light, and we see everything clearly from that particular angle. And then, absolute darkness. Then we read another aphorism, and another flash from another direction lights up another quarter of the sky, so that again everything is revealed, before the darkness descends once more.

Lightning-flashes seem to show us different landscapes. At some level we know that they are all the same landscape, but it is difficult to piece together the glimpses the lightning reveals into one coherent, all-embracing visual composition. The same goes for the writings of Nietzsche: they are inspiring reading, but very difficult indeed to expound systematically.

What this does mean, however, is that we can consider Nietzsche's aphorisms singly, without necessarily relating them to the rest of his work, and this is how I propose to proceed here. The aphorisms I shall be looking at in this chapter are those concerning his idea of the 'superman', 'self-overcoming', and the 'Will to Power'.

I have put the word 'superman' in quotation marks for two reasons; firstly, to indicate that it is not a literal translation of Nietzsche's original German term; and secondly, as a warning not to attach to Nietzsche's concept certain dubious connotations which have gathered around it ever since the Nazis made use of it for their own purposes (and of course to distinguish it from the comic-book hero of that name).

The term used by Nietzsche is *Übermensch*, which literally means not superman but overman; or even over-and-above-man. The Übermensch is the man who stands over and above – who transcends – human beings as they exist at present. One could even speak of the overman as 'transcendent man'. In other words, the Nietzschean superman is not just present-day humanity writ large, present-day humanity in a superlative degree, but a completely different type of humanity.

We will be stuck with the word superman as a popular rendition of Nietzsche's Übermensch for as long as George Bernard Shaw's play *Man and Superman* continues to be the English-speaking world's most prominent cultural expression of the Nietzschean concept. The chances of Shaw's work being supplanted in this respect were more or less nullified by the regrettable fact that after his death Nietzsche's whole way of thinking was hopelessly corrupted and debased in the popular understanding. It was debased, first of all, at the hands of his sister, and after that at the hands of those who tried to associate Nietzschean ideas with Nazi ideology. It is only in comparatively recent years that Nietzsche's thinking has been rescued from the most gross of these misinterpretations, and at last interpreted more accurately, notably by Walter Kaufmann.[57]

To begin to get a true flavour of Nietzsche we need to look at how he goes about presenting his material, which, as the title *Thus Spoke Zarathustra* intimates, is quite individual. Nietzsche's Zarathustra has very little to do with the Zarathustra – or as he is often known, Zoroaster – who is the historical founder of the ancient Zoroastrian faith. Nietzsche's Zarathustra is fictional; he is simply the mouthpiece for Nietzsche's own ideas. However, what the two Zarathustras do have in common is that they have a message for mankind.

The opening section of the work, entitled 'Zarathustra's Prologue', represents him as coming down from the mountain; this is of course symbolical and meant to be so. Zarathustra has been on the mountain for ten years, thinking and meditating, and now his wisdom has ripened and he wants to share it with mankind. On the way down he is recognized by a saintly hermit who has been living in the forest at the foot of the mountain for a long time, and who remembers seeing him years earlier on his way up. The hermit tries to persuade Zarathustra not to leave the mountain: 'People are so ungrateful, and distracted. Don't waste your time going down among them; better to be a hermit, to live in the forest with the birds and the beasts, to forget the world of men and simply worship God.' But Zarathustra leaves the hermit at his prayers in the forest, and as he goes on his way he says to himself, 'Could it be possible that this old saint in the forest has not yet heard anything of this, that God is dead?'[58]

The thunderous observation that God is dead constitutes one of Nietzsche's most important insights, and it has echoed down the twentieth century, giving rise to a whole 'death of God' theological movement. Nietzsche was the first to see that God was no longer up there in the heavens. In fact he saw clearly something that many people have since come to see as well, although others would still declare that he was entirely wrong. He saw that orthodox Christian teaching, with its belief in a personal God, a Supreme Being, a Creator, and its doctrines of sin and faith, justification and atonement, and resurrection, was dead, finished, irrelevant. His declaration heralded the beginning of what some people would identify as a post-Christian age. And if God is dead, then the Christian conception of man is dead as well. The conception of man as a fallen being – a being who, having been disobedient and sinful, needs grace to redeem him, a being who will be judged and perhaps punished – is no longer relevant. All the old dogmas are exploded.

So we need a new conception of who and what we are as human beings. We find ourselves in a universe without God – we are on our own – and therefore have to try to understand ourselves afresh. We can't accept ready-made answers any more. We find ourselves here and now, in the midst of the starry universe, standing on the earth, surrounded by other living beings like ourselves, with a history behind us, and perhaps a future before us, and we each have to ask ourselves – not anybody else because there's nobody else to tell us – the crucial question, 'Who am I? What am I?'

Now that the old definitions are gone, we have to define ourselves anew, discover ourselves, know ourselves. This, anyway, is what

Zarathustra has done on the mountain. He has thought, meditated, and contemplated for ten long years, and now he knows what man is, and he is bringing the message of what he has learned to humanity. So Zarathustra comes to a town on the edge of the forest, he enters the town, and there in the market square he finds people gathered together. They haven't assembled to listen to him – they didn't even know he was coming. They have come to see a travelling tightrope-walker. But as this entertainer hasn't turned up yet, Zarathustra seizes the opportunity and speaks to them.

His initial statement, addressing the people in that market square, and through them all humanity, is this: 'I teach you the overman. Man is something that shall be overcome.' Then he asks, 'What have you done to overcome him?' – by which he means 'What have you done to overcome yourself?' Through the words of Zarathustra in this prologue, Nietzsche points out that evolution never stops. In the course of evolution every kind of being has created something beyond itself, given birth to something higher than itself in the evolutionary scale – and there is no reason to suppose that this process will stop with human beings. Nietzsche's view of evolution is rather primitive here, but it does not have to be taken literally for his conclusion to strike home.

As the ape created human beings, so, in a more daring and glorious leap, we ourselves must now create a new kind of being. We do this by overcoming ourselves, and we begin to do that, Nietzsche goes on to say, by learning to despise ourselves, to be dissatisfied and discontented with ourselves. Only when we begin to look down on ourselves can we begin to rise above ourselves and be higher and greater and nobler than we were.

It should be emphasized again that Nietzsche's overman is not the product of evolution on anything resembling Darwinian lines. For Nietzsche the overman is not produced automatically, as a result of the general blind functioning of the evolutionary process. Nietzsche distinguishes sharply between what he calls the Last Man and the overman himself. The Last Man is simply the latest human product of the general, collective evolutionary process, not a higher type. The overman, by contrast, will be the product of the individual man or woman's effort to rise, even to soar, above himself or herself. It is on account of his distinction between the Last Man and the overman that Nietzsche is able to dissociate himself from superficial nineteenth-century ideas of human progress as an ongoing collective social development. As far as Nietzsche is concerned, we have to do something about it ourselves, by our own individual choice.

Nietzsche is not always explicit on this point, but he seems to be saying that whereas Darwinian evolution is collective, this higher evolution, as I call it, is individual. He has a dramatic vision of humanity as a rope or bridge stretched over an abyss between the beast on the one hand and the overman on the other.[59] In other words, he is saying that there is an element of risk attached to being truly human. We represent something transitional, rather than a fixed end point. We must therefore live with insecurity, even live dangerously. We must not hanker after cosy comfort. We must live for something other than ourselves, if we are to be truly ourselves. This something other, for the sake of which each and every individual should and must live, is the overman.

For Nietzsche the turning point, the great watershed of the evolutionary process, comes not between animal and man, but between man who is still an animal and man who is truly human. The distinction is a sharp one; in fact, Nietzsche's views on what constitutes humanity are rather too radical and demanding for a Buddhist to be able to subscribe to them. He says, in fact, that the majority of human beings are not human at all, but animals.

From a Buddhist point of view, the human realm includes a wide range of development in terms of self-consciousness, or awareness. Most human beings regularly veer between their animal nature and states of mind characterized by human sympathies, and even occasionally the finer, more integrated states of mind that are traditionally associated with the realms of the gods. Nietzsche's definition of humanity is a lot narrower, and not very flattering to the average person, obviously. People don't like to hear that they fall short of true humanity.

It is therefore not surprising that when Zarathustra speaks to the people in the market place about the 'overman' they just laugh at him, and take more interest in the tightrope-walker. For Nietzsche the category of the truly human, the human realm proper, includes only philosophers, artists, and saints. And the overman, apparently, is superior even to them. Kaufmann, expounding Nietzsche, says of him, 'He maintains in effect that the gulf separating Plato from the average man is greater than the cleft between the average man and a chimpanzee.'[60]

In fact, Nietzsche distinguishes three categories. The first consists of the animal realm, including the majority of human beings – honorary human beings, we may say. The second consists of the human realm proper. And the third is the category of the overman. Nietzsche also speaks of what he calls 'prefatory men', who seem to be intermediate between the human realm and that of the overman; that is, they are those who are bent on seeking in all things for that aspect of themselves which must be overcome. However, he is not very clear about how they might differ from the already narrow category of the truly human. If the overman is Nietzsche's ideal, the truly human seem to be those who aspire to it, and are engaged in the process of self-overcoming – i.e. artists, philosophers, and saints.

One does this, one overcomes oneself, by 'giving style to one's character'.[61] By this, Nietzsche means not accepting oneself ready-made. He complains that most people's characters have no particular style, almost as if they were somehow factory-made, or even no more than the raw materials out of which a real individual style might be formed. But the attitude he is advocating is one of treating one's life and character as so much raw material, and making something of it.

Usually we think of our character, our temperament, our personal characteristics or qualities, as a set of givens. We imagine that we are stuck with who we are for the rest of our lives. If we have a tendency to get angry quickly, that is how we are, we're stuck with it. If we are sensitive or shy, again, that is how it is with us – it's no different in principle, we think, from being tall or short. But according to Nietzsche, we may have come off a long production line, consisting of our genetic inheritance and parental influence, our general social and educational conditioning, but we still have a long way to go. We are not the finished product. In fact, this is merely what we begin with.

Nietzsche says in effect that we should work upon ourselves, create ourselves out of whatever condition we find ourselves in, just as a potter makes something beautiful out of a lump of clay. Just as it is possible to take a heavy, sticky mass, get your fingers into it, and start shaping it into something, in the same way you can shape yourself. If you start by being honest with yourself and admitting that you are more or less unformed as a human being, you can start to form this untidy, shapeless, dough-like stuff into something better.

As an example of someone who gave style to their character, Nietzsche cites Goethe. Goethe, who lived from 1749 to 1832, was the greatest of German poets, a notable dramatist and novelist, as well as a thinker, scientist, and mystic, but Nietzsche admired him most of all for this particular quality – that all the time he was trying to make something of himself. He was – as we have already observed – an individual. It is evident from biographies, and from the records of his conversations, that throughout his long life, more than eighty years, he was always working upon himself, just as one might work upon a poem, a novel, or a scientific treatise. This was evident also to his contemporaries. When Napoleon saw Goethe for the first time, he exclaimed, quite spontaneously, 'Look, there is a man!' Considering that Napoleon had conquered Europe, while Goethe's political status was negligible (he was merely an ex-minister of a small German state), this suggests that Goethe succeeded in the central aim of his life. From the unpromising bundle of rakish passions and wild ideas that was his youthful self, Goethe created a man in the fullest and truest sense, as Napoleon observed him to be.

We have seen that Nietzsche arrived at the concept of the overman by a consideration of the general nature of the evolutionary process. According to the way he understood the nature of existence, life – not just human life, but all life – is that which must always overcome itself. It is never satisfied with itself. It must continually, at every stage, go beyond itself. Life, we may say, is a self-transcending process.

This innate urge is what Nietzsche calls the Will to Power.[62] This term, which Nietzsche introduced comparatively late in his writings, like 'superman' has been much misunderstood and lamentably misinterpreted as having dubious political or even military resonances. But by Power – with a capital P – Nietzsche does not mean anything material at all. Certainly he means nothing to do with politics. The Will to Power is the will to a more abundant, noble, and sublime mode of being, a qualitatively, dimensionally different life. Especially, it is the will to the realization of the overman.

Nietzsche emphasizes that this higher degree of being is attainable only to the extent that the lower degree of being is left behind, negated, even destroyed. This brings us to a vital aspect of the Will to Power, and Nietzsche's approach generally, which is that it involves an uncompromising iconoclasm. Nietzsche looked at commonly accepted values, generally held ideas of good and evil, and he called quite categorically and peremptorily for them to be thrown away as so much rubbish. Otherwise, he said, the overman cannot be brought into existence.

Nietzsche is therefore utterly ruthless and uncompromising in his condemnation of the average man and his subhuman requirements. We are accustomed to thinking of the Hebrew prophets – Amos, Jeremiah, and the Second Isaiah, for example – as terrible enough in their fulminations against the vanity of men, but they are mildness itself compared with Nietzsche. He is for shattering – as he puts it – all the old tablets of the law. He has no time whatever for the whole of modern civilization and culture. Nietzsche is almost certainly the most devastating – in the full, literal sense of that term – critic of itself that the human race has ever produced. He is wholesale and unmitigated in his denunciation of human beings as we know them, and all their works, and all their ways. He says simply that they must all go – not just out of personal negativity, but simply because they get in the way. They must be transcended; they must make way for the overman.

It is crucial to Nietzsche's iconoclasm that in negating existing values and modes of thought, there is no question of negating something external to oneself. It is a question of negating not other people's values but one's own. It is oneself that one must overcome. It is with oneself that one must ruthlessly engage in battle. Nietzsche's fondness for the terminology of warfare is another source of misunderstanding, but the enemy is always oneself.

From the *Dhammapada* we have the Buddha's own exhortation to join this uncompromising struggle: 'Though one should conquer a thousand men in battle a thousand times, yet he who conquers himself has the more glorious victory.'[63] But how much further can we press a resemblance or even a comparison between the teaching of Nietzsche and that of the Buddha? Nietzsche did know something of Buddhism, but in his day very few Buddhist texts had been translated, and he did not know enough to be in a position to arrive at a balanced judgement about it. He had little conception, for example, of the positive content of the ideal of Buddhahood, and there is little such positive content in his conception of the overman. This is hardly surprising, in view of the fact that Nietzsche's overman is the product of thought. It is the product of a brilliant intellect, penetrating to the point of intuitive genius, but it is still an intellectual intuition, not the product of transcendental realization. Hence the conception of the overman by no means equals that of the Buddha – of Enlightened humanity.

However, the conception of the overman certainly points in the same general direction, and Nietzsche's rope stretched over the abyss between the beast and the overman therefore corresponds in a general way to the Buddhist path, because this path is ourselves. We are not static entities, but evolving, developing beings. According to Buddhism as well as Nietzsche, we follow this path by continually overcoming ourselves and rising to successively higher levels.

If we want to be bold, we can even say that the Will to Power corresponds in a general way to the Will to Enlightenment. Both are active. Both are powerful volitions. Both are concerned not just with thinking about the highest realizable ideal, but with actually attaining it. One is the ideal of the overman, while the other of course is the ideal of Buddhahood, Supreme Enlightenment for the sake of all living beings. And the achievement of both ideals requires the overcoming of our lesser identities, our lower selves, our smaller values, baser ideas of every kind.

With this clear similarity established, we can make out two equally clear differences. The Will to Enlightenment, the *bodhicitta*, is more altruistic, more other-regarding, more cosmic.[64] It is the manifestation in the individual of a universal, cosmic principle. Of course, the figure of Zarathustra, who is meant to exemplify the overman, does want – presumably as an essential aspect of his attainment – to share his wisdom with mankind. But the Will to Power is essentially more individualistic than the Will to Enlightenment.

The second difference between the Buddha's teaching and Nietzsche's thinking is to do with method. Nietzsche brings out the necessity for discontent with ourselves, and for overcoming ourselves so that the overman may be created, with blinding clarity, more so than any other Western philosopher or thinker. But he fails miserably – though nobly – to show us how to do it. He says, 'Overcome yourself,' but he doesn't say anything about how to go about it. There are no practical instructions – we are left with the empty exhortation. Buddhism, on the other hand, as an ancient spiritual tradition, has many methods, exercises, and practices for self-overcoming.

This makes a big difference. It is not so difficult to see that someone is ill, but only a skilled physician can prescribe the method of treatment they need to get well. Nietzsche certainly paints a grim and vivid picture of the disease of modern humanity, the disease which, in a sense, *is* humanity, and he also gives us an acute diagnosis. He then goes on to paint a glowing and inspiring picture of the patient restored to perfect health. But nothing is offered to link these two compelling pictures together. Nietzsche is not alone in this; almost the whole of modern Western philosophy suffers from the same missing link. It is rich in abstract thought, and some of this thinking, like Nietzsche's, pulses with intellectual energy, but it generally lacks any practical content.

Fortunately, in Buddhism we find not only the abstract ideal but also practical means for its realization; a way of life is prescribed. Nonetheless, Buddhists can learn a great deal from Nietzsche's uncompromising vision of human potential, rightly understood. Nietzsche's powerful vision allied with Buddhism's clear path of practice and supportive conditions (the sangha) together give us the possibility of the complete transformation of humanity that Nietzsche so desired. This is just one of the ways in which co-operation between Western philosophy and Eastern spiritual traditions can bear precious fruit.

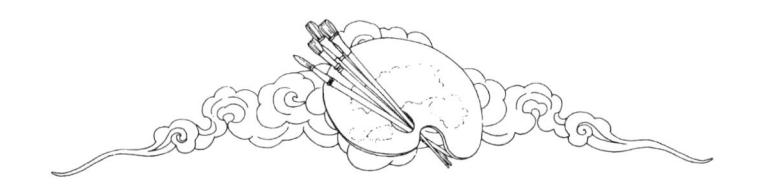

12

THE ARTIST AS THE TRUE INDIVIDUAL

IN THE LAST few chapters we have begun to build up a picture of the true individual. We have seen the emergence of the individual in the context of evolutionary growth and change. We have also noted two contrasting, even apparently contradictory, stages in the growth of the individual: first, the necessity to acknowledge and integrate all aspects of oneself, including those one would rather *not* acknowledge; and then, on the basis of that integration, the need to set about going beyond oneself – 'self-overcoming', as Nietzsche put it. Moreover, we have seen that Buddhism can be considered as the path of the higher evolution, and as offering specific methods and practices whereby the individual can form himself or herself.

It may seem strange to be placing so much emphasis on the qualities of the individual in a book about spiritual community, but, as we have seen, in its essence the sangha is not about organizations or ecclesiastical status, but purely and simply about communication between individuals. It is thus of the greatest importance that we understand the nature of individuality.

In the final part of the book, we will broaden our field of enquiry to explore the kinds of relationships that are part and parcel of the life of any individual Buddhist – a consideration of sangha in the broadest sense. But before we do so, I want to introduce one last aspect of individuality. We have seen that the true individual is characterized by self-consciousness or awareness, positive and refined emotions, independence of mind and freedom from group conditioning, creativity and free-flowing energy, aloneness and frequent unpopularity. It strikes me that these characteristics can be said to be shared by a kind of person who is perhaps not generally associated with spiritual matters: the artist.

As we have seen, it was the artist (together with the philosopher and the saint) whom Nietzsche identified as being capable of self-overcoming. But why? What is the connection between art and spiritual growth? (The term art should be taken in this context to cover all the fine arts – painting, sculpture, poetry, music, architecture, and so on.) I want to suggest that, as well as being related to the spiritual life through the production of works of art with sacred significance, the artist represents a particular aspect or manifestation of the higher evolution itself. This is not of course to say that one cannot participate in the higher evolution of humanity without being an artist. But one cannot be an authentic artist of any kind without at the same time participating in the higher evolution, in the spiritual life.

This may seem like a glorification of the artist which is quite hard to swallow. Many people don't see that art and artists are of much value in comparison with what they recognize as important or serious activities. The arts are sometimes seen as glamorous but trivial activities – 'not a real man's work' – or as the arcane luxury of a privileged élite, and of little relevance to the rest of us. It has to be said that a consideration of the lives of various artistic coteries, past and present, does seem to bear this view out. For example, there was the multi-talented Sitwell family, who seem to have formed a literary set all by themselves, and are captured in the many-volumed autobiography for which Osbert Sitwell is chiefly known. His upbringing among a brilliant and eccentric family in a vast and rambling old mansion provided him with some good stories to tell, and he tells them very well. But one of his little stories illustrates just how alienated the work of the artist had become from the values of most ordinary people.

It seems that Osbert lived in one wing of this mansion, while his sister Edith lived in another, with half a mile of corridors in between, regularly traversed by a small regiment of servants. One morning he rang the bell to call a maidservant and passed her a note to give to his sister 'if she isn't busy'. 'But,' he warned the maid, 'if she is doing something, don't disturb her; just bring the note back to me.' About fifteen minutes later, the maidservant returned without the note, and Osbert asked her, 'Was my sister unoccupied, then?' To which the maid replied, 'Yes indeed, sir, she wasn't doing anything at all; she was just writing.'

Despite the respect accorded to certain great works of art of the past, for most people creative work still does not count as 'doing anything at all', and the activity of the artist is therefore misunderstood. Certainly it is seldom understood that – as I believe – art is part of the spiritual life, and that the artist is, or at least can be, the true individual. But a little thought reveals that the great artist does indeed share the characteristics we have identified as being aspects of individuality.

First of all, the artist is more alive than other people. The evidence for this is in the artist's sensitivity in the best sense of the term. The painter, for example, is much more keenly aware of differences of shape, contour, and colour, than are other people. If you go for a country walk in the company of an artist, you will notice that they tend to see more than you do. They will call your attention to the outline of a tree against the sky, or the precise colours of a fallen leaf, or a withered flower, or the blue shadows cast by trees on the grass. The painter awakens the rest of us to our surroundings with a sharper awareness of what is going on in the outside world of shapes and forms and colours.

The musician has a correspondingly keen ear. He or she can detect distinctions of musical pitch and rhythm that hardly exist for the rest of us. For example, the subtleties of the tabla-playing in Indian music can be astonishingly difficult to follow, even for a trained ear. The drum can be played with such unbelievable delicacy and refinement that it sounds like whispering voices, moving occasionally into a sort of grumbling, interspersed with other, sharper voices. If one has the training and the sensitivity to hear it, one can get the definite impression that the drum is speaking, communicating, while someone without that degree of aural development will be unable to hear its language.

The poet, of course, is equally sensitive to the different tones and rhythms of words. We all use words all the time, but we tend to use them in a careless, coarse way, without being fully aware of their meanings and sensuous qualities, their textures. Edith Sitwell, for example, described the different values of words in a way that revealed her exceptional sensitivity to them. Some words, she said, were 'rough' or 'hairy' or 'heavy', while others are 'smooth' or 'light'; such awareness of the distinctive qualities of words goes well beyond the range of most of us.[65]

Not only are artists acutely aware of the external world of sensuous impressions; they are particularly aware of their own responses to all these things, their own mental and emotional states. It isn't just that they reflect upon these states more than other people do – they actually experience them much more intensely. Furthermore, the artist is usually more aware of other people. This is graphically displayed in the work of the great portrait painters, dramatists and novelists, in which people are truly alive. There is a kind of spiritual biography in a great portrait. For example, the famous portrait of Pope Innocent X by Velásquez is a detailed reading of a very wicked man. You feel you can see in that face – in his cold eyes, the texture of the skin, the shape of the mouth, and his grim, fixed expression – everything he had ever done. Such a face can belong only to someone who has got where he is by corruption; and yet you can see, too, that his path of advancement is built out of a wealth of other human qualities and frailties. The painter has seen it all and put it down on the canvas.

In the plays of Shakespeare and the novels of George Eliot is to be found the same ability to see with such intensity as to be able to realize with absolute conviction the life of another human being. Turning briefly to an artist who comes somewhere in between being a painter and a novelist, I must confess that when I was much younger, I used to imagine that Hogarth's serial depictions of the London life of his time, like the *Rake's Progress* and *Marriage à la mode* were caricatures, that in his satires he was exaggerating for effect, laying it on a bit thick. But after I had seen a bit more of life and observed people a little more closely, I came to the conclusion that Hogarth was being deadly accurate, and that people really were like that. He saw people as they were, and as they were he depicted them in his paintings and engravings, with terrifying candour.[66]

The artist, therefore, is aware of the external world, of himself or herself, and of other people. And the artist is also aware of something beyond all these things. He or she is aware in some incomprehensible way of reality itself – not in the sense of considering the concept of reality with a capital R, but in the sense of being deeply and resonantly sensitive to the meaning and mystery of existence. The artist feels the presence of this mystery of existence, whether cosmic or human.

As a result of this heightened and cultivated sensitivity and awareness, the artist is distinguished by positive and refined emotions, particularly an ability to empathize with others, and to capture his or her own most fleeting and subtle mental impressions.

The true artist is also independent in spirit, and to a large extent free from group conditioning. Artists don't hesitate to go their own way, to be themselves. In fact, they have long been notorious for flouting convention, rocking the boat, refusing to conform, refusing to do what is expected, or what will cause least fuss. In taking this kind of attitude, they are not just being eccentric or perverse or difficult. They are simply trying to lead their own life and to be themselves.

Then, of course, the artist is creative. This goes without saying. Most importantly, the artist is creative of new values, such as did not exist or which were not experienced or perceived before. However, as well as this, artists are quite simply productive, and in the case of the very greatest artists, immensely productive. Their energies flow with extraordinary vitality. Quantity does tend to go with the very greatest quality (though not vice versa, of course). Shakespeare, Goethe, and Lope de Vega were all prolific writers, and the ancient Greek dramatists produced very many more plays than have survived intact. Bach, Handel, Haydn, Mozart, and Schubert all turned out a more or less unstoppable avalanche of music, while Titian, Rubens, and Rembrandt each left behind them a huge number of canvases.

Reading the life of any great artist, one is struck, sometimes with wonder, by the spectacle of this uninterrupted flow of creativity. You wonder how on earth they managed to fit all that work into what is in so many cases, like that of Mozart, a very short lifetime; or in other cases, like that of Bach, who fathered twenty children, a very busy lifetime; or in the case of a great many artists, altogether rather unfavourable domestic circumstances. Whatever way you look at it, such creativity implies a great deal of hard work. These artists did not twiddle their thumbs waiting for inspiration to strike. They just got on with it, morning, noon, and night. They were at their desks or easels at first light, and they would work all the hours that their affairs allowed them, every day, in some cases without a break for years on end, right into old age.

Finally, artists are essentially alone, isolated from the masses on account of their greater awareness, their greater individuality and even their greater creativity. Only too often the ordinary person cannot understand why the artist should take such pains with words, with sounds, with line and colour and form. Surely one word or shade of colour will do as well as another very similar word or shade – why take so much trouble over it? Does the precise detail of that musical progression really matter, in the larger scheme of things? If you put that comma in or take that full stop out, what difference does it really make? Isn't it all a bit petty and precious? But to the artist, these things are all of the first importance.

As a result of the almost total lack of sympathy and understanding ordinary people have for what he or she is doing, the artist is usually unpopular, and sometimes not recognized at all. In one way or another, the greatest artists are ahead of their time, even ahead of other comparatively ordinary artists. Sometimes it takes the rest of humanity centuries to catch up. Only too often we find that the artist is condemned in his or her own generation only to be praised in generations to come. It is as though the voice of the ordinary people will honour an artist only after he or she is dead, as though the only good artist is a dead artist. This is all so well known that it is not necessary to insist upon it. The artist will often feel even more alone than does the religious genius or mystic.

If we look at what makes a true individual we find that the true artist tends to have essentially the same characteristics. But what defines someone as an artist? The definition will of course depend on the nature of what he or she creates. So – to plunge straight into one of the most vexed and debated questions in the history of Western thought – what is art?

This question has also been discussed in the East, especially in India, but the debate there has followed such different lines that one cannot even begin to compare it with Western arguments on the subject. It is a question that used to occupy a good deal of my own time and energy in the days before I took on responsibilities that put a limit on the amount of reflection I could devote to such an issue. I found that there are numberless definitions of art, some of them quite extraordinary. The eminent art critic Herbert Read came up with 'Art is an attempt to create pleasing forms.' Even more succinct is Clive Bell's definition, very famous indeed in its day, and the subject of his best-known work: 'Art is significant form.' As for the great Italian critic and statesman, Benedetto Croce, his offering seems a little vague: 'Art is intuition.' Indeed, all the definitions I found seemed rather unsatisfactory – too broad, too narrow, or just incomplete. So eventually I decided to formulate my own.

I wrote my own short work on the subject, *The Religion of Art*, in the early 1950s, when I lived in Kalimpong, and in it I defined art as follows: 'Art is the organization of sense impressions that express the artist's sensibility and communicate to his audience a sense of values that can transform their lives.'[67] The reason I find this definition particularly satisfying is that it takes a definitely spiritual perspective on art. It is from this angle specifically that I want to examine it here in a little more detail.

The primary assertion – 'Art is the organization of sensuous impressions' – should be obvious enough, but it is still worth making. One book on poetry that I consulted began by saying that we must never forget that poetry consists of words (and if there are people who do forget this, no doubt this author is right to remind them). But let us go even further: if poetry consists of words, of what do words consist? What is the raw material of poetry? Words consist of sounds, vibrations in the air, sounds associated in varying degrees – and sometimes only marginally – with conceptual meaning. The raw material of painting is simply visual impressions: shape and colour, light and shade. Likewise, music is made of auditory impressions: sounds and rhythms, whether loud or soft, harmonious or discordant. Indeed, all the arts have sensuous impressions as their raw material, their basic stuff. This is where art begins, with the impressions pouring in upon us all the time through our five physical senses (to which the Buddhist tradition adds mental activity as a sixth).[68]

The artist organizes this chaos of impressions into a pattern, a shape, something whole, and in so doing creates a world, which is the work of art. There are various ways of organizing sensuous impressions, some very simple, others highly sophisticated. The key point is that the resulting work of art does not exist apart from the artist; it does not hang suspended in mid-air, so to speak. The artist's shaping of sensuous impressions expresses his or her sensibility. That is to say, works of art express or embody the awareness of artists, their experience of life as a whole, their experience of themselves, of other people, and even of reality.

The sensibility expressed in the work of art reflects the level of consciousness of the individual artist. Not all artists have access to particularly high levels of consciousness. But even simple folk art – making and building things oneself, broadly following traditional patterns – expresses the rudiments of an artistic sensibility in a way that mass-produced goods do not. And just a few artists may be said even to penetrate, at least occasionally, beyond the furthest reaches of ordinary human consciousness, into the experience of transcendental consciousness.

The true artist has access to higher levels of consciousness, awareness, and even understanding, than the ordinary person. He or she is further advanced in the evolutionary development of humanity, and this is one of the reasons why he or she is an artist. At this point, I expect some readers will be shaking their heads with bemusement at the bold claim that the true artist represents a higher type of humanity than the ordinary, decent citizen. They will say that my rosy-tinted idea of the artist is fiction, and that only too often the artist is wicked, depraved, and selfish. Perhaps we should look into this question a little.

Admittedly, painters, poets, and musicians can be rather difficult to live with. This, I think, is often due to the fact that artists are rightly concerned to safeguard their privacy and working conditions from intrusion. There will always be well-meaning people who will try to make artists conform, make them behave, dress, look, talk, and even write or paint like other people. It is only natural that in such circumstances artists will rebel – sometimes even violently – against the efforts of kindly folk who only want them to be happy and successful. Rather ungratefully, the artist will insist upon being himself.

Besides this, the artist is, more often than not, in revolt against conventional morality. This is especially conspicuous in the case of a poet like Shelley, who flouted the moral canons of his day, and was ostracized for so doing. The real question is not whether the artist is immoral, but whether flouting conventional morality is wrong. Only too often it is clear that conventional morality itself is at fault, and that the artist's rejection of it is simply an expression of his or her own healthier and more balanced mental attitude.

Not, of course, that the artist is always 'balanced'; far from it. We have seen that we all tend to be – at least until we have embarked on the process of integration – not a unified self, but a bundle of selves. This is all too true of the artist. Indeed, the artist is only too often a deeply divided person, and sometimes it seems that the greater the artist is, the more deeply divided he is within himself. This deep cleft in the depths of his own being can make him tense and unbalanced, bordering even on madness. The artist can be said to have access to deeper states of consciousness than almost anyone else, but this does not mean that he has access to them all the time. As Shelley says in his 'Song', 'Rarely, rarely, comest thou, Spirit of Delight.'

This spirit of delight – the experience of a higher mode of being and consciousness – does indeed visit the creative artist all too rarely. The artist does not enjoy such states continuously, and in this he differs from the true mystic, who tends to dwell in them much of the time. Slipping and veering between these higher states and more ordinary states of mind, it can seem as though the artist were two people. It is a sad but unfortunately common experience to read a wonderful book and then find that the author is nothing like as wonderful in person as his book led you to believe he would be. You finally get to meet him, and you approach him full of gratitude and admiration, with the sense that certain books give you that the author is practically a friend already, that they have already revealed their soul to you, but then you are confronted with some dry, withered, mean little man, and you are sorry that you ever set eyes upon him, you are so disappointed.

It is as though the artist has two separate identities – an artistic self and an ordinary self. Hence the idea of the artist's inspiration coming down to him from on high, that it is not his own work. The eighteenth-century composer Haydn apparently had precisely this experience. Listening to a performance of his oratorio *The Creation*, written in his old age, he cried out, 'Not I, but a Power from above created that!' Now that he was back in his ordinary state of consciousness, Haydn the ordinary person had to disclaim the achievement of Haydn the artist.

This is also one of the reasons why we traditionally refer to the artist – and anyone who depends on some kind of higher power – as a genius. The word genius originally meant one's guardian deity, which translated into Christian terms as one's guardian angel. A genius represented the higher powers overshadowing you and guiding you, directing your steps; to put it another way, it represented your own higher self, conceived of as an independent or quasi-independent personality that was your ordinary self's source of guidance and inspiration. The same idea lies behind the classical concept of the Muses. At the beginning of the *Iliad*, for example, Homer invokes the goddess to 'sing of the baneful wrath of Achilles'. The *Odyssey*, likewise, begins: 'Tell me, Muse, of the man of many wiles....' For any classical poet this was the conventional opening. Following in their footsteps, Milton does likewise at the beginning of *Paradise Lost*, except that he invokes what he calls the heavenly muse, which he distinguishes from the profane muse. But the idea is the same. You are invoking some higher power which seems to be outside you but which in truth is your own highest self, whence any true artistic creation proceeds.

Nowadays the word genius tends to be used very freely, with no awareness of its original significance, and is applied to any moderately gifted person. Asked whether he saw himself as a genius, the novelist Vladimir Nabokov replied:

> *The word 'genius' is passed around rather generously, isn't it? At least in English, because its Russian counterpart,* geniy, *is a term brimming with a sort of throaty awe and is used only in the case of a very small number of writers – Shakespeare, Milton, Pushkin, Tolstoy. To such deeply beloved authors as Turgenev and Chekhov, Russians assign the thinner term,* talant *– talent, not genius. It is a bizarre example of semantic discrepancy – the same word being more substantial in one language than in another. Although my Russian and my English are practically coeval, I still feel appalled and puzzled at seeing 'genius' applied to any important story-teller, such as Maupassant or Maugham. Genius still means to me, in my Russian fastidiousness and pride of phrase, a unique, dazzling gift – the genius of James Joyce, not the talent of Henry James.*[69]

Whether or not one agrees with his estimation of Henry James, the force of the distinction he is making between talent and genius is very much in line with the kind of revaluation of what art means and what it means to be an artist that I am attempting here, in my own definition of art.

We have seen that art is the organization of sensuous impressions that express the artist's sensibility (at whatever level of refinement that may be). The definition goes on: 'and communicate to his audience a sense of values that can transform their lives'. How does this happen? And what is meant by 'a sense of values that can transform our lives'?

If we agree that the artist experiences a higher level – that is, a more comprehensive, more powerful degree – of awareness than ordinary people, then the work of art expresses that degree of awareness – not only expresses it but communicates it, in the sense that when the communication succeeds, we experience for the time being, to a lesser degree, the state of consciousness in which the artist produced it. This is the communication of the artist. Temporarily at least, we are raised to his or her level; we become a true individual. Temporarily, we share his or her sense of values and insight, and this can transform our lives.

This is ultimately what the evolution of our humanity is about. Transformation *is* evolution. It is not an outward change but a change of level. Artists, therefore, are not only more highly evolved themselves but, through the art by which they communicate their experience of themselves, they contribute to the higher evolution of other people.

Enjoyment of great works of art broadens and deepens our own consciousness. When we listen to a great piece of music, see a great painting, read a great poem – when we really experience it, allow it to soak into us – we go beyond our ordinary consciousness. We become more generous in our sympathies; our whole life is subtly but deeply modified. If we persist in pursuing an interest in the arts, our whole mode of being may be affected, and our lives may even be transformed.

Today, traditional religion – in the form of Christianity, at least – has lost its unquestioned hold on the minds of people in the West. The astonishing architectural monuments to Christianity are still around us, but however glorious some of them may be, for most people they are empty shells. For the vast majority of people, orthodox religion is no longer a means of grace. We don't get anything from it. It means nothing to us. It no longer uplifts us, or moves us, or transforms us, much less still transfigures us. People aren't even against it any more.

As the title of my own book on art is meant to suggest, for many people the place and function of religion has been taken over by art. This is one of the reasons, I think, for the immense popularity today of all the fine arts – for despite all the grumbling one hears about the decay of culture, the fine arts are hugely popular as they have never been before. Formerly the enjoyment of works of art was the privilege of a few. Five hundred years ago in England, most of us would have been living in miserable hovels. We would never have seen any paintings except perhaps one or two in the local church, and we would have heard little music of any quality. As for reading, hardly anyone read for pleasure, or even at all. Enjoyment of high culture was the privilege of no more than a few wealthy ecclesiastics and noblemen. Even as late as the eighteenth century, how many people heard the works of Bach, Haydn, or Mozart performed? A few tens of thousands at the very most – and sometimes only a few hundred bored aristocrats.

But nowadays the artistic heritage of the ages is within the reach of practically everyone. The music of the great composers may be heard and enjoyed over and over again, by millions of people throughout the world. High culture is being disseminated on an unprecedented scale. What results this is likely to have we can only guess, but there must be some possibility that the sudden mass availability of high culture will start to exert a slow and steady refining influence on a considerable and influential section of the population.

If it is true that the arts have taken the place of religion, this is because they form an integral part, not of religion in the narrow sense, but of the spiritual life. And if I am right in this analysis, we should encourage all the fine arts, as an integral part of the spiritual life and the evolution of our humanity.

One final question remains to be addressed, and it concerns the psychology of artistic creation. How and why is it that, for the artist, the production of works of art should be a means – even *the* means – of higher evolution? What happens when the artist creates?

In brief, when artists create, they objectify. And when you objectify, you can assimilate. This is not unlike what happens in the process of traditional Buddhist visualization exercises. When, for instance, in meditation, we visualize the Buddha, we close our eyes and we see – we try actually to see rather than just think about – first, an expanse of green, with an expanse of blue sky above it, and in between, a bodhi tree. Then at the foot of the bodhi tree, we see the figure of the Buddha in orange robes. We see the supremely peaceful features, the golden complexion, the gentle smile, the curly black hair, the colours of his aura. We see all this as vividly as if the Buddha himself was sitting before us. And in what we visualize we recognize the spiritual qualities of the Buddha; in his face we see wisdom, compassion, tranquillity, fearlessness, and so on. Drawing gradually nearer to the visualized image, and thus to those qualities, we feel as if the visualized image was drawing nearer to us. We feel that we are absorbing within ourselves the Buddha's own qualities.[70]

If we persevere in this exercise, if we keep it up not just for a few days, but for months, even years, eventually a time will come when we fully assimilate all these qualities of the Buddha, and become one with him in that meditation experience. When that happens, the unenlightened being is transformed into the Enlightened Being, and we realize our own Buddha nature. But in the course of this practice, in the process of this exercise, what has really happened?

What has happened is that our own potential – that is to say Buddhahood – which was there all the time, unknown and unrecognized, in the heart of our own being, the depths of our own nature, has become actual; it has been realized. But it has been realized by being objectified, by being seen 'out there' (even though it is 'in here'). Having been objectified in this way, it has been gradually assimilated, more and more, until we become one with it.

The same sort of thing happens in the case of artistic creation. When we say that the artist creates out of his or her experience of some higher level of being, it is not quite as simple and straightforward as that makes it sound. It is not that the artist has the experience itself fully and perfectly and completely before creating anything. Someone who did that would not be an artist at all, but a mystic, which is something else and, at least potentially, something higher. The artist's starting point is a vague sense of something that he or she clarifies and intensifies in the process of creating the work of art. The original creative experience of the artist is like a seed which is bursting with life but whose nature is fully revealed only when the flower blooms, when the work of art itself stands complete and perfect. But however fine the objects one creates, whatever their transforming power, the highest aim of any artist must be the same as that of any human being. Each of us must aim to be ourselves our own finest work of art, to 'give style to our character' in Nietzsche's phrase – to become, that is, a true individual.

PART 3

The Network of Personal Relationships

INTRODUCTION

SOME VERSES I once composed for the dedication of a Buddhist shrine-room include the aspiration: 'May our communication with one another be Sangha.'[71] This reflects the very great importance that has always been given in Buddhism to the quality of communication both between members of the sangha and in the context of all the relationships an individual Buddhist has with other people. The Buddha had a great deal to say about communication – about the importance of truthful, kindly, meaningful, and harmonious speech, and about the necessity to pay attention to one's relationships in general, making sure that one is relating in ways that accord with one's Buddhist principles.

The reasons for this are quite obvious. To be human is to be related to other human beings. We cannot live our lives in isolation; whatever efforts we make to develop as individuals are continually tested in the fires of our relationships with other people. However calm, kind, and wise we may feel in the privacy of our own hearts or shrine-rooms, the true test of how fully we have developed these qualities comes when we are faced with the realities of life as represented by the challenges 'other people' represent.

The first human being to whom we are related is of course our mother. That relationship is very intimate, and it affects us for the whole of our lives. After that, our father comes into view, and perhaps brothers and sisters as well, together with grandparents, if we are fortunate. A little later we may also become aware of aunts, uncles, and cousins. This is usually the extent of our family circle. But then there are neighbours – next door, up the street, over the way – and from the age of four or five there are teachers, schoolfellows, and friends. Later, there may be a husband or wife, and perhaps children. On top of these relationships we will probably have connections with employers and workmates, perhaps even employees. And we will also, sooner or later, have to have relationships of a kind with government officials, bureaucrats, even rulers, whether in our own country or abroad. By the time we reach maturity, we will find ourselves in the midst of a whole network of relationships with scores, perhaps hundreds, of people, and connected indirectly or distantly to very many more.

This network of relationships is the subject-matter of a Buddhist text known as the *Sigālaka Sutta*, which is to be found in the *Dīgha-Nikāya*, the 'Collection of Long Discourses', in the Pāli Canon.[72] It is a comparatively early text, the substance of which, we can be reasonably certain, goes back to the Buddha himself. It is called the *Sigālaka Sutta* because it is a discourse given by the Buddha to a young man called Sigālaka. One translator describes the sutta as 'Advice to Lay People'. In it the Buddha lays down a pattern for different kinds of relationships, explaining how each should be conducted. All this is set forth with such clarity and succinctness that it remains of considerable interest today – and we will be using it as the framework for this final section of our consideration of the question 'What is the Sangha?'

Sigālaka is a young brahmin, which means that he belongs to the priestly caste, the highest and most influential caste of Indian society. The introduction to the sutta reports that the Buddha happens to meet Sigālaka early one morning. Sigālaka's clothes and hair are still dripping wet from his purificatory ritual bath. (This is something you can still see today – brahmins standing in the holy River Ganges at Varanasi, dipping into the water and reciting mantras.) Having taken his bath, Sigālaka is engaged in worshipping the six directions: north, south, east, west, the zenith, and the nadir.

He is doing this, so he informs the Buddha, in obedience to his father's dying injunction, in order to protect himself from any harm that might come from any of the six directions. The Buddha thereupon tells Sigālaka that although worshipping the six directions is right and proper he is not going about it in the right way, if he wants such worship to protect him effectively. He then proceeds to explain what the six directions really represent.

The east, he says, means mother and father (in Indian languages mother comes before father) because one originates from them just as the sun – or at least the day – originates in the east. So the first relationship the Buddha refers to is that between parent and child. As for the other directions, they refer to the other key relationships in life: the south to the relationship between pupil and teacher; the west to that between husband and wife; the north to friends and companions; the nadir to the relationship between 'master and servant' (employer and employee, in modern terms); and the zenith to the relationship between lay people and 'ascetics and brahmins'.

True worship of the six directions, the Buddha explains, consists in carrying out one's duties with regard to these six kinds of relationship. Such ethical activity is naturally productive of happiness, and it is in this sense that one protects oneself through this kind of 'worship'. Here the Buddha envisages the individual as being at the centre of a network of relationships, out of which he enumerates just six. The Buddha seems to give equal emphasis to these six primary relationships, which represent a fairly wide spread of human interaction, and in this respect he is characteristic of his culture, that of north-east India in the sixth century BCE.

But most other cultures emphasize one kind of human relationship rather more than the others. For example, a similar list to the one the Buddha gave Sigālaka can be found in Confucianism, according to which there are five standard relationships: between ruler and subject (sometimes described as prince and minister), between parent and child, between husband and wife, between brother and brother, and between friend and friend. But in ancient China particular emphasis was always placed on the relationship between parents and children, and especially on the duties of children towards parents. According to some Confucian writers, filial piety is the greatest of all virtues, and in classical times sons and daughters who were conspicuous examples of it were officially honoured by the government with a title, or a grant of a large piece of land, or a monument erected in their honour. The whole idea can only seem rather strange to us now, living as we do in very different times, when independence from one's parents is the goal as far as most people are concerned.

Turning to the ancient Greeks, we find no particular list of significant relationships. However, if we take Plato's account of the teachings of

Socrates as representative of the highest Greek ideals, it is clear that for them the relationship between friend and friend was the most significant. The moving description of Socrates' death puts this emphasis into stark perspective. Some time before his death we find him bidding a rather formal farewell to his wife and children, who are nevertheless described as sobbing bitterly. He then dismisses them, and devotes his last hours to philosophical discussion with his friends.[73]

In medieval Europe, on the other hand, the emphasis was placed on the relationship between master and servant, particularly that between the feudal lord and the vassal. Such was the centrality of this relationship that a whole social system was built around it. In the feudal system the great virtue was loyalty, especially to the person directly above you in the social pecking order. If you were a great lord it would be the king; if you were a small landowner it would be the local lord; if you were an ordinary servant or serf it would be your knight. And you would be prepared and willing to die for your feudal superior.

In the modern West, of course, we find the main emphasis placed upon the sexual or romantic relationship. One may move from one such relationship to another, but through all these ups and downs, their current sexual relationship nevertheless remains the central relationship for most people, giving meaning and colour to their lives. The romantic relationship is the principal subject-matter of films, novels, plays, and poems, and as an ideal it is all-consuming – lovers commonly declare that they cannot live without each other, even that they are prepared to die for each other. Thus for most people in our culture, the sexual/romantic relationship is the central and most important one – an idea which people of the ancient civilizations would probably have found ridiculous. This is not to say that they would necessarily have been right, but we can at least remind ourselves that people have not always felt as we feel today.

In the modern West other relationships often tend to be superficial because they are simply not given the same weight. We tend to neglect our relationships with our parents and with our friends, rarely taking these relationships as seriously as we do our romantic liaisons. That, we think, is the way things are meant to be. We tend to think that the tremendous value we give to this particular relationship compared with the lesser value we accord to others is perfectly normal; indeed, we are apt to assume that it has always been like that everywhere in the world. But that, as we have seen, is not really the case. On the contrary, our position is a distinctly abnormal one – no other society has raised the sexual relationship so high above all others.

Quite apart from the neglect of other relationships, our attitude has the unfortunate result of overloading the romantic relationship. We come to expect from our sexual partner far more than he or she is able to give. If we are not careful we expect him or her to be everything for us: sexual partner, friend, companion, mother, father, adviser, counsellor, source of security – everything. We expect this relationship to give us love, security, happiness, fulfilment, and the rest. We expect it to give meaning to our lives, and in this way it becomes like an electrical cable carrying a current that is too much for it. The result is that the poor, unfortunate sexual relationship very often blows a fuse – it breaks down under the strain. The obvious solution is to work at the development of a greater spread of relationships, all of which are important to us, and to all of which we give great care and attention.

But one can see it the other way round too. As well as contributing to the decline of other relationships, the present-day centrality of the sexual or marital relationship also reflects the fact that other relationships have become more difficult or have tended to fall into abeyance. Teacher–pupil, employer–employee, and ruler–subject relationships have all been seriously depersonalized – indeed, often they are not seen as relations that should involve a personal element at all. But this was not the case in older societies. Centuries ago – as little as 150 years ago, in some areas of Europe – if you were a servant or an apprentice, you would probably have lived with your master under the same roof. You would have shared in his day-to-day existence, eating the same food at the same table, just as though you were a member of the family, albeit one who knew his or her place. Under the traditional apprenticeship system, a very close personal relationship could grow up between master and apprentice or servant, or in modern terms, between employer and employee.

The novels of Dickens, which date from the 1840s, by which time the industrial age was well under way, could still portray the relation between master and servant in distinctly feudal terms, because those terms were still a reality for many people. When in *The Pickwick Papers* Sam Weller, Mr Pickwick's faithful servant, wants to get married, Mr Pickwick naturally offers to release Sam from his service. Sam declares his intention to stay with Mr Pickwick, who says, 'My good fellow, you are bound to consider the young woman also.' But Sam says that she will be happy to wait for him. 'If she don't, she's not the young woman I took her to be, and I give her up with readiness.' His duty, he says, is to serve Mr Pickwick.'

In this way he was harking back to the situation where you served a feudal chief who led you in battle, who was more powerful than you, who protected you, and to whom you were unconditionally loyal. This commitment made it a truly personal relationship, and very often the most important relationship in a man's life, even emotionally, and one for which other relationships would be sacrificed if necessary.

This attitude was still around to some extent in the East when I was there in the 1950s. In Kalimpong I sometimes had to engage Tibetan or Nepalese cooks, handymen, or gardeners, and it was noticeable that they quickly became very loyal. They weren't interested in just getting the money at the end of the month. Some of them didn't even want to work for money at all. They were much more concerned to have a decent relationship with a good master.

Nowadays, for better or worse, all this is on the way out, with the steady incursion of Western values. The very word 'master' makes people today feel slightly uneasy. The result is that you cannot generally have any truly personal relationship with your employer. You work not for a master but for a department in a company, and your work is overseen by people who have more power than you have, but no loyalty or commitment to you. Only in truly archaic situations, like an army regiment, in which loyalty and devotion to duty is the key to success, do you still find anything like this sort of relationship. Likewise, we have a very remote, impersonal relationship with those who are meant to protect our interests, and we certainly don't think in terms of serving them. You may, once or twice in your lifetime, get round to shaking hands with your local Member of Parliament or Congressman, but usually that's about as close to them as you are likely to get.

One might think that the relation between teacher and pupil would be a naturally personal one; it certainly can be so in the tutorial system of some universities. However, in general, teaching these days is a business-like process of passing pupils from one teacher to another in the hope that a balanced ingestion of facts will result. Under the usual classroom system, one teacher sometimes has to address as many as forty pupils, and then moves on to teach another large group of pupils. A relationship is necessarily an individual thing, and it is virtually impossible to develop such relationships with every pupil in your care in such circumstances. Nor can you have favourites, as this will lead to resentment.

Anyway, most of us come in contact with teachers only when we are comparatively young, so that any relationship we might have with a teacher never gets a chance to mature. We don't generally think in terms of learning anything beyond the point at which we stop accumulating qualifications; that is the end of the teacher–pupil relationship for us, although certain relationships later on may involve an unofficial mentoring element which can have a profound effect on our development.

In modern life, relationships between friends are not, in the case of men anyway, meant to go deep enough to produce problems. We tend to keep such relationships at an easygoing, undemanding level, probably because in many people's minds there is a fear of homosexuality. Any strong emotional relationship between two people of the same sex, especially between two men, tends in our times to be rather suspect.

We can also say that relationships among brothers and sisters are much less important than formerly. One obvious reason for this is that some of us don't have brothers and sisters. It is all too common to find oneself an only child – very different from the large families of earlier times, when (especially before the advent of the Welfare State) members of the family would be expected to care for one another.

The fact that these various kinds of relationship have become more superficial means that we are left with only two effective personal relationships in our lives nowadays. The ancient Indians had six, the ancient Chinese had five, but we, for all practical purposes, have two: the parent–child relationship, and the husband–wife or boyfriend–girlfriend relationship. And of these two, it is the second that is for many people by far the more important.

Of course, there are various complicating factors in sexual relationships, the most obvious one being sex itself. Under the conditions of modern life, sexual needs are not only biological but also psychological. For example, a man will tend nowadays to associate the expression of his manhood less with his activity in the world than with his sexual activity, particularly if his work is fairly meaningless and undemanding.

Another complicating factor is that, as in most civilizations, the man–woman relationship is institutionalized – whether as marriage or as cohabitation. Apart from the parent–child relationship (which is on a rather different basis), marriage is the only one of our relationships that we legalize and institutionalize in this way. It is not just a personal understanding between two people; it involves a legal obligation, which under certain circumstances is even enforceable in a court of law. It is not always easy to make changes in such a relationship, and this can lead to difficulties.

When a conflict arises between our need to develop as an individual on the one hand and our sexual relationship on the other, the psychological pressure can build up to create intense distress. Indeed, any personal relationship has the potential to get in the way of our attempts to grow spiritually. There is something of a paradox here. On the one hand, personal relationships are absolutely necessary for human development. On the other hand, if we are committed to spiritual development, it is much easier to sustain a personal relationship with another person who is also trying to lead a spiritual life. Problems are likely to arise – especially in the context of a sexual relationship – when one of the two people wishes to engage in spiritual practice and the other does not, and such problems are difficult to resolve because we are unlikely to be completely wholehearted in our commitment to the spiritual life anyway. Part of us, so to speak, is likely to side with the other person against our spiritual aspiration, so that we may find ourselves agreeing that setting aside time to meditate, for example, is simply selfish.

Some people find that as they get involved with spiritual practice, the importance to them of their old personal relationships diminishes, at least for a time. This can be very difficult to accept. It sounds unbearably harsh to say that as you grow, you just have to leave family and friends behind in some sense. But in a way this is only to be expected. Spiritual life does involve an element of going forth, as we have already seen. And if you are interested in things that your friends and family have little or no knowledge of or interest in, you can't help losing contact with them to some extent.

However, many people find that as they mature in their spiritual practice, their increased positivity, sensitivity, and sense of gratitude brings them into much deeper and closer relationship, especially with their families, and this is very much to be welcomed, and indeed consciously worked on. After all, as the Buddha reminded Sigālaka, our parents gave us this life, which we increasingly feel to be very meaningful and precious; great love and respect is due to them for that, whatever has happened since. At the same time, as we move more deeply into spiritual practice, we will be forming new personal relationships with other people who are trying to live a spiritual life – in other words, we are likely to join or help form a spiritual community.

In the following chapters, we shall take a look at each of the six relationships which the Buddha encouraged Sigālaka to associate with the six directions. Each chapter looks at the relationship in question from a particular angle, so this is not intended to be a comprehensive account (which would hardly be possible in any case), but simply to give an opportunity to pause and reflect on the nature of each relationship in turn. Having considered all six relationships, we will consider something that pertains to all of them, and is also a quality of the true individual: gratitude. We will conclude with two chapters that offer some thoughts on the individual Buddhist's relationship with the wider world. After all, far from being a rationalization for selfishness, as some people assume it to be, the Buddhist life can only be fully lived in the light of the realization of our interconnectedness with all life, and the commitment to act with compassion and vigour on that basis.

13

BEING A BUDDHIST PARENT

ACCORDING TO THE BUDDHA'S advice to Sigālaka, one of the six relationships to be honoured and respected is that between parents and children. We get a sense that this was something Sigālaka already knew something about, in that he was worshipping the six directions in the first place in deference to his father's wishes, but there is a great deal to be said about the duties of children to their parents. Here, however, I will be focusing on the duties of parents to their children.

I am not a parent myself, but I have certainly had occasion to observe the nature of parenthood, through my communication with friends and disciples who are parents, through my observations of what goes on around me, and through my reading and contact with the media generally. Perhaps the saying that the onlooker sees most of the game is relevant here. On the basis of such experience – albeit vicarious – as I have had, I will venture to offer a list of points that any Buddhist parent would do well to consider. I will not be going into the question of whether one should or should not have children. It is simply an established fact that many people, including many Buddhists, have them, and that there is a need, therefore, to consider how best to handle this important relationship.

The observations I want to make – many of which are simple common sense – are expressed in the form of fifteen points, the first of which is this:

1. REMEMBER THAT YOU ARE A BUDDHIST FIRST AND A PARENT SECOND

If one is both a Buddhist and a parent, it is important to think of oneself as a Buddhist who is a parent, rather than as a parent who happens to be a Buddhist. There is a great deal of difference between these two positions. In saying this, I am certainly not encouraging Buddhists to put their children second. If you want to go on retreat and your son or daughter happens to be ill, I am not suggesting you should leave him or her to someone else's tender mercies and go off on retreat. Not at all. Buddhism comes first in the sense that it is from Buddhism that you derive the very principles in the light of which you are trying to be a *Buddhist* parent, not just a parent.

Human beings share parenthood with practically the entire animal species; just becoming a parent is no great achievement, and almost all human beings do it. But although it is easy to become a parent, to be a good parent is very difficult indeed, and to be a Buddhist parent is still more difficult, because it involves applying, or trying to apply, Buddhist principles to your relations with your children. This point underlies all the others I want to make.

2. DON'T BE AFRAID TO TEACH YOUR CHILDREN BUDDHISM

These days there is a great deal of confused thinking about what children should be taught. People often say that we mustn't interfere with anybody's thinking; we should encourage people to think for themselves. Children should not be indoctrinated, but should be allowed to grow up with open, free, almost blank minds. Then, when they are old enough, they will decide for themselves whether they want to be Christian or Buddhist or agnostic or Muslim or Hare Krishna, or whatever appeals to them.

This way of thinking is totally unrealistic. While you are carefully refraining from teaching your children about Buddhism, refraining from indoctrinating them, as you may see it, all sorts of other agencies are going to be hard at work indoctrinating your children with quite different values from your own, whether you like it or not. Children are indoctrinated all the time: in school or playgroup, by television, by films, by the general atmosphere of our society. Don't think that if you refrain from 'indoctrinating' your children, they will be completely free to make up their own minds about things when they reach the age of discretion, whenever that happens to be (if, indeed, it is ever reached).

Don't be afraid, therefore, to teach your children Buddhism – or rather, to communicate to them something of the spirit of the Dharma. Society in the broadest sense is going to be communicating all sorts of other messages, some of which may have a definitely negative effect on them, so don't hold back from giving them the positive influence of the Dharma. You don't have to try to teach them abstruse Buddhist doctrines like the law of conditioned co-production. You don't have to get them reading *A Survey of Buddhism* at a tender age. You can start very early by showing them picture books about the life of the Buddha, or the traditional stories of the Buddha's previous lives. Every child loves stories, and it is to be hoped that television is not excluding storytelling in the home altogether. In this way you can introduce them to the world of Buddhist culture, and give them something of the feel of Buddhism.

Something else you can do – indeed, something you should do – is set an example. When, as your children get older, you begin to communicate your values to them – perhaps your commitment to ethical speech – it is important that you yourself should be demonstrating that commitment in the way you live. As any parent will know, children are very quick to pick up on discrepancies. It's no use telling your son or daughter that it's wrong to tell lies and then saying, when someone comes to the door, 'Just say I'm not in.'

You also communicate to your children something of the spirit of the Dharma through the atmosphere that prevails in your home. It is important that when children come home from school or some other activity, they should feel that home is a good place to be: perhaps peaceful or perhaps quite lively, but happy and positive, with an atmosphere of affection and security. Perhaps they will eventually realize that this atmosphere has something to do with the fact that you are a Buddhist and that you meditate; but whether or not they make this connection, they will feel the benefit of living in a positive environment.

3. REALIZE THAT YOU ARE UP AGAINST IT

No parent will need reminding that as a parent one is up against it in the sense that bringing up children is expensive, or that children can be difficult, or that one has sleepless nights. But one is up against it in other senses too – up against the world in the broadest sense. As a Buddhist parent, you are trying to bring up your children in accordance with Buddhist principles. But those principles are far from being acknowledged in the outside world. You are saying one thing, as it were, to your child, but the world is usually saying something quite different, even quite opposite.

Any Buddhist has to fight to sustain their principles in this way, but as a parent you have to fight the battle on your children's behalf as well as your own. The extent to which children should be shielded from outside influences, especially when they are very young, is a big question; and in any case it is only possible to shield them to a certain degree. But it is important and helpful to acknowledge that to try to bring children up in accordance with Buddhist principles is a tremendous challenge, because the outside world – consciously or unconsciously, intentionally or unintentionally – is all the time having a quite different influence on them, and on you as well.

4. JOIN A PARENT–TEACHER ORGANIZATION

Here we come to something much more specific. Sooner or later, your child will start going to school. My fourth point is therefore: join a parent–teacher organization. Don't just leave the education of your children during school hours to their teachers. It could almost be said that education is too important to be left to teachers, just as it is sometimes said that politics is too important to be left to politicians. The teachers may well be doing an excellent job, but they are up against it too – being a teacher is in some ways just as difficult as being a parent.

If you have school-going children, it is a good idea, therefore, to make contact with their teachers. Talk to them about your children, and children in general at the school, and also discuss with them the problems they themselves face as teachers. These days teachers have a very difficult time. There are more and more cases of teachers being physically attacked by students, and this sort of thing makes life very difficult for them indeed. If you join a parent–teacher organization or association, you can have some input, contribute some ideas and suggestions, so that the school may become a better place for all the children who are attending it. You may even get the opportunity to become a school governor, and thereby an even greater opportunity to influence the school in a positive and creative way.

5. COMMUNICATE WITH YOUR CHILDREN

Some people would say that this point should be addressed more to fathers than to mothers, but I am not going to make any such distinction. It is very important, if you are a parent, to communicate with your children. Talk to them seriously – don't talk down to them. If they ask a question, take it seriously. If you do so, you may be surprised to find how difficult it is to answer. Even quite small children are intelligent and perceptive, and can come up with quite extraordinary questions sometimes.

One of my happiest memories of my own childhood, back in the late 1920s and early 1930s, is of my father spending time talking to me. He would get home from work – when he was in work, because those were days of unemployment – at about six or seven o'clock, and come to my room – I'd be in bed already – and sit on my bed and talk to me for half an hour or an hour. Sometimes my mother would get impatient because she had his dinner ready and it was getting cold, but he was more interested in talking to me. He used to talk about all sorts of things, especially his wartime experiences – he had been seriously injured in the Great War, which had ended only a few years before. Not only did my father talk to me; as I grew older, I always found it very easy to talk to him.

So, talk to your children. Share your serious thoughts with them, to the extent that they are able to understand them. That means finding time to spend with them. Don't be too busy to talk to your own children. Even set aside a time, if you're very busy, just as you would set aside time to see a friend. Not, of course, that you should sit the children in front of you and say, 'Come on, we're going to have a little talk.' You must catch them on the wing. They may not always feel like talking when you've got time.

6. RESTRICT TELEVISION

It is difficult, if not impossible, to sustain a clear and positive mental state – to remain mindful, as Buddhists would say – unless you do something to limit the extent to which you absorb all the stimulating input of modern life. And, of course, nowadays a lot of input comes from television. There is a big debate going on as to whether or not there is a causal connection between violence as seen on television and violence in the home and in the street. Some experts say there is no real connection, others say there is, and it is very difficult for the layman to know the truth of the matter.

But from a Buddhist point of view we can be sure of one thing. Whether or not seeing violence on television results in actual violence, it certainly does not improve the mental state of the viewer. To spend several hours every week, or even every day, watching programmes that contain a large component of violence can only be to the detriment of one's mental state, whether one is an adult or a receptive and susceptible child.

Some people will say that children have rights, including the right to watch television whenever they like. But, as I have mentioned elsewhere, I think it is better not to use the language of rights, but instead to think in terms of duties. And parents – Buddhist parents especially – have a duty to restrict the television viewing of their children.

The restriction should apply not just what to they watch, but also to how much time they spend sitting in front of the television set. Surveys have found that many children in the West are overweight. This is partly because of an unhealthy diet – that is the subject of my next point – but also because they don't take enough exercise. And they don't take enough exercise because – apparently – it is much more interesting to be parked in front of the television set. Tests have shown that watching television also impairs the imagination – essentially because while one is passively taking in whatever the television producers choose to present, one is simply not having to use one's imagination.

Of course, restricting the watching of television is going to be difficult. One Buddhist mother I know said her children felt deprived because they didn't have a television set in the house, and therefore felt different from all the other children at school because they couldn't join in discussions about what they had been watching the previous night. In the end their mother reluctantly had to give in to their persistent pressure, although she did manage to restrict their viewing to some extent. Obviously strong forces are at work. Nonetheless, one should take a firm line on this matter.

7. GIVE YOUR CHILDREN A HEALTHY DIET

This point may seem obvious, but again, contemporary conditions are against it. Living in the city and keeping my eyes open, one of the things I notice is children eating in the street. And, of course, they are usually eating junk food: chocolate, ice creams, burgers, and chips. Parents need to do what they can to counter this widespread habit. There is no need to be faddish or fanatical in the way we were in the sixties, when we were all into macrobiotics. But whoever does the cooking for the family should try to give the family a balanced diet, and discourage snacking between meals.

And, of course, children should be discouraged from smoking. Another thing I notice as I walk around is how many schoolchildren smoke. I see them coming straight out of school – they can't be more than twelve or thirteen – and they pull out a packet of cigarettes and light up straightaway. So again, Buddhist parents need to take a firm line with their children when they come to that particular age.

It was very different when I was a child. I hadn't even thought of smoking when I was young, but when I reached the age of sixteen, my father said to me, 'Son, you're sixteen now. You can smoke if you want to.' I didn't, though – not until I joined the army. Even then I only smoked for a short while, because I didn't enjoy it, and I haven't smoked since. It's really very discouraging to see such small children, both boys and girls, already having acquired the smoking habit. So please discourage your child from smoking – well, don't discourage them, just stop it. Exert your parental authority. I know that parental authority has been reduced to shreds and tatters these days, but whatever pitiful remnants of it are left, exert it in this respect.

8. SOCIALIZE YOUR CHILD

This is a point I particularly want to emphasize. Your children don't belong just to you. They aren't just members of the family. They are, or will be, members of society, part of the wider community, and they need to be brought up, even trained, in such a way that they can function in a positive manner as members of that society. Again, this obviously involves the exercise of a certain amount of discipline. Children have to be brought up, for example, to respect other people's property, and to consider other people's feelings. Otherwise, they are going to have a very tough time in the world later on. You may put up with tantrums and bad behaviour and inconsiderate conduct, but the world will not.

So socialize your children. And don't inflict them on other people. One does see parents doing this. Little Jimmy or Mary is misbehaving, and being very inconsiderate where other people are concerned, but the parents just smile indulgently – 'Oh, that's little Mary' or 'That's little Jimmy' – and other people are supposed to put up with it, or even think it's sweet. In fact, of course, other people are much more likely to be thinking, 'What a dreadful little brat!'

Good manners are rather unpopular nowadays, associated as they are with bourgeois values, middle-class upbringing, and all that sort of thing; the tendency is to throw the baby of good manners out with the bathwater of sociological fashion. But we have to do what we can to retrieve the baby. Recent research has even identified a definite connection between bad manners and juvenile crime, and this suggests that the aspect of socialization which consists in teaching children good manners is not to be underestimated.

9. DON'T BE POSSESSIVE

Of course, your child is your child, with all that that means, and you are legally responsible for him or her up to a point. But try to avoid thinking, 'This is *my* child.' Don't develop the attitude that no one else is allowed to speak to your children, or tell them off if they are misbehaving. In a healthy, positive community, it should be possible for any adult to tell off any child who is misbehaving anywhere. Unfortunately, in Western society at present, this is not possible. One sees it happening in India, but in the West people seem to resent anybody interfering, as they would call it, with their children.

Buddhist parents obviously shouldn't have this sort of attitude, partly because as Buddhists we try not to be attached, or at least to reduce our attachments, and partly because Buddhist parents are part of the Buddhist sangha. You shouldn't mind if a fellow Buddhist thinks it appropriate to remonstrate with your child for some misdemeanour. If your child is visiting the Buddhist centre with you, and while you are doing something, the child is racketing around the centre, any fellow Buddhist should be able to say, 'Come on Tommy, don't make such a noise,' without your resenting it or feeling offended.

A very important aspect of non-possessiveness is letting your children go when the time comes for them to leave the parental nest and go forth into the wider world. You should have brought them up in such a way that they can go forth freely, easily, without feelings of guilt, and with self-confidence, while you feel – yes, a little sad, that's inevitable – but on the whole quite pleased and happy, even, perhaps, if you'll admit it, a little relieved to see them go, and willing and ready to put the old relationship on a new basis.

There is a very interesting verse on this subject in the Hindu *Manusmriti*. The verse refers to fathers and sons, but it applies to all parent–child relationships. It says, 'When your son is sixteen, cease to regard him as a son, and treat him as a friend.' And that, of course, becomes all the more possible when the child leaves home. When your son or daughter comes to visit you, try to see him or her not as your child returning to the nest for a bit of comfort, but as a good friend coming to see you for a good talk.

10. TEACH YOUR CHILDREN TO SPEAK PROPERLY

Sometimes when I'm out and about and I overhear people talking – not only children but adults as well – I am astonished at the sheer poverty of their vocabulary. Standards do seem to be dropping as regards language and verbal communication in general. It is therefore very important that children should be encouraged to extend their vocabulary and speak grammatically. Speech is our principal medium of communication with one another; unless we master it, we will simply be unable to communicate beyond a certain level.

Make sure, therefore, that your children grow up not just talking, but really *speaking* their language, speaking correctly and elegantly, with some attention to grammar and the correct use of words. Don't be afraid of correcting them. Some teachers maintain that children should never be corrected, because that would undermine their self-confidence, but it's a rather puny self-confidence that can be undermined in that way. If one is not corrected, one will go on making mistakes, and mistakes will become habits. So correct your children when they pick up incorrect expressions from school friends – and, of course, when they show any tendency to use bad language.

Speech is such a wonderful thing, one of the greatest creations of the human race. We should use it, and teach our children to use it, as fully and effectively and beautifully as we can. Teaching our children to speak properly gives them access to something that is very precious indeed.

11. TAKE YOUR CHILDREN TO SUITABLE BUDDHIST FESTIVALS

It is best to steer a middle course here. Rather than invariably leaving your children at home when there is a Buddhist festival on, or invariably taking them with you, try to find out which festivals or celebrations might be suitable. Not all of them will be. A programme involving a lot of meditation, for instance, will not suit small children; it is unfair to expect them to sit still for such long periods of time, or even more than a few minutes.

But children do like to join in, and they like to do things, so if the celebration is going to include a festive puja, by all means take them along – in consultation, obviously, with whoever is organizing the festival. I have noticed that children like to make offerings to the shrine: that's something they can do, it's simple and poetic, and they enjoy it. They could even prepare the offerings themselves beforehand and bring them along and offer them in their own way.

Don't insist that the children should take part in everything – there are certain occasions when it may not be appropriate – but whenever possible, include them. Perhaps there could even be a special children's festival occasionally.

12. INTRODUCE CHILDREN TO YOUR BUDDHIST FRIENDS

This may seem obvious, but it doesn't always happen. With reference specifically to English people, there is a saying that an Englishman's home is his castle, and we tend not to let down the drawbridge. It's part of our English character that we tend to keep a bit separate from other people, and to keep our domestic life separate from our social life. But if you have children, it's a good idea to make sure they spend time with your Buddhist friends, or at least have some contact with them. Very often this happens naturally and spontaneously, but one may need to make some effort to make sure it does.

It is important partly because it helps compensate for the nuclearness of the nuclear family. In some parts of the world – India, for example – most parents still live as part of an extended or joint family of ten or fifteen or more members. But, in England, our castles have become very small indeed. The nuclear family is getting more nuclear every day, it seems, and that isn't healthy, either for the parents or parent, or for the children or child. Some families these days consist of just two people: one parent and one child – a rather constricting, even claustrophobic, situation. Introducing your children to your Buddhist friends helps to modify the potentially claustrophobic nature of the nuclear family.

Being accustomed from an early age to meeting adults from outside the immediate family circle definitely helps children develop self-confidence, and that is obviously a tremendous asset. One of the things I noticed when I came back to the West after many years in Asia was that people generally seemed to lack self-confidence. Parents have to do whatever they can to make sure that their children grow up with plenty of self-confidence – not the sort of confidence that finds expression in antisocial activity, but self-confidence of a positive and even creative kind. And it does help in the development of a child's self-confidence if he or she is accustomed to interacting with adults from beyond the family circle.

13. TEACH CHILDREN TO CARE FOR THE ENVIRONMENT

Children are quite often to be seen blithely discarding sweet wrappers and so on in the street, apparently unaware of what they are doing, or perhaps accustomed to thinking that someone else is going to tidy up after them, that it isn't their responsibility to keep the streets litter-free. And this, of course, is symptomatic of an attitude that potentially has far-reaching consequences for the environment.

Even in the planet's greener days, at the time of the Buddha, the environment was very much a concern for the practising Buddhist, and the Buddha himself had quite a lot to say about it. As a Buddhist parent, one will want to bring up one's children to care for and respect the environment, which is after all *their* environment. As they get older, you can discuss environmental issues with them – as well as issues of other kinds, of course, but environmental issues do have a very immediate practical application.

14. TEACH CHILDREN TO EMPATHIZE

This is very important indeed. In recent years in England there has been much discussion of the distressing case of James Bulger, a toddler who was murdered by two very small boys. In a radio discussion after the trial, someone said that the reason the two boys had committed that terrible crime was that they had not been brought up to know the difference between right and wrong. But there was a woman psychologist taking part in this discussion, and she disagreed. She pointed out that the two boys had been found guilty of murder – in other words, it had been ascertained that they knew the difference between right and wrong. And she went on to make the very important point that it isn't enough to know the difference between right and wrong; one has to be able to empathize with other people, with other living beings. Without empathy, one's recognition of the difference between right and wrong will be purely abstract and conceptual, and will not necessarily influence one's behaviour.

Of course, you can't give lessons in empathy; it can't be made part of the school curriculum. Here again the example of parents comes in. Children can be taught to empathize with people, and with animals too, taught to realize that animals feel pain just as they do themselves. There is an incident in the Pali Canon where the Buddha finds some boys tormenting a crow, and says to them, 'If you were tormented in that way, how would you feel?' Of course, they say they wouldn't like it. And the Buddha said, 'Well, if you would feel pain if you were treated in that way, don't you think the crow feels pain too?' And they have to admit that yes, it does. In other words, they start empathizing with the crow.[74]

In the well-known series of engravings by Hogarth called 'The Four Stages of Cruelty', the first engraving depicts some boys tormenting a dog and a cat. In the next stage, one of the boys commits a murder. In the third stage, the boy who committed the murder is being hung. And in the last stage, his body is being dissected by some surgeons. Hogarth seems to be saying that this life of violence, which ends in the hanged man experiencing violence himself, begins with tormenting animals, having a lack of empathy with other living things.

Some people are so sensitive that they feel empathy even with plants, not liking to pick flowers because they feel that the plant is being injured in some way. Not everybody can empathize to that extent, but we should at least empathize with animals and with other human beings. This is one of the most important things we can teach our children.

15. DON'T FEEL GUILTY IF YOU HAVE MADE MISTAKES

It isn't easy being a parent. Even though I'm not a parent, I know that very well, because sometimes parents do confide in me, and I keep my ears and eyes open. It's very difficult being a parent, whether a mother or a father – more difficult now than ever before, in some ways at least. There are so many variables, so many decisions you have to take without being able to know all the relevant facts. And things may go wrong, despite your good intentions.

Even apart from that, children are individuals. They bring their own karma with them. You may bring your child up beautifully, and he or she may turn out to be a monster; you may bring them up very badly, and they may turn out very well. I have seen this, because I have lived long enough now to be able to see karma descending from one generation to another. For example, I have known children who were brought up very badly but who were themselves very good parents.

So there is karma to take into account. Quite apart from chromosomes, you don't know what karma your child brings with them. Things may turn out very differently from the way you expected them to turn out. Even apart from that, you yourself are a fallible human being. You're not omniscient. Maybe you mustn't tell your children that too early, but even parents don't know everything, and they can make mistakes.

Provided that you have really done your best for your children, and at every stage have made what you felt at the time was the best decision, if things do seem to have gone wrong, try to learn from that, but don't blame yourself too much. Don't feel guilty. If later on in life your child does something dreadful, don't agonize about it. Don't think that if only you hadn't done this or hadn't done that, it might have turned out different. You don't know. You can't work it out. You just have to do the best you can in the present, here and now. The rest is karma, chance, circumstances, society. So don't feel guilty if it does turn out that you've made mistakes. And don't even be too ready to think that what happens *is* due to your mistakes. Maybe it isn't. You don't know. But either way, don't blame yourself. You did your best at the time. That should be sufficient for you and for others.

Some parents feel they have to apologise to their children for the way they have brought them up. If you've done something definitely, unmistakably wrong, which has clearly caused the child suffering – well, all right, say you're sorry when the child is old enough to understand. But apart from that, bear in mind that once your children reach the years of discretion, they are responsible for their own lives. If anything goes wrong, or if your son or daughter does something wrong, he or she can't blame you for that. Your children are responsible for themselves, just as you are responsible for yourself. You are responsible for them only to a limited extent, and for a limited period of time.

These are just a few things to be considered about the relationship, from a Buddhist point of view, between parents and children. It goes without saying, I hope, that all these considerations are to be understood within the overall understanding that as a Buddhist parent you relate to your child with love and care, and that everything you try to do – including the times you need to bring in some discipline – is done in that loving spirit.

14

IS A GURU NECESSARY?

THE SECOND OF THE RELATIONSHIPS that 'protect the six directions', as the Buddha tells Sigālaka, is the relationship between pupil and teacher. Here we will be considering in particular the relationship between the disciple and the spiritual teacher, often thought of as a 'guru'. But is a guru necessary? This question connects with some of our earlier considerations about whether it is necessary to live one's spiritual life in the context of a spiritual community. The question is not likely to have occurred to Sigālaka or any of his contemporaries; at that time, the first question anyone would ask you would have been 'Who is your teacher?', not 'Do you think a teacher is necessary?'

But this question will inevitably arise sooner or later for any modern Westerner who genuinely tries to develop as an individual, to be authentically himself or herself. In particular, it is likely to arise if one attempts quite specifically and consciously to follow what we usually refer to as the spiritual path, and it will demand an answer all the more imperatively when one tries to follow that spiritual path in one or another of its oriental forms.

However, before we address the question itself, we must banish the haze of imaginative associations that gather around the magic word 'guru'. We must, unfortunately, dispel the vision of brilliant blue skies, beautiful white snow peaks, and, just above the snow line, the snug little caves which are in the popular imagination the natural habitat of that rare creature, the guru. We must come down to earth from those inaccessible valleys of Shangri-la in which benign and wise old men with long white beards and starry eyes pass on the secret of the very highest teaching to a very few devoted disciples. We must ruthlessly dismiss any notion of those lucky disciples effortlessly floating up to nirvāṇa on the strength of having secured the most advanced techniques from the most esoteric lineage holder.

We need to consider the whole question of the guru in as sober and matter-of-fact a fashion as possible, and try to understand what a guru is, and what a guru is not. On that basis, it should become clear to what extent and in what way a guru is necessary, if at all. We can also consider the attitudes it may be appropriate to adopt in relation to the guru.

Let us begin by seeing what a guru is not. First of all, a guru is not the head of a religious group. By a religious group I do not, of course, mean a spiritual community, but rather a number of non-individuals organized into a power structure around the forms or conventions of some kind of religious practice. Religious groups are of many kinds – sects, churches, monasteries, and so on – and they each have someone at their head. Such heads are regarded with great veneration by other members of the group, but there is likely to be something unfocused or off-key about this devotion. They are venerated not for what they are in themselves, as individuals, but for what they represent, what they stand for, even what they symbolize.

It might seem obvious that they should stand for or symbolize something spiritual; and in a superficial sense they do. But in fact they represent the group itself. That they are the head of a group is their principal significance. It is easy to see when this is the case; you just have to wait for the head of a group to be criticized or even vilified, as in course of time will inevitably happen. Members of groups usually feel that an attack on the head of their group is an attack on them. Any disrespect shown to the head of the group by those outside the group is interpreted by group members as lack of respect for the group itself.

The Buddha refused to countenance any such attitude among his followers. The *Brahmajāla Sutta* of the *Dīgha-Nikāya* tells the story of how the Buddha and a great crowd of his followers were once travelling on foot between Rājagaha and Nāḷandā, and found themselves in company with a wanderer called Suppiya and a follower of his, a young man called Brahmadatta. These two, in the hearing of the Buddha and his followers, began to argue, and kept arguing as they walked. And the subject of their argument, one can imagine, must have upset some of the Buddha's disciples considerably. For Suppiya, the text tells us, was finding fault in all sorts of ways with the Buddha, the Dharma, and the Sangha – though Brahmadatta was praising them just as strongly. All the travellers found themselves staying in the same place overnight, and still Suppiya and Brahmadatta kept on arguing.

Not surprisingly, when dawn came, the Buddha's followers gathered together and started talking among themselves about this disconcerting behaviour on the part of their fellow travellers. Coming to join them, the Buddha asked them what they had just been talking about, and they told him. Reading between the lines here, we can gather that they were somewhat upset, even angry, at what had happened. But the Buddha said:

'Monks, if anyone should speak in disparagement of me, of the Dharma or of the Sangha, you should not be angry or displeased at such disparagement; that would only be a hindrance to you.'

Nor did the Buddha let the matter rest there. He said: 'If others disparage me, the Dharma or the Sangha, and you are angry or displeased, can you recognize whether what they say is right or not?' And the monks had to admit that, in those circumstances, they would be in no state to think about things objectively.

So the Buddha said, 'If others disparage me, the Dharma or the Sangha, then you must explain what is incorrect as being incorrect, saying: ''That is incorrect, that is false, that is not our way, that is not found among us.''[75]

If one reflects on this episode, one realizes that the Buddha is pointing out to his disciples a tendency that is all too human. If they had become angry, they might have thought that their anger had arisen because the Buddha was being criticized, but in fact it was much more likely that anger had arisen because the group to which they belonged was being criticized, and so, in effect, *they* were being criticized. A disciple in that position might well feel that his wisdom in being a member of that group, and a follower of the person being criticized, was being called into question.

Examples of such sensitivity are not confined to the Pāli Canon. I have come across Buddhists who would hunt through books on comparative religion, dictionaries of religion and philosophy, and the like, to see if they could find unfavourable references to Buddhism. When they found them, they would write off to the publishers, call public meetings, and organize protests and demonstrations. It seemed that little short of stringing up the unfortunate person responsible for the offending comments could pacify them. The most interesting aspect of the whole business was that the Buddhists who thus spluttered and seethed with rage were invariably convinced that they were thereby demonstrating their devotion to the Dharma. What they were exhibiting, however, was their group spirit – a thing that has nothing to do with the spiritual life or the Buddha's teaching.

Hence a guru is not the head of a religious group. Nor is he an ecclesiastical superior, someone higher up in the power structure of a religious group. When prominent religious personalities come from the East, they are sometimes heralded by advance publicity in which one is told that this particular personality is in charge of an important group of monasteries, or that he is second-in-command of an ancient and historic temple. Sometimes in India one is told simply that he is very wealthy. I was once in Calcutta at a time when preparations were being made for the arrival of a monk from a famous temple in Sri Lanka, and I was told by the head monk of the temple where I was staying that I ought to go and see him, as he was very important and influential. Naturally I asked, 'In what way is he important?' The head monk replied, 'He's the richest monk in Sri Lanka.' It was on that basis that I was expected to go and pay my respects to him.

This is an extreme example, but it is representative of a general expectation that one should be impressed by people who are higher up in the ecclesiastical structure, and regard them as gurus. But a guru is not this sort of figure at all. Someone who is organizationally important or influential is not thereby a guru.

A guru is not a teacher either – a statement that may come as something of a surprise. It is comparatively easy to understand that a guru is not the head of a religious group, but it is quite usual to think that a spiritual teacher is just what a guru is supposed to be. But what is meant by a teacher? A teacher is one who communicates information. A geography teacher teaches facts and figures about the earth; a psychology teacher teaches facts and figures about the human mind. In the same way, a teacher of religion may teach the general history of all the different religions of the world, or the theology or doctrinal system of a particular tradition. But a guru, as such, doesn't teach religion. In fact, he or she doesn't necessarily teach anything at all.

People may ask questions, and he may answer those questions – whether or not he does so is up to him. But he has no vested interest in teaching. If nobody asked him any questions, he probably wouldn't bother to say anything. The Buddha himself made this perfectly clear. In several places in the Pāli scriptures he is reported as saying that he has no *diṭṭhi* – no view, no philosophy, no system of thought. 'There are lots of other teachers,' he says, 'who have this system of thought to expound, or that philosophy to teach; but I have none. I have no "view" to communicate. The Tathāgata (Buddha) is free from views, liberated from doctrines, emancipated from philosophy.'[76]

Outside the Pāli Canon the Buddha is further reported as saying that he has no Dharma to impart. The great *Diamond Sūtra* describes innumerable Bodhisattvas and disciples sitting and waiting for the Buddha to teach them the Dharma. But the Buddha tells them, 'I have nothing to teach.'[77] In another celebrated Mahāyāna text, the *Laṅkāvatāra Sūtra*, the Buddha goes so far as to say that he has never taught anything. 'Whether you have heard me speaking or not, the truth is that from the night of my Enlightenment, all through the forty-five years until the night of my parinirvāṇa, the night of my passing from the world, I have not uttered a single word.'[78] So the Buddha, the ultimate Buddhist guru, has no view, no teaching to impart. He is not a teacher.

Something else that the guru is not relates to one of the most striking facts about the human race as a whole, which is that the majority of its members do not grow up. People develop physically, of course, and they also develop intellectually in the sense that they learn how to organize their knowledge more and more coherently. But they don't grow up spiritually, or even emotionally. Many people remain emotionally immature, even infantile. They want to depend on someone stronger than themselves, someone who is prepared to love and protect them absolutely and unconditionally. They don't really want to be responsible for themselves. They want some authority or system to make their decisions for them.

When one is young, one depends on one's parents, but as one grows older, one is usually obliged to find substitutes for them. Many people find such a substitute in a romantic relationship, which is one of the reasons marriage is so popular, and also, often, so difficult. Others find their parent-surrogate in a concept of a personal God. One might even follow Freud in saying that God is a father-substitute on a cosmic scale. The believer expects from God the kind of love and protection that a child expects from his or her parents. It is highly significant that in Christianity, God is addressed as 'our Father'.

The role of father-substitute is often played by a guru – or rather a pseudo-guru. Mahatma Gandhi, for instance, was a great Indian politician, thinker, activist, even revolutionary, but it is rather significant that as a religious figure for much of his life he was addressed by his disciples as Bapu, 'Father'. Nor was this sort of title at all unusual in India. When I lived there I was in contact with quite a number of religious groups and their gurus, many of whom liked to be addressed as Dadaji, or 'Grandfather'. Their disciples, it seemed, were only too happy to fall in with their wishes in this respect.

This rather amused me, and when I was in Kalimpong and had some pupils of my own – most of them Nepalese rather than Indian – I asked them out of curiosity how they regarded me. At that time I was about thirty, and they were in their late teens and early twenties, so when they clasped their hands together and said with great fervour, 'Oh sir, you are just like our grandfather,' I was taken rather by surprise.

In India I also met a number of female gurus, and they were invariably addressed as Mataji, 'Mother', or even Ma, which means 'Mummy'.[79] One of these gurus, who was well into middle-age when I first got to know her, was surrounded by young male followers, most of whom, as I discovered later, had lost their mothers. In the evenings they would gather in the meeting-hall to sit gazing up at 'Mummy' and singing in chorus the word Ma – nothing else, just that word, 'Mummy' – to the accompaniment of drums and cymbals. They would keep it up for two or three hours at a time: 'Ma, Ma, Ma, Ma, Ma'. They believed that what they called 'Ma-ism' was a radical new development in religious history, and that the worship of Mother – this particular mother, anyway – would be the future religion of humanity. I was not at all surprised to find that there was intense competitiveness and jealousy among her disciples, as if they were all vying with one another to be the favourite, if not the only, son. It was also noticeable that they tended to disparage other groups. In the same way that children will say, 'My daddy is much stronger/richer than your daddy,' or 'Our house is bigger than your house,' they would maintain that in comparison with their own guru, other gurus were insignificant.

Fortunately, I have known gurus who knew how to manage their followers in a much more healthy manner – particularly certain Tibetan gurus. A story about three great lamas I knew personally in Kalimpong will illustrate this. All three were eminent lamas of deep and genuine spiritual experience, and they all had many disciples. Though they all belonged to the predominantly 'Red Hat' tradition, their characters were very different. One wore a sheepskin robe, dyed red, and was always on the move, so that it was difficult to catch him. Another lived with his wife and son, and gave initiation to thousands of people – initiations that were said to be particularly powerful. The third was the scholarly head of an important monastery.

The story I was told by one of their disciples – and they had a number of disciples in common – was that a discussion had once arisen among the disciples as to which of the three gurus was the greatest. In the end, one of the bolder spirits plucked up courage and approached one of the gurus. He said, 'Look, there's been a lot of discussion as to how the three of you would place yourselves with respect to each other. We all have immense veneration for all three of you, but we would appreciate it if you could clear up this point: Which of you is the greatest? Who has gone furthest? Who is nearest to nirvāṇa?' So the guru smiled and said, 'All right, I'll tell you. It is true that among us three there is one who is much more highly developed than the other two. But none of you will ever know which one that is.'

A real guru does not fall into the role of a father figure. This is not to say that people do not need father-substitutes, at least for a while. Such a projection may be necessary for their psychological development. One must also allow that the function of the guru is analogous to that of the true father: the guru fulfils the same function on a spiritual level that the true father fulfils on the ordinary human level. But the guru is not a substitute for a father where the father has been lacking, or where he is still required.

Neither should a guru be taken for a problem-solver. This brings us to a distinction that I find it helpful to draw between a problem and a difficulty. The difference is that a difficulty can be overcome or resolved with effort, whereas a problem cannot. If you put a lot of effort into what I call a problem, you only make it more problematic. It's like finding a knot in a piece of string and pulling on the two ends in order to untie it. You can pull as hard as you like, but you'll only succeed in tightening the knot. The genuine guru may help people overcome their difficulties, but he will not attempt to grapple with their problems.

There are fundamentally two kinds of problem: doctrinal problems and personal, usually psychological, problems. The problems of Westerners tend to be of the second type, whereas in the East people's problems are often doctrinal – they want to resolve technical questions to do with nirvāṇa, the *skandhas*, the *saṃskāras*, and so on. However, even such doctrinal problems are very often psychologically motivated, or at least psychologically oriented. One asks even the most abstract theoretical question ultimately for personal psychological reasons, though usually one is not conscious of this.

If you have a problem, it embodies a self-contradictory situation; it cannot be solved on its own terms. But if you bring it to your guru, you are in effect asking him or her to solve the problem on its own terms. For instance, a woman comes along in great distress, so upset that she can hardly speak. Eventually she tells her guru that she just can't live with her husband any longer. She's had enough. If she has to put up with any more, she'll go stark staring mad. She's just got to leave him. But her problem is that if she leaves her husband, she will have to leave her children too – because the children cannot be taken away from their father – and leaving her children is no less impossible than continuing to live with her husband. She will go mad if she has to stay with her husband, but she will also go mad if she has to leave her children. 'What am I to do?' she asks her guru expectantly.

Then somebody else comes along and complains of lack of energy: 'I'm always tired,' he says. 'I feel exhausted all the time, constantly at a low ebb, totally depleted. I can't do a thing. I don't seem able to work up any interest in anything; I just lie around all day like a limp, wet rag. I can watch a bit of television or listen to the radio, but that's it. I feel utterly drained all the time. There's just one thing that I know will help: meditation. I can get energy through meditation – I'm convinced of that.' So the guru says, 'Well, why don't you meditate?' And the unfortunate disciple replies wearily, 'I just don't have the energy.'

But if the guru has to send this person away with his problem still unresolved, there are still more problems waiting in the wings. To take yet another example, someone comes along and says that he just wants to be happy. That's all he asks from life. And he feels that he could be perfectly happy if only someone would give him a satisfactory reason for being happy. He has examined all the reasons offered by religions, philosophies, and friends, but none of them has proved truly convincing. Can the guru do better? If anyone has the answer, surely the guru will. Surely a guru is there to provide the answers to the big problems. Of course, the guru knows quite well that every reason he can produce will be rejected as unsatisfactory. But still the man demands a reason.

If you asked any of these people what they are really looking for, all of them would say that they want to find a solution to their problem.

That is why they have come to the guru. They firmly believe he can solve their problems if he chooses to do so. But, in fact, this is not the situation at all. What these people really want to do is defeat the guru. They present their problem in such a way that the guru cannot solve it without their consent or co-operation – which they have no intention of giving.

Such people are sometimes very cunning. Especially in the East they will very often approach the guru with a great show of devotion and humility, bearing presents, making offerings, bowing, and declaring their unshakeable faith in the guru. They say, 'I've taken this problem of mine to lots of other gurus, to all the most famous teachers and masters, and not one of them could solve it. But I've heard so much about you, and I'm sure that you are the one person who can.'

Only a guru who lacks experience, or isn't a true guru, will be taken in by all this. The true guru will see what is going on at once, and will refuse to play the role of problem-solver, even if, as is very likely, the person with the problem goes away disgruntled, and starts saying that the guru cannot be a true guru because he hasn't got the down-to-earth compassion to deal with his disciples' problems. Some gurus are rewarded with quite damaged reputations for refusing to play this sort of game.

So a guru is not the head of a religious group, or a teacher, or a father-substitute, or a problem-solver. This does not mean that he or she may not, from time to time, function in these ways, and in many others. A guru can function, for instance, as a physician, a psychotherapist, an artist, a poet, a musician, or even just a friend. But he or she will not identify with any of these roles.

The guru may be the head of a religious group, although this rarely happens, because the qualities that make a guru are not those that assist promotion within an ecclesiastical system. Much more often, particularly within the Buddhist sangha, the guru may be a teacher – that is, he or she may function outwardly as a teacher. But it remains important to distinguish the teacher from the guru as such. Some gurus may be teachers, but by no means all teachers are gurus. A guru may even function as a provisional father-substitute or problem-solver, but the emphasis is on 'provisional'. As soon as possible, he or she will discard this role and function as a guru.

But if the guru is none of these things, what is a guru? It has been said that there are many different ways of being wicked, but only one way of being good (which in the eyes of some people makes goodness seem rather dull). One could also say that there are many misconceptions about the guru, but only one true conception. There is therefore much that can be said about what a guru is not, but comparatively little to be said about what he or she positively is. Of course, this doesn't mean that it is any less important. Indeed, from a spiritual point of view, the more important a thing is, the less there is to be said about it.

Perhaps, above all, the guru is one who stands on a higher level of being and consciousness than ourselves, who is more evolved, more developed, more – in a word – aware. Also, a guru is someone with whom we are in regular contact. This contact may take place at different levels. It may take place on a higher spiritual plane – that is, telepathically – as the direct contact of mind with mind. There may be contact between the guru and the disciple in dreams or during meditation. But for the ordinary disciple, it generally takes place on the physical plane – that is, on the ordinary social plane, in the ordinary way. The relatively undeveloped disciple will need regular and frequent physical contact with the guru. According to Eastern tradition, ideally he or she would be in day-to-day contact with the guru, even living under the same roof.

Contact between the guru and the disciple should be 'existential' – that is, there should be real communication between them – not just the sharing of thoughts or ideas or feelings or experiences, even spiritual experiences, but communication of being, or, if you like, action and interaction of being. The guru and the disciple need to be themselves as fully as possible in relation to each other. The guru's business is not to teach the disciple anything, but simply to be himself in relation to the disciple. Nor, as the disciple, is it your business to learn. You simply have to expose yourself to the being – and to the effect of the being – of the guru, and at the same time, be yourself in relation to him.

Spiritual communication, like integration, can be thought of as being of two kinds: 'horizontal' and 'vertical'. Horizontal communication takes place between two people who are on more or less the same level of being and consciousness. Because their states of mind fluctuate from day to day, sometimes one of them will be in a better state of mind than the other, but the next day it may be the other way round. Vertical communication, on the other hand, takes place between people one of whom is on a consistently higher level than the other, quite apart from any ups and downs. It is such vertical communication that takes place between guru and disciple.

In all communication, whether horizontal or vertical, there is mutual modification of being. In the case of horizontal communication, in the course of communication anything one-sided or unbalanced in one's nature is corrected. People who really communicate gradually develop a similarity of outlook, responding to things in the same spirit; they have progressively more in common. At the same time, paradoxical as it may seem, they become more truly themselves.

Suppose, for example, a very rational person were to engage in true communication with a very emotional person. If they sustained this communication long enough, the emotional person would become more rational, and the rational person more emotional – each rubbing off on the other. At the same time, if you are the rational person (to take that example) you do not just have emotionality added to you from without. Through communicating with the emotional person, you are enabled to develop your own undeveloped emotionality which has been there all the time (as it were) beneath the surface. A quality emerges that was there, but not active. The communication has simply enabled you to become more yourself, more whole, more complete. And it's the same, obviously, if you are the emotional one of the two.

Vertical communication is different. The disciple grows in the direction of the guru's higher level of being and consciousness, but the guru does not become correspondingly more like the disciple. The principle of mutual modification of being does not mean that the guru slips back in his development as a result of his communication with someone less developed. He does not meet the disciple halfway, as it were. In the intensity of his or her communication with the guru, the disciple is in a sense compelled to evolve. He or she has no choice, unless they break off the relationship altogether, and a real disciple cannot even do that. It is said that the true disciple is like a bulldog puppy. When offered a towel, the puppy will snap at it and not let go, even if he was lifted off the ground with his jaws still attached to it. The true disciple has that sort of tenacity.

As a result of his vertical communication with the disciple, the guru also grows spiritually. The only guru who doesn't do this is a Buddha, a fully and perfectly enlightened one, and even among gurus a Buddha is extremely rare. It is sometimes said in Tantric circles that disciples are necessary to a guru's further development, that nothing helps a guru so much as having a really good disciple – not an obedient, docile disciple, but one who really engages in communication, one who is really trying to grow. A good disciple may give the guru quite a lot of trouble, sometimes more trouble than all the other disciples put together. It also occasionally happens that the disciple overtakes the guru, and a reversal of roles takes place. This situation is less problematic than it might seem from the outside, because the relationship is not one of authority or power, but of love and friendship.

So is a guru necessary? Well, to grow spiritually without any contact with a guru is extremely difficult. Generalizing, one might say that for most people spiritual growth does not take place without at least two factors being present: the experience of suffering, and contact with a more highly developed person or persons. Why? Because personal relationships and real communication are necessary to human development. Not only that – we need real communication that includes a vertical element. Through communication with our friends, we develop horizontally – we become more whole, more ourselves. But most people seem to need communication with a guru to enable them to rise to a higher level of being and consciousness. Just as a child develops into an adult mainly through contact with his or her parents, regular contact with at least one person who is more highly developed than we are is necessary for our spiritual development. Not that it is absolutely impossible to make progress without being in contact with such a person, but that kind of contact certainly speeds up and intensifies the whole process.

But if a guru is necessary, how do you go about choosing one? How do you know whether someone is more highly evolved than you are? Obviously, it is important not to make any mistake in this matter. The problem is that it is very difficult indeed to know if someone is really more advanced – perhaps impossible, without prolonged contact. Some gurus in the East say not only that it is impossible for the disciple to choose the guru, but that it is quite presumptuous for the disciple to think that he can do so, or that he can know whether someone is more developed than himself. What actually happens, they say, is that the guru chooses the disciple. You may think that you are choosing a guru, but in fact the only choice you are capable of making is of a religious group (with the guru as its head), or a religious teacher, or a father-substitute or problem-solver. You are not choosing a guru as such, because you are not equipped to see who is of greater spiritual attainment.

As a would-be disciple, what are you to do? All you can do is make as much progress as possible by yourself so that you can recognize and make contact with a spiritual community (as distinct from a religious group). Then you must hope that some member of that community will take you on as a friend, or refer you to somebody else who can. In any case, you should always be ready and receptive for the advent of the guru.

Sometimes the guru just grabs you by the scruff of the neck, as it were. You may not even have thought about the spiritual life; you may not have any interest at all in religion; you may not have any problems; you may be quite happy as you are; but the guru sees your potential, and takes you on anyway – he makes you a disciple regardless of your protests.

There is a well-known story of the Buddha himself adopting a disciple in such a peremptory manner. On the receiving end, so to speak, was his own cousin, a young man called Nanda – nicknamed Sundarananda, or 'Handsome Nanda'.[80] The occasion was Nanda's marriage to a very beautiful girl, and it seems that the Buddha had been invited to the marriage feast. The Buddha had produced his begging-bowl and been served along with everyone else; then after the feast, he prepared to go back into the depths of the forest. Calling for Nanda, he said, 'Nanda, would you mind carrying my bowl just a little way for me?' And, rather pleased to get this special attention from his illustrious relation, Nanda followed him, carrying his bowl.

As the Buddha paced sedately on, Nanda came after him rather less sedately because he kept looking back at his brand-new wife, entranced by the long shimmering tresses of her hair as she waved to him. After a few hundred yards, he found himself going deeper and deeper into the forest. He started to become a little uneasy, having heard all sorts of strange stories about his cousin. A mile or so into the forest he became really worried, but he was too much in awe of the Buddha to say anything, so he just stumbled on after him, still clutching his bowl. Mile after mile they went on in this way until eventually they emerged into a clearing where they found a circle of huts occupied by a group of the Buddha's disciples.

Wasting no time on introductions, the Buddha took the bowl from his cousin – who was by that time trembling with fear and confusion – and directed the other monks to ordain him. So they seized hold of Nanda, forced him down on to his knees, shaved his head, and stripped off his white robes, giving him yellow ones to wear instead. Finally he was instructed in the rules of the order of monks and taught how to meditate, and then left to sit under a tree and get on with it.

The story does, however, have a good outcome for Nanda, in that after undergoing further trials he eventually becomes an Arhant, an Enlightened One. Thus it is possible for a guru, if they know what they are doing, to go so far as virtually to hijack someone – an extreme example of the basic principle that it is the guru who chooses the disciple, not the other way round.

In a way, the guru cannot be overvalued. Nothing can be more valuable than the person who helps you to develop spiritually. All the same, it is true to say that in the East the guru often tends in a sense to be overvalued, while in the West he is usually undervalued. What can happen in the East is that a false and inflated value is attached to the guru. People in India sometimes say that the guru is God. This is asserted not just as a figure of speech, but quite literally. If you are sitting in front of the guru, you are not just looking at a human being, seated on a cushion on the floor. You're sitting in front of God – in fact, all the gods rolled into one, the all-powerful, the all-knowing himself. He may look just like an ordinary human being, but he knows everything that is going on in the whole universe, including everything going on in your mind. He can read your thoughts like an open book. If you've got a problem, you don't have to tell him – he knows already. He can do anything he likes. He can bless you, give you riches, promotion, fame, children, all with just a word of blessing. He can give you Enlightenment if he wants to. It is all in his hands – it's all the 'grace of the guru', as they say.

All the disciple has to offer is faith in the guru, faith that the guru is God. If the disciple only has enough of this kind of faith, the guru can work miracles on his behalf. Such faith is therefore regarded as of the very greatest importance. There are, of course, little difficulties. It sometimes happens that the guru appears not to know something, or to forget something you have told him, and you may get a bit upset by this. But the true disciple isn't bothered at all because he knows that these apparently human limitations and failings are tests of faith. The guru is only pretending to have slips of the mind to see if your faith is still firm and sound, just as a potter taps a pot after it's been baked, to see whether or not there's a crack in it.

It is no wonder that over the years the disciple comes to inhabit a fantasy world in which whatever happens is seen to do so on account of the guru's 'grace' and the guru's will. If the guru isn't careful, he may come to inhabit this fantasy world too, especially if he isn't a real guru. After all, it isn't easy to escape such a fantasy world if you yourself are at the centre of it. If someone comes and tells you that their child was sick and has now recovered due to your blessing, you may not be inclined to dispute that interpretation, even if you hadn't given the child a moment's thought.

The problem from the guru's point of view is that sooner or later it will dawn on certain of his more perceptive disciples that he isn't really God. While he may have a deep level of insight and spiritual experience, he also has some quite human limitations. Perceiving this, they are likely to conclude that he isn't a true guru, and go off to look for someone else, someone who is a true guru, someone who *is* God. If they do that, the same thing will inevitably happen all over again. They will start noticing little discrepancies, get disillusioned, and see that this guru too is 'only' a human being after all. And so the merry-go-round continues.

This happens among Buddhists as well to some extent. A Tibetan friend of mine, a lama and guru living in Kalimpong, recalled that when he first arrived there, the local Nepalese Buddhists used to flock to see him, bringing him wonderful offerings and eager to take initiations from him. But after a few years they got a bit tired of him. They continued to come to pay their respects, but he was amused to observe that they didn't bring quite such big offerings as before. Then a new lama arrived on the scene (he was a friend of the first one) and everybody abandoned my friend to get their new initiations from the new lama – to the amusement of both lamas. Eventually, as the Chinese communists seized power in Tibet, more and more gurus started to arrive in town, which was very bewildering for the local community. No sooner had they identified a supremely powerful guru and rushed to make him offerings, than another one arrived, who – according to some people – was even more eminent and accomplished. In the end they must have run through perhaps twenty gurus, looking for the 'real' one.

Clearly, the guru is overvalued in this manner in the East because he is regarded as an idealized parent figure: all-knowing, all-powerful, infinitely loving and tolerant. The disciple in such cases wants to adopt an attitude of infantile dependence. Gurus are usually very popular in India, but there is one thing demanded of them, regardless of almost anything else: they must always be kind and affectionate, soft-spoken and gentle. What they teach and how they live are side-issues by comparison.

In the West we have traditionally gone to the opposite extreme. Here, far from overvaluing the guru, we have hardly any concept of the guru at all. This is no doubt largely due to the influence of Christianity. On the one hand you have belief in God with all his various attributes, and on the other you have submission to the head of the particular religious group to which you belong, your ecclesiastical superior, but there seems to be no room for the guru in the true sense.

The gurus who do appear – who may eventually be identified as saints – are usually subject to the rule of the ecclesiastical authorities. In medieval times, even a great saint sometimes had to submit to a bad pope. Perhaps that didn't do the saint much harm, but it was bad for the pope, and for the Church as a whole. However, we must not imagine that the Christian tradition is the only spiritual tradition the West has ever known. Nor should we accept the assumption that the concept of the guru in the Eastern sense is alien to the Western mentality. There were certainly gurus in ancient Greece and Rome – for example Plato, who maintained a sort of school or academy, Pythagoras, who founded spiritual communities, Apollonius of Tyana, and above all perhaps, Plotinus. From Porphyry's life of Plotinus, especially the description of his later life in Rome, one gets the definite impression of a sort of spiritual community, set up more along the lines of an Indian ashram than in a manner typical of the kind of institution one might think of as characteristic of the later Roman Empire.[81]

Such great figures of classical times were gurus in the true sense of the term. And in modern post-Christian times there are signs that the importance of the guru is again beginning to be appreciated in the West, despite our democratic and egalitarian prejudices, our modern belief that no one should be seen as better than anybody else. Even in modern cultures so apparently hostile to the possibility of spiritual development, there are signs that people are beginning to appreciate the significance of those who are more highly developed than the average person.

Such people may not be appreciated in spiritual terms; more often they are lauded as geniuses or heroes. A noticeable phenomenon in the United States is the academic guru figure, who travels from one university campus to another and attracts crowds of students to his lectures. Young people who may have no interest in gurus from the East are beginning to feel or even think quite consciously that there is not much to be gained from books, and that the conventional voices of religion, politics, and even the arts, don't say very much to them.

They are therefore looking for some kind of guru figure. They want to be taught by someone wiser than themselves, someone they can look up to, someone who will shed a clear light to guide them on their path. There are some obvious examples of this phenomenon from the sixties – Buckminster Fuller, Allen Ginsberg, Timothy Leary, and Richard Alpert, who went on to become a guru in an overtly Eastern sense as Baba Ram Dass. Today, the 'guru' is a widespread feature of Western intellectual life.

As Buddhists, we have to follow a middle way. We have to recognize above all that we are capable of evolving from our present state of being and consciousness to a more fully developed degree of self-consciousness and even to a realization of transcendental consciousness, leading to what, without really being able to understand it, we can only call absolute consciousness. In order to do this, we have also to recognize that different human beings are at different stages of this great process of spiritual development. Some are lower down than we are, while others are higher up, even a great deal higher up. We have to recognize that those who are higher up in the scale of the evolution of humanity are in a position to help us, and that we will develop through communication with them. It is gurus in this sense whom we need to recognize as being superior. The kind of guru we don't need is one to whom we give an unrealistically inflated value, and on to whom we project our desire for an idealized father-figure. It is a great mistake to expect from a guru what we can only get, ultimately, from ourselves.

The Buddha did not ask anybody to regard him as a god or as God. He never asked anybody to have faith – much less to have absolute faith – in him. In fact, this is a very important aspect of Buddhism. The Buddha never said, 'You must believe in me, and believe what I say, if you want to be saved, or if you want to realize your own true nature.' Again and again in the Buddhist scriptures he is presented as saying, 'Let any reasonable man come to me, one who is willing to learn; I will teach him the Dharma.'[82] All he asks is that we should be rational and open-minded. All he requires is reasonable and receptive human contact. He seems to have been quite convinced that he could introduce anyone to the spiritual life without making any appeal for absolute faith and devotion, but purely by rational and empirical means. On this basis alone he could awaken anyone to the truth that the path to Enlightenment is the most worthwhile thing to which as human beings we can possibly devote ourselves.

15

FIDELITY

KALIMPONG IS SITUATED in the foothills of the Himalayas in the state of West Bengal, some four thousand feet above sea level. This is where I spent most of my time in India, within almost daily sight of the snows of the Himalayas for some fourteen years. Kalimpong was, and to a lesser extent still is, rather off the beaten track. Nevertheless, over the years I had plenty of visitors. At first they came from no further afield than Darjeeling, Calcutta, and other parts of India, but eventually I began to get a steady trickle of visitors from Europe, America, and Australia.

Some of these visitors, both from India and abroad, left a strong impression, and few more so than a certain elderly Punjabi, who came from the town of Wardha, right in the middle of India. He had been a Buddhist monk for a good many years, but he was better known in India as a Hindi journalist. He was a frequent visitor to Kalimpong, and when he was in town he invariably used to come and see me.

He had one characteristic that distinguished him from the great majority of his countrymen. Most Indians tend to avoid any form of exercise, but he loved his afternoon walk, and he certainly kept up this part of his routine whenever he was in Kalimpong. As well as his afternoon walk he also loved to talk, and if he could combine the two activities, that was all the better. But casting around Kalimpong for company for his afternoon walks, he found few takers among his Indian friends, which is how, when he came to understand that I wasn't averse to a walk, he latched on to me. He would stop by at about four or five o'clock of an afternoon, and we would walk along the roads that wound around the hillside for an hour or more.

I came to look forward to these walks, as he was an entertaining companion with an unending flow of anecdotes and opinions. He was not what one could call monkish – it was something of a mystery as to why he had become a bhikkhu at all – but one has to imagine him, a man in his early fifties, in yellow robes and with a shaven head, striding along with walking stick in hand, talking.

From him I gleaned information about Indian social life and politics, about developments in Indian Buddhism and Buddhist politics, and about the Hindi-speaking world and its literature. Among the many fascinating stories he had to tell, the following made a particularly strong impression on me at the time. It relates to something that had happened in Calcutta shortly before he made this particular visit to Kalimpong, and he spoke of it in the course of our first walk on that occasion, it being fresh in his mind.

He had heard it from a friend of both the parties concerned, who were students at the University of Calcutta. Central Calcutta is something of a university city, in which tens of thousands of young people of different backgrounds are brought together as students. And, as sometimes happens even in traditional India, two particular students – both Bengalis, both science students – fell in love. They were conducting experiments together in the laboratory, their eyes met over the test tubes, and that was that.

But in India, as in Shakespeare's Verona, the course of true love never runs smooth, because true love has no official sanction. What is still rather quaintly called 'free love' hardly exists at all. Marriages aren't made in heaven in India; they are arranged on earth by your parents and grandparents, who are careful to choose someone of the right background and, most crucially, of the same caste, or, to be exact, the same sub-caste. In the case of this couple even this basic requirement could not be fulfilled, as they happened to come from quite different castes. Hence there was no question of their love leading to marriage. There was no conceivable possibility of their parents consenting, and without the consent of parents there is no marriage in India.

What could they do? They felt that they couldn't live without each other, so they decided on a suicide pact. They agreed to commit suicide at the same time – but for one reason or another, they were not able to do so in the same place. On the appointed day, and at the agreed hour, the boy kept his side of the pact and swallowed poison – but the girl did not do likewise. Sadly, the day after her lover committed suicide, she was seen laughing and chatting with other male college students.

I have never been of a romantic disposition, but this story lingered in the back of my mind as a sort of recurring echo until I laid it to rest by turning it into a short story, which I entitled 'Fidelity'. It didn't come out very well, so it was never published, but much later, when I was back in England, I was reminded of what I had heard from my friend on that walk round Kalimpong by certain developments in the personal relationships of friends of mine – in some cases, people I had ordained – which reflected the theme, if not the dramatic conclusion, of that tragic sequence of events.

It is this story that gives me the angle I want to take on the third of the six relationships discussed by the Buddha and Sigālaka: the relationship between husband and wife. One of the five ways in which, according to the *Sigālaka Sutta*, husband and wife should 'minister' to each other is by not being unfaithful; and fidelity is our theme here. I do not propose to treat the subject exhaustively, or even systematically; I just want to put together a few observations. As well as commenting on the nature of the relationship between husband and wife (or the modern equivalent), I want to explore the theme of fidelity because – to return to our earlier theme – I have come to the conclusion, the more I have thought about it, that fidelity should be one of the qualities of what I call the true individual – that is, of one who is trying to become a truly human being.

So far as I can see, all the different kinds of fidelity can be included under three main headings: fidelity to oneself, fidelity to ideals, and fidelity to other people. Arguably, one could make fidelity to one's given word into a fourth heading, but this is perhaps best considered as an aspect of fidelity to oneself, although it obviously involves fidelity to others as well. Fidelity to oneself could also be described as being true to oneself, as in the famous advice of Polonius to his son Laertes, in Shakespeare's *Hamlet*:

This above all: to thine own self be true,
And it must follow, as the night the day,
Thou canst not then be false to any man.[83]

Being true to oneself means consistently acting, speaking, and thinking in accordance with what is best in oneself. It involves seeing oneself objectively – not in a cold-blooded fashion, but in the sense of seeing clearly one's own real interests, in the highest and fullest sense, and being consistently faithful to them.

Fidelity to ideals is not so easy to explain. It does not necessarily mean fidelity to ideas. In fact, to understand what it does mean we have to be clear about the difference between an ideal and an idea. An ideal may be defined as a regulative model for human existence. But – and this is the important point – this model is not imposed upon human existence from outside. It is derived from human existence itself. An ideal brings the basic trend, the true nature, of that existence more clearly into consciousness, and thus intensifies, or even elevates, that basic trend. Ideals, therefore, are instruments of human development.

Ideals – or rather, human beings holding those ideals – can of course lose touch with the concrete situation, become detached from human experience, and when that happens ideals cease to function as ideals. They become dead ideals, and thus not really ideals at all. Dead ideals are simply ideas, and as such they should indeed be rebelled against and rejected.

So fidelity to ideals means consistently acting, speaking, and thinking in accordance with the regulative models of human existence, being true to the basic trend or true nature of that existence, especially as that trend is reflected, intensified, and amplified in consciousness or awareness. Fidelity to ideals eventually becomes virtually indistinguishable from fidelity to oneself. It is, one might say, the objective counterpart of fidelity to oneself.

Fidelity to other people is perhaps easier to understand, at least superficially. In feudal society, as we have seen, there is the fidelity of the retainer to his overlord. In domestic life there is the fidelity of wife and husband to each other, and of servant to master. And in the broader sphere of social life there is fidelity between friends. Fidelity to other people means consistently behaving, speaking, and thinking in accordance with the way in which one has defined oneself in relation to those other people. It means behaving as one has undertaken to behave towards them.

Fidelity is thus the consequence of a voluntary act. One can speak of a good mother or a good slave, but one cannot speak of a faithful mother or a faithful slave, because the relation of mother to child or of slave to master is not one that is entered upon voluntarily. It is imposed – by nature in the one case, by society in the other.

But what makes fidelity a quality of the individual, or, indeed, part of the very way in which we should define the true individual? We have seen that the first and most fundamental quality, the essence, of the individual is self-awareness or reflexive consciousness, the ability to see oneself objectively. Being self-aware is seeing ourselves as others see us – not quite in Robert Burns's sense, perhaps, but in the sense of seeing ourselves in the same sort of way that others see us, as an object of awareness. We can become the object of our own thought.

Thought is not limited, in the way that our body is limited, by time and space. Through thought we can abstract ourselves from the conditions under which we at present exist. In particular, we can form an idea of ourselves as having existed in the past and as having an existence to come in the future. Self-consciousness therefore involves a degree of separation from the present, a sort of standing back from it. It is because we have self-consciousness that we can project our idea of ourselves into the future; and it is because we can do this that we can say in the present that we will do something in the future. In other words, it is because we have self-consciousness that it is possible for us to make a promise.

When we say that fidelity involves consistency – consistently behaving in a certain way – this implies continuity in time. Consistency means behaving in the same way over a period of time. Indeed, it means more than this. It means consciously and deliberately behaving in the same way over a period of time. And to be able to do this, we must have self-awareness, we must be individuals.

If our self-awareness is weak, we will not be able to keep a promise. We may say the appropriate words because they are expected of us, but they will not have the significance of a promise if we are not able to keep that promise. If we don't keep a promise it is because in truth we never made it in the first place.

It is lack of self-awareness, lack of individuality, that gets in the way of our being faithful. This applies to our capacity to be faithful to ourselves and our ideals, but here I will discuss it in terms of fidelity to other people – in fact, in terms of fidelity to one other person. And, of course, the form of fidelity to another person with which we are most familiar, and about which we are usually most exercised, is sexual fidelity.

We all know what sexual fidelity means, at least in a superficial sense. It means confining one's sexual activity to one person. Most of us would also agree that the antithesis of fidelity is promiscuity. There are, of course, degrees of promiscuity, and most people understand the precise degree to be determined by the number of sexual partners one has (at different times in one's life, usually). But properly defined, promiscuity consists not in the multiplicity of one's sexual relations, but in non-continuity. The essence of promiscuity is that one does not have sexual relations with the same person twice consecutively. The most completely promiscuous person would therefore be the one who, over however long a period, never had sexual relations with any partner more than once.

With respect to sexuality, there are three possible lifestyles: the monogamous (or polygamous where that is an option), the promiscuous, and the celibate. The degree of approbation accorded by 'the group' towards the way people express their sexuality is based, by and large, on these choices of lifestyle. (The group may also reserve degrees of disapprobation for what it considers to be perverse expressions of sexuality.) But so far as the development of the individual is concerned, there are just two forms of sexual lifestyle: a neurotic form and a non-neurotic or psychologically healthy form. Someone who is trying to be an individual may follow any one of these lifestyles, provided he or she follows it in its non-neurotic form.

But how does this square with the idea that fidelity is a quality of the true individual? It would seem that there is a certain contradiction here. Are we, or are we not, saying that it may be ethical for the individual to follow a sexually promiscuous lifestyle? The difficulty is more apparent than real. The essence of the matter is that it is quite impossible for all the relationships of one's life to be continuous. However, some of them must be, otherwise one can hardly be self-aware at all. To the extent that one limits the continuity of one's relationships, to that extent one will not continue to grow as an individual. Having sexual relationships which are non-continuous need not be a problem if we have non-sexual relationships that are central to our life and which are continuous – i.e. in relation to which we practise fidelity. At the same time, if our non-continuous sexual relationships are more important to us than our continuous non-sexual relationships, we are obviously in serious difficulties.

But – to return to our main theme – how does one sustain fidelity to one person? There are two enemies of such fidelity: a 'near enemy', attachment, and a 'far enemy', distraction.[84] Distraction could be described as something that forces itself on our attention when we do not really want to pay attention to it. Of course, we experience distraction almost every time we try to meditate. We may be trying to concentrate on the process of our breathing, but the noise of the traffic outside intrudes and it seems that we just can't help listening to it. Sometimes the thing that forces itself on our attention is something to which at another time we would be very glad to pay attention. It may be something of which we are very fond or even something by which we are fascinated, something that appeals to our most basic interests and desires. I hardly need spell out the kinds of thing this might be. The distraction then becomes very difficult to resist.

In meditation, the distractions that present themselves to us come in the form of memories and fantasies, but in daily life we are confronted by distracting objects that are all too obviously and literally present. This is what makes it difficult for us to practise fidelity. The distracting object – or, generally, person – is present, whereas the person to whom we intend to be faithful may not be. Of course, the impression produced by something present is very vivid, by comparison with the impression produced by something that is not present (other factors being equal). Thus, a person who is present may cause us to forget – at least for the time being – a person who is absent, or even to act as if the absent person did not exist at all. There occurs a breach of continuity in our relationship with that other person, and this is the essence of infidelity. Present impressions have triumphed over our sense of continuity, in respect of our relation with that other person through past, present, and future.

We usually say that someone who yields too easily to the impressions of the moment has a weak character. They have very little continuity of purpose and, being so easily distracted, they don't have much individuality either. Such a person cannot practise fidelity. Of course, the reality of the situation is not neat and abstract in this way, although it can be described so succinctly. We are talking about some of the messier aspects of human life, and the human messiness involved should not be forgotten.

The near enemy of fidelity is attachment. It is called the near enemy because fidelity and attachment look very much alike, at least to the superficial observer. But where there is a neurotic degree of attachment to another person, there can be no fidelity, because there is no real self-awareness in that attachment, and therefore no real individuality. One's attachment to someone in the present excludes consciousness of past or future, and is simply prolonged indefinitely. One does not experience such a relationship as persisting through time. One is therefore incapable of fidelity.

But how does one know if one is capable of being faithful? How is fidelity tested? A test is a situation or experience that exposes the true nature of a thing, which reveals whether it is the genuine article or only a poor imitation. Thus, for example, fire reveals whether a certain yellow metal is gold or just something that looks like it.

Our fidelity to another person is, of course, tested by physical separation. When we are separated from someone, the relationship is transferred, at least for the time being, from the physical to the mental plane. Its continuity becomes exclusively mental (the term 'mental' being understood as including the emotional aspect of the psyche). It is much more difficult to live on the mental plane than on the physical plane, because sense consciousness is much stronger than self-awareness. Consequently, when as a result of separation our relationship has to exist on the mental plane, it is only too easy for that relationship to be interrupted by a relationship with someone else on the physical plane. In other words, it is only too easy for us to be unfaithful. Fidelity is possible only to the extent that we can envisage our relationship with the person from whom we are separated continuing into the future. This ability to project ourselves into the future is in turn possible only to the extent that we are self-aware.

Thus separation is also the test of self-awareness. Indeed, it is because it is the test of self-awareness that it is the test of fidelity. Separation reveals the level at which our relationship with another person really exists – whether it is predominantly physical or both physical and mental; and fidelity is possible only to the extent that a relationship is mental (and emotional). Physical separation can therefore be taken as an opportunity for developing and intensifying the non-physical side of a relationship along with one's self-awareness. This in turn will enhance one's individuality in the true sense of the term.

The most extreme form of separation, obviously, is death, and death is therefore the ultimate test of fidelity, as it was for those Bengali students. One might even say that fidelity includes awareness of death, as indeed does self-awareness. If you can imagine yourself existing in the future, you can also imagine yourself not existing in the future. To be self-aware, to be human, to be an individual, is therefore to be aware of death.

Fidelity is also tested by isolation, in the sense of being in a minority, even in a minority of one. This kind of test applies particularly to fidelity to ideals, although it can also apply to fidelity to another person. It is very difficult really to stand alone. It is very difficult to hold on to your ideals – whatever those ideals may be – when everyone around you is trying to persuade you to abandon them, because they think those ideals are wrong, or inopportune, or out of date, or no fun. You are in a very difficult position when your most precious values cut you off from everyone else, whether from your family, your neighbourhood, your country, your culture – even, it may sometimes seem, from everyone in the whole world. If you happened to believe in God and your ideals also seemed to cut you off from him, so much the worse. Human beings will do almost anything to avoid the terrible isolation of being derided by others on account of their ideals, and most people will be tempted to give up those ideals under that sort of pressure.

A good example of isolation as the ultimate test of fidelity to ideals is to be found in Milton's *Paradise Lost*. In one passage, the angel Abdiel finds himself by a mischance among the rebel angels, and thus in the uncomfortable position of disagreeing with their rebellion against God. He is in fact the only one in the whole vast assembly of millions of rebel angels who so disagrees. After Abdiel, all alone, denounces Lucifer and the rebel angels, Milton comments on his noble fidelity, thus:

> *So spake the seraph Abdiel, faithful found.*
> *Among the faithless, faithful only he;*
> *Among innumerable false, unmoved,*
> *Unshaken, unseduced, unterrified,*
> *His loyalty he kept, his love, his zeal;*
> *Nor number, nor example, with him wrought*
> *To swerve from truth, or change his constant mind,*
> *Though single, from amidst them forth he passed,*
> *Long way through hostile scorn, which he sustained*
> *Superior, nor of violence feared aught;*
> *And, with retorted scorn, his back he turned*
> *On those proud towers to swift destruction doomed.*[85]

I will end this chapter with two stories. Like the one that opened the chapter, they are concerned with both fidelity and death. The first comes from Beethoven's opera *Fidelio*, which was composed at the beginning of the nineteenth century. Fidelio means 'faithful one', and it is the name assumed by Leonora, the wife of a Spanish nobleman called Floristan. Floristan has aroused the enmity of Pizzaro, the governor of a gloomy medieval fortress which functions as a prison for political offenders, and Pizzaro seizes him and casts him in the deepest and darkest dungeon of the fortress, meanwhile spreading abroad a report of Floristan's death. Everybody believes this report – everybody, that is, except Leonora. Refusing to accept that her husband is dead, she plans a ruse to gain entry to the fortress and save him. Disguising herself as a young man, taking the name of Fidelio, she gets work in the fortress as assistant to the chief jailer, called Rocco. Of course, Rocco has a daughter who falls in love with the supposed young man, giving rise to the mandatory operatic complications. It is at this point that the opera opens.

Condensing the story to its essentials, it runs as follows: Pizzaro learns that Fernando, the minister of state, is coming to inspect the fortress, and decides to murder Floristan before Fernando arrives. He posts a trumpeter on the battlements to give warning of Fernando's approach, and orders Rocco, the chief jailer, to kill Floristan. Rocco refuses. Pizzaro then orders him to go and dig Floristan's grave and says that he will kill Floristan himself, with his own hands. So Rocco digs the grave ready for Floristan, and Fidelio (Leonora) as his assistant has to help him dig it, although she is digging the grave of her own husband. The scene then changes to Floristan's cell, where Pizzaro is on the point of stabbing Floristan. At this moment Leonora throws herself in front of him and says he must kill her first. As she does so, the famous trumpet call is heard. The minister of state arrives, Pizzaro is arrested, and Floristan and Leonora are reunited.

It has been said that 'as a drama and as an opera *Fidelio* stands almost alone in its perfect purity, in the moral grandeur of its subject and in the resplendent ideality of its music'. As for the moral grandeur of its subject, this obviously refers to the opera's exploration of the theme of fidelity. When Floristan disappears and is rumoured to be dead, Leonora doesn't start looking for another husband, but goes in search of Floristan and risks her own life to save him. Her fidelity is tested by death in more ways than one, and she passes the test. The opera is not staged very often, although the various 'Leonora' overtures are familiar orchestral fare. Whether this is because the 'moral grandeur of its subject' is a bit much for modern audiences, and fidelity is out of fashion, it is impossible to say. But if so, perhaps the fact is of significance. If we want to cultivate the qualities of the true individual, we may not get very much help from our society as far as fidelity is concerned.

Passing from a Western story to an Eastern one, and from an opera to a sūtra, we come again to the *Amitāyur-Dhyāna Sūtra*, the sūtra of the meditation on Amitāyus, the Buddha of Infinite Life.[86] Here we find another fortress, another dungeon, another prisoner, and another faithful wife – added to which we get some extra ingredients: the Buddha, the Dharma, and the Sangha. We have encountered this story before, in our consideration of the spiritual community and the Pure Land. As we have already seen, when this sūtra opens – in Rājagṛha, the capital of Magadha – King Bimbisāra has just been deposed by his wicked son Ajātasatru, who has shut him up in prison, hoping that there he will starve to death. In fact, he isn't just hoping – he conveniently forgets to give orders that his father should be supplied with food. But Vaidehī secretly takes food to her husband and keeps him alive day after day, week after week, month after month. In other words, she remains faithful.

Eventually, Ajātasatru becomes suspicious about the fact that his father is not dying as expected. Setting watch on the comings and goings at the prison, he eventually discovers that he has his mother to blame for his father's irritating survival. Ajātasatru is clearly not a dutiful son at the best of times, and in his fury he draws his sword on his mother, and is only restrained from matricidal violence by his ministers. They say, 'In our royal traditions there are many records of kings who have killed their fathers, but none yet of a king who has killed his mother. Desist from this unspeakably bad action.' Ashamed, the king sheathes his sword and contents himself with ordering that his mother should be imprisoned too. In prison she prays to the Buddha – for she is not only a faithful wife, but also a faithful disciple of the Buddha – and begs him to send his disciples, Ānanda and Mahāmaudgalyāyana, to visit her.

Hearing her plea with his divine ear, the Buddha does more than she asks. Together with Ānanda and Mahāmaudgalyāyana, he appears before her, resplendent with rainbow light, filling the darkness of the prison cell. Vaidehī tells him that she is dissatisfied with this world (as well she might be) and asks the Buddha to teach her how to meditate on a better world. The Buddha does as she asks, and the description of these meditations makes up the greater part of the sūtra.

In this story too we see how fidelity is tested by separation, even by death. Vaidehī remained faithful to Bimbisāra even at the risk of her own life. Possessing the quality of fidelity, she was an individual; and because she was an individual, she could go for Refuge to the Buddha, the Dharma, and the Sangha. She could see the Buddha and his disciples before her, and she could hear the Dharma. Ultimately, in fact, fidelity means fidelity to these three ideals. Fidelity to oneself is ultimately fidelity to the Buddha. Fidelity to ideals is ultimately fidelity to the Dharma. And fidelity to other people is ultimately fidelity to the Sangha.

Fidelity of this supreme kind is embodied in the figure of the female Bodhisattva Tārā, sometimes called Samayatārā (which, according to Lama Govinda, translates as 'the faithful Tārā'). All Bodhisattvas, however, are embodiments of perfect fidelity. They are faithful to all beings, and their fidelity is without limit in space and time. They are, we may say, individuals in the fullest and highest sense.

Hence if we want to be Bodhisattvas, if we want to be individuals, we should practise fidelity. We should be faithful to ourselves, to our word, to our promise. We should be faithful to our ideals, to our experience, to our work, to the path of human development. We should be faithful to other people: not just to our lovers, but to our friends, fellow workers, and teachers. And ultimately we should be faithful to the Three Jewels. Without fidelity there is no continuity, without continuity there is no development, and without development there is no spiritual life. Fidelity is a human need because development is a human need. And fidelity is part of human nature because development is part of human nature.

16

THE MEANING OF FRIENDSHIP

IN THE MODERN WORLD, friendship is arguably the most neglected of all the primary human relationships. But as we have seen, according to the Buddha himself, friendship has a direct connection with the spiritual life. Speaking to Sigālaka on the subject, he says that friends and companions are to be served and looked after in five ways.[87] In other words, we have five duties towards our friends, and if we perform these, our friendships will flourish.

First of all, it is our duty to be generous. We should share with our friends whatever we have. This should ideally be taken quite literally. Some Buddhist residential communities live on the basis of a common purse, pooling all their resources. This isn't easy to do, of course – some people find it difficult even to share a book – but it reflects the ideal relationship between friends. Ideally, your friend should not even have to *ask* you for money. If you take the principle of sharing seriously, you share everything: time, money, resources, interest, energy – everything. You keep nothing back for yourself.

The second duty is never to speak harshly or bitterly or sarcastically to our friends, but always kindly and compassionately. Speech is taken very seriously in Buddhism. The five basic Buddhist precepts include just one speech precept – to refrain from false speech – but it is not enough just to speak truthfully, and this is reflected in the ten precepts taken by some Buddhists. These include no less than four speech precepts, because it is so easy to fall into harmful, destructive speech, to speak in an indifferent, careless, or even callous way.

Our third duty to our friends is to look after their welfare, especially their spiritual welfare. As well as seeing that they are all right in terms of their health and economic well-being, and helping them with any difficulties they have, we should help them in whatever way we can to grow and develop as human beings.

Fourthly, we should treat our friends in the same way we treat our own self. This is a very big thing indeed, because it means breaking down the barrier between oneself and others. One of the most important Mahāyāna texts, the *Bodhicaryāvatāra* of Śāntideva, deals with this topic in great depth and considerable detail.[88]

And fifthly, we should keep the promises we make to our friends. We should keep our word. If we say we will do something for a friend, we just do it, come what may. If we are careless about fulfilling our promises, it is usually because we make them carelessly. We therefore have a duty to make our promises so mindfully that we treat them as serious obligations. Once we have given our word, that should be that.

Just as we have these five duties towards our friends, they have the same duties towards us; it's a two-way thing. Our friends and companions minister to us, serve us, reciprocate our friendship. Having listed our duties towards our friends, the *Sigālaka Sutta* therefore gives a list of five ways in which our good friends look after us. Firstly, according to the sutta, they take care of us when we are sick. Secondly, they watch over our property when we are neglectful; in other words they take more care of our possessions than we do ourselves – that is a sure sign of friendship. Thirdly, they are our refuge in time of fear: they can allay our anxiety, and if we have genuine cause for fear they help us deal with the situation. Fourthly, they do not forsake us when we are in trouble; as the proverb says, 'A friend in need is a friend indeed.' And lastly, they show concern for our dependants. If we have children, our friends are just as concerned for their welfare as we are ourselves, and the same goes for the welfare of our disciples, if we happen to have disciples.[89]

These, in brief, are the duties of a friend. Clearly they represent a very high ideal of friendship, and they repay careful reflection. Here I will just point out one or two salient features. It is interesting, for example, that the first four duties are identical with another well-known list that occupies an important place in Mahāyāna Buddhism: the four *saṁgrahavastus*, usually translated as the four elements of conversion.[90] These form part of the seventh *pāramitā*, the seventh of the ten Perfections to be practised by the Bodhisattva: *upāyapāramitā*, the perfection of *upāya* or skilful means. The four *saṁgrahavastus* are thus an aspect of the Bodhisattva's skilful means.

The fact that these elements of conversion are the same as the first four duties of a friend says something deeply significant about how the sangha operates at its best. It suggests that the best way of converting people is simply by being friends with them. Some people try to convert others to their point of view or their religion almost forcibly, but this is not the Buddhist way. Buddhists should convert people – if that is really the right word – simply by being friendly. We make friends and that's an end of it. There is no need to preach to people, to knock on their doors and say, 'Have you heard the word of the Buddha?'

As a Buddhist one should not be thinking about 'converting' someone, or in any way manoeuvring them on to the path that one follows oneself. One's business is just to be a friend, to be generous, to share whatever one has, to speak kindly and affectionately, to show concern for one's friend's welfare, especially their spiritual welfare, to treat them in the same way that one treats oneself, and to keep one's word to them.

However, the fact that these four things are elements of conversion means that in themselves they constitute a communication of the Dharma. You communicate the Dharma itself by practising friendship in this way. One could even go so far as to say that friendship *is* the Dharma. William Blake, the great English poet, artist, and mystic, said, 'Religion is politics.' But he went on to say: 'Politics is brotherhood.'[91] Religion, therefore, is brotherhood. We can say, following him, that the Dharma is friendship. If you are practising friendliness you are not only practising the Dharma, but communicating it.

One further issue raised by the duties of friendship has particularly important implications. It concerns the fourth duty: treating our friends and companions like our own self. The Sanskrit term, here, is *samānārthatā* – *samān* meaning equal. A friend is one whom you treat equally. But what does this mean? A clue is to be found in the etymology of the word friend, which is apparently cognate with the word free. Friendship is a relationship that can exist only between two or more free people – that is to say, people who are equals. Understanding this, the Ancient Greeks maintained that there could be no friendship between a free man and a slave.

We can take this metaphorically as well as literally. Friendship, we can conclude, can never involve any kind of power relationship. The relation between master and slave is based upon power, and where one person has any kind of power over another, there can be no friendship, because friendship is based upon love – to use the word love in the sense of the Pāli term *mettā* rather than in the sharply differentiated sense of the term *pema*, which is love as sticky attachment or possessiveness. *Pema* is fundamentally selfish, and it can easily turn into hatred; sexual love, of course, is often of this kind. But mettā is unselfish or non-attached, concerned only with the happiness and well-being of others.

The Pāli word for friend, *mitta* (Sanskrit *mitra*), is closely related to the term *mettā* (Sanskrit *maitrī*). And mettā is of course the quality developed in one of the most important Buddhist meditation practices, the mettā bhāvanā, the development of friendliness towards all living beings. This practice begins with the development of mettā towards yourself. In the next stage you develop mettā towards a near and dear friend (not a sexual partner or someone to whom you are sexually attracted). In the third stage you direct that same feeling of mettā, which by this time should be quite well-established, towards a neutral person – someone you know fairly well but whom you neither particularly like nor dislike. Next, in the fourth stage, you develop that same mettā towards an 'enemy' – someone whom you regard as an enemy or perhaps who regards you as an enemy, or both. It might sound incredible that you could develop deep friendliness towards an enemy, but anyone who has done the mettā bhāvanā practice with any regularity will know from their own experience that it is possible.

Finally, in the fifth stage, you develop mettā towards all these four people – to yourself, your friend, the neutral person, and the enemy – and then you start expanding the range of your mettā, cultivating it towards anyone upon whom your attention falls. You start with people who are close by – those meditating with you, or those in the same house or street – and then allow your mettā to radiate further and further, to include everyone in the neighbourhood, the city, the whole world. You can include within the scope of your mettā all kinds of people as well as other living beings, even gods and animals.

With the help of this meditation practice we can develop a friendly attitude. In other words, we shift from operating in the power mode to operating in the love mode. There are many ways of operating in the power mode – that is, focusing on getting what we want in a situation that involves other people. Usually, if we are clever enough, we don't have to use force. Subtly and indirectly we manipulate other people into doing what we want them to do, not for their good but for our own purposes. Some people are very good at this. They are so subtle, they seem so unselfish and so frank, that you hardly know that you are being manipulated, and it's so indirect that they may not even realize they're doing it. But in one way or another we deceive people, and ourselves, as to our real motives. We cheat, we lie, we commit emotional blackmail. But in mettā, in friendship, there is none of this, but only mutual concern for each other's happiness and well-being.[92]

Thus, friendship has a definitely spiritual dimension, and the Buddha has other things to say on the subject in other places. In chapter four of the *Udāna*, which may be an even earlier text than the *Sigālaka Sutta*, we find the Buddha staying at a place called Cālikā, accompanied by his attendant, who is at this time a monk called Meghiya. The two of them are alone together one day when Meghiya, who seems to be quite a young monk, happens to see a lovely grove of mango trees. In India you often get these on the outskirts of a village; the trees are very beautiful, with an abundance of dark green leaves, and they grow close together, so that as well as producing mangoes, they provide cool shade in the hot Indian summer.

Meghiya thinks to himself, 'What a beautiful grove of mango trees! And what a very fine place in which to sit and meditate – so cool and refreshing!' He therefore asks the Buddha if he may go and spend some time there. The Buddha, however, asks him to wait a while until some other monk arrives, because, for one reason or another, the Buddha needs someone to be with him. But Meghiya is not concerned with what the Buddha needs. Instead, he comes up with a clever and apparently unanswerable argument. He says, 'It's all very well for you – you've reached the goal of Enlightenment – but I have a long way to go in my practice. It's such a beautiful mango grove, I really want to go there and meditate.' In the end the Buddha has to agree, and off Meghiya goes, leaving the Buddha on his own. However, although Meghiya has got what he wanted, and the mango grove turns out to be just the fine, peaceful place he thought it was going to be, he finds that he can't settle into his meditation at all. Despite his enthusiasm and energy, as soon as he sits down his mind is overwhelmed with greed, jealousy, anger, lust, false views – the lot. He just doesn't know what to do.

In the end he trudges back to the Buddha and reports on his abject failure. The Buddha doesn't scold him, but he gives him a teaching. He says, 'Meghiya, when you are spiritually immature there are five things that conduce to spiritual maturity. And the first of these is spiritual friendship. The second thing is the practice of ethics; and the third is serious discussion of the Dharma. Fourthly, you need to direct energy towards eliminating negative mental states and developing positive ones. And fifthly, you must cultivate insight in the sense of a deep understanding of universal impermanence.'[93]

The Buddha marked out these five things as necessary for the spiritually undeveloped, and of course he was implying that Meghiya should put spiritual friendship first. If you have a spiritual friend, whether the Buddha or someone much less eminent, they cannot be disregarded in the careless way that Meghiya has brushed off the Buddha. But like Meghiya, we are often unaware of the extent to which we are dependent spiritually on having personal contact with our spiritual friends, particularly those who are more developed than we are. It is very difficult to make any spiritual progress without them. The Buddha himself is no longer around, but most of us, like Meghiya, would not be ready for such a friend anyway. We would probably act rather as Meghiya did.

We may not have the Buddha, but we do have one another. We can help one another, encourage one another in our practice of the Dharma. We can confess our faults and weaknesses to one another. We can share our understanding with one another. We can rejoice in one another's merits. In these ways we can make a practice of spiritual friendship.

No one else can practise the Dharma for us; we have to practise it ourselves. But we do not have to practise it *by* ourselves. We can practise it in the company of other like-minded people who are trying to do the same, and this is the best way – in fact, the only effective way – to practise.

As the Buddha was to say to his disciple and cousin Ānanda, some years later at a place called Sakka, 'Spiritual friendship is the whole of the spiritual life.' But how are we to take this? We can understand that friendship is important, but the idea that friendship, even spiritual friendship, should be the whole of the spiritual life, does seem hard to swallow. But let us look a little more closely at what is being said here.

The Pāli word I have translated as 'spiritual life' is *brahmacariya*, which sometimes means celibacy or chastity – that is to say abstention from sexual activity – but in this context it has a much wider meaning. It consists of two parts. *Brahma* means high, noble, best, sublime, and real; it also means divine, not in the theistic sense but in the sense of the embodiment of the best and noblest qualities and virtues. And *cariya* means walking, faring, practising, experiencing, even living. Hence *brahmacariya* means something like 'practising the best' or 'experiencing the ideal'; we could even render it 'the divine life', or just 'spiritual life', as I have done.[94]

There is a further aspect to the term *brahmacariya* that brings us to a deeper understanding of what it means in this context. In early Buddhism there is a whole series of terms beginning with *brahma*, and one of these is *brahmaloka*, which means the sublime realm, the divine world, or simply the spiritual world in the highest sense. So the *brahmacariya* or spiritual life is that way of life that leads to the *brahmaloka* or spiritual world. But how is it able to do this? For the answer, we must turn to yet another early Buddhist text: the *Mahāgovinda Sutta*. Without going into the background to this sutta – it's a long story – we find in it this very question being asked: 'How does a mortal reach the immortal brahma world?' In other words, how can one pass from the transient to the eternal? And the answer given is short and simple. 'One reaches the brahma world by giving up all possessive thoughts, all thoughts of me and mine.' In other words, one reaches the brahmaloka by giving up egoism and selfishness, by giving up all sense of 'I'.[95]

Thus the intimate connection between spiritual friendship and spiritual life starts to come into focus. Spiritual friendship is a training in unselfishness, in egolessness. You share everything with your friend or friends. You speak to them kindly and affectionately, and show concern for their welfare, especially their spiritual welfare. You treat them in the same way you treat yourself – that is, you treat them as being equal with yourself. You relate to them with an attitude of mettā, not according to where the power between you lies. Of course this is very difficult; it goes against the grain, because we are naturally selfish. The development of spiritual friendship is very difficult. Leading the spiritual life is very difficult. Being a Buddhist – a real Buddhist – is very difficult. We need help.

And we get that help not only from our teachers but also from one another. We can't be with our spiritual teacher all the time, but we can be with our spiritual friends all the time, or at least much of the time.

We can see them regularly, perhaps live with them, perhaps even work with them. If we spend time with spiritual friends in this way, we will get to know them better, and they will get to know us better. We will learn to be more open and honest, we will be brought up against our weaknesses, and in particular we will be brought up against our natural tendency to operate in accordance with the power mode. If we have spiritual friends, they will try not to relate to us in this way and they will expect us to operate in the love mode as well, to relate to them with mettā. Learning to relate to our friends in this way, we will gradually learn to respond to the whole world with mettā, with unselfishness. It is in this way that spiritual friendship is indeed the whole of the spiritual life.

17

BUDDHISM AND BUSINESS RELATIONSHIPS

THE PRINCIPLE of non-exploitation should ideally hold good in all the relationships of life. It should be possible for us to take what we need, whether food, clothing, education, or anything else, and give whatever we can. There is no need for there to be any connection between what we give and what we receive. Unfortunately, however, the way things usually work is that each person involved in any transaction, whether as the giver or as the receiver, thinks only of himself or herself, giving as little as possible in exchange for as much as possible. This is how ordinary life generally works: we negotiate transactions in which what we give is determined by what we can get for it, not by any regard for the consequences of the transaction for other people.

Beyond a certain point, any commercial profit made is necessarily at the expense of someone else; but the plight of the losers in the game does not generally bother the winners. A particularly brazen form of this universal phenomenon is to be found in poor places like India, where hugely wealthy dealers in grain, especially rice, hoard their stocks, refusing to admit that they have anything to sell, so as to force prices up. This may go on for weeks at a time, especially in remote parts of the country, to the point where people are actually starving, yet the merchants will hold on to those stocks as long as they possibly can, before slowly releasing them at extortionate prices on the black market. The poor have then to scrape together every penny in order to buy enough food to live on. Such exploitation happens – albeit usually in more subtle ways – in all walks of life, in all parts of the world.

The idea of non-exploitation is clearly related to the second of the five precepts (the precepts which form the basis for the ethical life of all Buddhists). In trying to live in accordance with the second precept, one undertakes not to take what is not given.[96] This is more than simply a roundabout way of saying 'not to steal'. Not stealing isn't enough. It leaves too many loopholes. Someone may be a perfectly honest person according to the letter of the law, but they may still build up their business in all sorts of irregular, dubious, or downright shady ways. Thus a great deal of wealth is amassed through highly unethical means without the breaking of any conventional ethical codes.

But the Buddhist precept is an undertaking not to take something unless those who are its present owners, whether individuals or the community as a whole, are willing and ready to give it to you. If it has not been given to you, you do not take it. I mentioned that there should be no connection between what we give and what we take. However, what we take must at the same time be given – in this respect giving and taking are two aspects of the same action. In some Buddhist countries monks are supposed to be so strict in the observance of this precept that when food is given to them on formal occasions, they are not allowed to eat it unless the plate containing the food is lifted up and actually placed in their hands.

The same principle finds application in the fifth stage of the Buddha's Noble Eightfold Path: right or perfect livelihood.[97] The very fact that right livelihood is included in the list gives an idea of the importance given within Buddhism to the way one earns one's living. People may talk of getting the perfect job, but we can guess that this is not what is meant by 'perfect livelihood'. But how does something so apparently mundane as employment find a place in this august collection of ideals?

We all have to earn a living – those who are not monks, anyway – but however we do it, no harm should come either to others or to ourselves through the work we do. The early scriptures even offer a rough and ready guide to right livelihood in the form of a list of occupations which are prohibited for those following the spiritual path.[98] The first of these concerns any commercial activity that involves trading in living beings, whether humans or animals. Slavery is and always has been condemned and prohibited in Buddhist countries – Buddhists did not have to wait until the eighteenth or nineteenth century for a clear line on this issue. Of course, trading in human beings still goes on in the world today, but even more widespread is trading in animals for slaughter, also prohibited in Buddhist societies: you will never find a Buddhist butcher or slaughterman. This form of livelihood is harmful not only to – of course – the animals being slaughtered, but also to those doing the slaughtering. To spend eight hours a day killing pigs, cows, sheep, or chickens will necessarily bring about some degree of mental or emotional damage to the slaughterman, as a result of stifling his natural feelings of compassion for other living beings.

Another early Buddhist prohibition was placed upon trade in poisons – not of course medicinal poisons, but poisons used to take life. Before the days of autopsies, this was an almost foolproof way to dispose of someone; a dealer in poisons would give you a phial of the requisite potion – whether fast or slow working, painful or painless – and you would then dose that inconvenient person's curry with it. Like slavers, dealers in poisons are, in a sense, found less frequently today than they used to be. But, of course, the modern equivalent – the widespread dealing in what are called class A drugs (like heroin and cocaine) – is just as harmful. Also, many people are involved in the manufacture and sale of cigarettes and other indisputably harmful drugs, including advertising them and dealing in shares in them.

The third prohibition was against making or trading in weapons. For the early Buddhists this meant bows and arrows, spears and swords. From these primitive beginnings of the arms trade, however, our more advanced cultures have made considerable progress – so they would say – in the development of wonderfully safe and refined methods of ensuring victory over the enemies of civilized values. But any involvement in making these means of destruction, however 'intelligent' they may be, is to be condemned as wrong livelihood. There is no question of justifying any war, any idea that weapons are a deterrent, any bombs, however 'smart'.

These prohibitions are of course directed at the laity, but there are also certain ways of earning a living which are forbidden specifically to monks. For example, various forms of fortune-telling, of which there were very many in the Buddha's day, are enumerated and roundly condemned in the scriptures. However, all over the Buddhist world monks to this day are relied on by the laity to foretell the future, and unfortunately many monks take advantage of this trust in their powers of prognostication.

Monks are also prohibited from earning a living through the display of psychic powers, or by promising psychic powers to others. The reason for this is obvious, really. People are naturally very interested in psychic phenomena, supernormal powers, and so on. Such things are generally taken more seriously on an everyday level in the East, but in certain circles in the West there is also an intense – and unhealthy – fascination with the idea of acquiring mysterious and occult powers that other people don't possess. If you dangle psychic powers in front of someone's nose, you can, if they are easily led, lead them almost anywhere.

I was once presented with the opportunity of doing this myself. When I lived in Kalimpong in the 1950s, an Englishman arrived on my doorstep one evening in the midst of the rainy season. I was quite accustomed to unexpected visitors, so I invited him in and he introduced himself. He was a medical man who had trained in Dublin. Quite soon I got round to asking him what had brought him to Kalimpong. He said straight out, 'I want to develop psychic powers.' This was not the first time someone had expressed to me this kind of interest, so I just said, 'What sort of psychic powers do you want to develop?' He said, 'I want to be able to read other people's thoughts, and to see the future.' He was not at all coy about it; he was quite open about what he wanted. I then asked him, 'Why do you want to develop these powers?' He simply said, 'It will help me in my work.' What that work turned out to be is not germane to this specific issue; I will mention only that he was a disciple – or had been a disciple – of Lobsang Rampa, who wrote a lot of books about the more fabulous and fanciful aspects of Tibetan Buddhism. Inspired by one of the most successful of these books, *The Third Eye*, my visitor was searching for a Tibetan lama who could perform an operation to open his third eye. It involved, he believed, drilling a little hole in the middle of his forehead and thereby endowing him with the clairvoyant vision he wanted.

One can see the temptation that this kind of person puts in the way of monks and lamas. He could have been milked by any unscrupulous teacher who was ready to pander to his desire for developing psychic powers. What he said to me made this very clear: 'If anyone can teach me these things I'm quite prepared to place at their disposal a very large sum of money.' He came to an untimely end, unfortunately, but before he did so, several people got quite a lot of money out of him in one way or another.

So much for general prohibitions as regards earning a living. However, the Buddha did not leave it at that, for, as we know, the economic relationship is one of the commonest fields of exploitation in the whole range of human life. Employers exploit employees if they can, and employees exploit their employers whenever they get the chance. We tend to think that problems of suspicion and exploitation between management and workforce, capital and labour, boardroom and factory floor, are peculiarly modern. But the Buddha gave considerable attention to this issue, in his advice to Sigālaka as recorded in the *Sigālaka Sutta*. In the section of the discourse devoted to the employer–employee relationship the Buddha enumerates five duties of the employer towards the employee, and five duties of the employee towards the employer.[99] Together, these amount to a general guide to capital and labour relationships, and a business code of economic ethics for Buddhists.

Taking the duties of the employer first, the Buddha says that the employer must give the employee work according to his bodily and mental strength – that is, work he or she can do without injury. Unfortunately, 2,500 years later, this principle is still not being observed – certainly not in India. In India today, thousands of men and women earn their living as coolies, that is, as unskilled labourers. They are treated as beasts of burden, carrying heavy loads on their backs, or more usually on their heads, and anybody who ever goes to India will see them at work. Coolies are at the very bottom of the economic ladder, and they have virtually no hope of rising above that level, even though they may have to support a growing family as well as themselves.

The problem from the point of view of the merchant hiring a number of coolies to carry, say, sacks of rice is that some coolies cannot carry as much as others, and they do not move as fast, particularly if they are old or unwell. It is shocking to say that the solution for a great many well-to-do merchants is to make sure they get their money's-worth out of all their coolies equally. This is a pitiable sight indeed – some old man, old before his time, staggering along, his veins standing out, muscles stretched like whipcord, and the perspiration streaming down, under loads which he has no business to be carrying at all. It's the same with the rickshaw pullers that you used to find all over Asia (though not any more, I am glad to say). Their life-expectancy was no more than a few years. They used to start pulling rickshaws when they were fifteen or sixteen; by the time they were twenty-five they usually had tuberculosis, and that would be the end of them within a few months. Their inadequate diet and the huge physical stress of their work quite literally killed them.

But for a very long time it was not an issue that bothered anyone. I remember vividly the first time I was in Sri Lanka, taking a ride in a rickshaw – rather against my will. As we moved smartly through the streets I kept telling the coolie to go slower, but he didn't understand me – he thought I was telling him, as most of his fares must have done, to go faster. The more I expostulated with him, the faster he went, until I had to tell him to stop altogether. Thereafter I used a rickshaw only in an emergency; and even then I would pick someone who was fairly strong and sturdy, and insist that he went at a reasonably leisurely pace. In retrospect, I should not, probably, have used them at all, but at the time it seemed there was no other work for them to do. However, the Buddha was quite clear that no human being should be hired to work beyond his natural capacity.

Secondly, the Buddha said that the employer should give the employee sufficient food and pay. This is still the custom in certain parts of India. If you employ someone you give them food and clothes, plus some cash, rather than a salary. But the operative principle is to give food and pay that is sufficient in terms of enabling the employee to live a full and decent human existence, not simply sufficient in relation to the work done. There shouldn't be any correlation between the amount of work done and the amount of pay received. Even if the employee is strong and healthy, and his output is prodigious, he should not get paid more than his weaker or even lazier fellows; he should just get what he needs by way of remuneration. We have become accustomed to thinking in terms of rewarding hard work and penalizing those who underperform: so much work done, so much pay received. But while this is an effective incentive to invention and enterprise, a Buddhist should ideally find that incentive somewhere else. If the incentive is greed, you are feeding that mental poison.

The employee is enjoined by the Buddha to work as faithfully as he can, and the employer is enjoined to provide for the employee's needs. These needs constitute not just a bare subsistence, but the means to live a richly human existence. We no longer have a society that divides quite so rigidly into employer and employee as the society of the Buddha's day, but the Buddha was not of course recommending the particular social structure of his day, he was simply pointing out the essential principle by which the people in his society could make an economic relationship an essentially human one.

We have to try to do the same within our own society. One radical plan that used to get an airing from time to time, and did seem to express the principle of non-exploitation very effectively, is the idea that on the attainment of their majority everyone should be given by the government a basic stipend to cover the cost of food, clothing, and shelter, regardless of whether they work or not. If they want more than this – if they want to travel, buy expensive electronic equipment, go out to cinemas and restaurants, have the luxury lifestyle that most people see as a virtual necessity – they will have to work. But in a luxury culture people should work because they want to – because they want to make a creative contribution to their society, or because they want a few extras, or both – not simply in order to live. In this way the state would support the spiritual community, enabling individuals who wanted to devote themselves to creative but financially unremunerative activity – to meditation, study, even the arts – to do so, if they were prepared to live a very simple, even monastic life.

Thirdly, the Buddha says that the employer should provide the employee with medical treatment and support after retirement. This we do have nowadays, with pensions, insurance, and so on, but it has taken two millennia for us to get round to this scheme of the Buddha's. Fourthly, the Buddha says that the employer should share with the employee any extra profit he makes. That is, you don't take the profits for your own purposes while telling your employees that they must make do with a basic level of support. Once again, we have caught up with this idea rather late in the day, in the form of bonus schemes. Fifthly and lastly, it is the duty of the employer, according to the Buddha, to grant the employee holidays and special allowances – and this, too, has something of a modern ring to it. However, we should not lose sight of the essential principle expressed in the Buddha's advice – that of establishing the human dimension of the economic relationship – which is not always what bonus schemes, holiday allowances, and pension schemes are about.

So much for the five points made by the Buddha for the guidance of the employer in relationship to the employee. The employee also has certain duties. The first of these is that he or she should be punctual. Indians are of course notorious for their lack of punctuality. Trains can be two or three hours late. Someone may say, 'I'm coming to see you at three o'clock,' and you'll see them the following week. A public meeting may be advertised to begin at eight o'clock sharp, but if you are naïve enough to turn up at that time, you may find the place deserted. The meeting has not been cancelled: if you wait until nine o'clock the organizers will arrive; by ten o'clock the platform is being erected. At eleven o'clock the audience is beginning to arrive, and at half past eleven you will be invited to begin your talk. In the West we are a lot more punctual than this; but the Buddha's principle is not just about clocking in on time, but of not needing to clock in at all. Indeed, the Buddha suggests that you try to be already working before your employer arrives: you are not coming to work simply to be seen to be working.

Secondly, the employee should finish work after the employer. You should try to become free of the whole clock-watching mentality. You don't fling down your tools as soon as the clock strikes. Thirdly, the employee should be sincere and trustworthy. This is quite obvious, as is the fourth point, which is that the employee should perform his or her duties to the satisfaction of the employer. Fifthly, the employee should speak in praise of his employer. The Buddha must have been aware of how readily workers abuse the boss behind his or her back, then as now. They may be dutiful and respectful during working hours, but what you hear outside the company gates can tell a different story.

The Buddha is reminding us that, as with any relationship, the economic relationship should not be one of antagonism, in which all you feel you can express is impotent frustration. Ideally, it is a happy, harmonious relationship, in which there is no exploitation on either side. Each takes from the other what he or she needs, without causing harm, and gives what he or she can. If you are an employer, you make use of the labour and skills of your workers, and also take responsibility for seeing that their needs are met. And if you are an employee, you work to the best of your ability and take what you need from that work situation. There is then no need for a grim, protracted bargaining between employers and unions, as though they were in opposite camps, arranging a truce between opposing armies. As the Buddha says to Sigālaka, 'In this way the nadir is covered,' (the nadir being the direction which denotes the relationship between 'master and servant') 'making it at peace and free from fear.'

18

NON-EXPLOITATION

As the bee takes honey from the flower,
Leaving its colour and fragrance unharmed,
So let the monk go about the village.[100]

This verse comes from the *Dhammapada*, an ancient and deeply loved anthology of verses which was the first Buddhist text to be translated from the original Pāli into a European language (in this case Latin). It is characteristic of Buddhist scriptures to draw all sorts of beautiful illustrations, metaphors, similes, and parables from day-to-day life in India, and so it is with this verse from the *Dhammapada*, which is taken from the chapter called 'Flowers', so-called because each verse mentions a flower of some kind, or flowers in general, by way of illustration.

Anyone who has lived in India or in any of the Buddhist countries of South-east Asia will be familiar with the timeless scene evoked in these lines – the monk going for alms in the village. It was a scene I participated in myself in my own wandering days as a monk, when I went around on foot from place to place. But I have seen it as an observer often enough, and will describe it here from that viewpoint. Usually the monks go out for alms very early in the morning, because in India there is no such thing traditionally as a midday meal. People eat what we would call lunch at about nine o'clock in the morning; it is a huge meal, consisting mainly of rice. After that – in the villages at least – people go off to work in the fields and don't come back home again to eat until five or six in the evening. So if the monk wants to fill his bowl, he has to be off at the crack of dawn, leaving the monastery and moving silently along the deserted streets, stopping briefly at each house.

The Buddhist custom is that throughout his alms collection tour, as it is called, the monk should stand silently at each door with his begging-bowl, not asking for anything. But people are usually on the lookout for monks at this time, so it may be that a child runs inside and says, 'Mummy, the monk is here,' and the mother says, 'All right, ask him to wait.' Then she quickly ladles out some rice and curry, and takes it outside to put in the monk's bowl. The monk then recites a verse of blessing in Pāli, and moves on to stand at the door of the next hut.

The idea is not to get the whole meal from any one house, but to take a little here and a little there. In India even today Hindu sadhus follow this custom. It is called *madhukari bhikṣā*, which means collecting alms just like the bee collects honey. Just as the bee collects a little pollen from each flower it visits, in the same way the monk accepts a little food from one house, a little food from another, until he has enough to sustain him for the day.

Food is just one of four things that the monk is traditionally entitled to expect from lay supporters. These four requisites or essentials are: firstly, food; secondly, clothing, especially in the form of the saffron robe; thirdly, shelter, whether a temporary hut, a monastery, or some arrangement in between; and fourthly, medicine. When the monk is ordained he is told that this is all he should expect from the lay people, and all he can accept from them.

The idea is that the monk or nun – that is, the person devoted to the religious life – should accept from lay supporters only what is necessary to keep him or her going, so that he or she can practise meditation, study, and teach the Dharma, and make progress towards Enlightenment. Inevitably, after 2,500 years of Buddhist history, a few things have been added to the list of requisites. The most significant addition is perhaps books; in modern times a collection of a few books tends to count as a fundamental requisite.

But Buddhist monks still generally lead an exceedingly simple life, making do with one or at most two meals a day, quite basic accommodation in cottages or huts, the minimum of clothing (easy enough in a tropical country), and very simple medicines. Incidentally, this medicine is supposed to be made of gallnuts and cow's urine. This is less bizarre than it sounds; you can make a sort of ammonia out of cow's urine which is efficacious in a number of ways. Many Buddhist monks take cow's urine religiously, so to speak, and swear by its curative powers. Indeed, a very orthodox Sri Lankan monk with whom I was in regular correspondence wrote to me while I was once lying ill, in Benares, and advised me in the strongest terms to take cow's urine, assuring me that if I did so I would never be sick again in my life. (Not having heeded his advice, I cannot vouch for this.)

But people in the West often say, 'Well, that's all very well. It's a great arrangement from the monk's point of view: he gets his food, he gets his clothing, he gets housed, perhaps in a beautiful monastery, he gets medicine when he is sick. Everything is provided for him, so that he can quietly get on with his studies, his meditation, his literary work, or his preaching, as he thinks fit. But what does he give in return?'

The traditional answer to this question is: nothing. He gets all he needs and he does absolutely nothing in return. Nobody even expects anything in return, and it does not occur to the monk that he should give anything in return. Anything you give to monks or nuns is given for the support of the sangha, not as payment for teaching. Correspondingly, teaching is not given in return for that support. The monk accepts what he needs, and he gives what he can, but there is no relationship between the two, no equivalence between what you give and what you get, no reciprocal relationship at all. You don't think of translating what you give into so many equivalent units of what you ought to receive. You keep the two things quite separate. When you can give, you give. When you need, you accept. There is no question of a bargain being struck. Just as the bee accepts the pollen it needs from the flower to make its honey, without injuring the flower in any way, in the same way, the monk quietly and gently accepts what he needs without doing any harm to the village. In both cases, there is no exploitation.

This, then, is ideally the nature of the relationship between the layperson and 'ascetics and brahmins' which the Buddha lists as the last of the six relationships to which Sigālaka (and all of us) should pay attention. But perhaps this relationship is more obscure to us than the others; Western Buddhists do not generally think along the traditional lines of monastic and lay, although we may find it easier to relate to the full-timer/part-timer distinction we considered in an earlier chapter. But there is a further aspect of this verse of the *Dhammapada* that most translations fail to draw out clearly, but which broadens out what is being said beyond the monastic–lay relationship. It concerns the term 'monk'.

The first problem with this word is that in Buddhism there is nothing resembling the Western conception of a monk. This problem is further compounded by the fact that 'monk' is the standard rendering of the term *bhikṣu*, whereas the word in this verse is not *bhikṣu* but *muni*. In some contexts *muni* means monk in the sense of bhikṣu, but not always. A *muni*, essentially, is a wise man, or holy man, or sage. The Buddha was not only called 'Buddha'; he was given many other titles, including Śākyamuni, 'sage of the Śākya tribe'. *Muni* is also related to the term *mauna*, which in Sanskrit, as well as in the modern languages of northern India, means 'silence'. So a *muni* is one who is silent, or even one who observes a vow of silence. In order to bring out this double meaning, some translators render *muni* as 'the silent sage'.

This combination of meanings reflects an interesting association of ideas: it suggests that silence and wisdom go together, that the wise man doesn't talk too much. Whether he is wise because he is silent or silent because he is wise, or both, it may be difficult to say. In any case, it is clear that we are talking about more than just monks here. It becomes clearer what *muni* means once we consider that this verse is very ancient, one of the earliest (along with some passages of the *Sutta Nipāta*) of all Buddhist scriptures. Some scholars believe that *muni* was the original term used by Buddhists for the disciple of the Buddha who is himself Enlightened. According to this theory, the word *arhant* – the term for this ideal which has become so familiar – came later.

We can therefore get a much broader, more universal meaning from this verse by replacing the line 'so let the monk move about the village' with 'so let the wise person live in the world'. In this way, what appears to be an injunction restricted to those who are at least technically monks becomes applicable to everybody who lives in the world. It is important that it does so because it establishes a fundamental principle of the ethical and spiritual life, which is that the wise person does not exploit anyone or anything. This may seem very simple to understand, but if it were to be thoroughly and systematically put into practice, the effects would be far-reaching indeed.

If we are wise, we take from society, from others, from our environment, what we objectively need in order to sustain life, to work, and to progress spiritually. But we do no harm to individuals, to society at large, or to the environment. And we give what we can. However unrealistic this ideal may seem, one does occasionally come across reflections of it in real working relationships, and there is no reason why it cannot be held up in the context of any working environment. Moreover, the principle of non-exploitation extends far beyond the field of economics. It has psychological and even spiritual implications which can be extended to cover the whole field of personal relationships, especially our more intimate relationships.

We don't just decide to like someone on a whim. We like them because they fulfil a certain need we have – a need of which we are not usually conscious, although we can become conscious of it if we try. If we don't try to become conscious of what our own needs are, we tend to rationalize our liking for someone: we say we like them because they are considerate and kind, or because they love animals as we do, or because they are interested in Buddhism as we are. But behind these rational appraisals there is often something quite different at work. Perhaps that person satisfies our need for attention, our psychological need to be at the very centre of things. As long as that need continues, we shall continue to want it to be satisfied. And if we get from someone the attention we need, then obviously we will want that relationship to continue.

But how are we going to ensure that it does continue? Most of us, whether we realize it or not, find that the best way of doing this is to find out what the other person needs, and make sure that we are the person who satisfies that need. They may have, say, a deep lack of self-worth that manifests as a craving to be appreciated. Latching on to this, we start saying, 'What a wonderful writer you are – I wish I had such a way with words!' or 'Did you really paint this yourself? How do you manage to achieve such magical effects?' We give them what we sense they need, so that they become dependent on us for the satisfaction we give them, just as we have become dependent on them for the satisfaction of our own needs. In short, together we create a relationship of mutual dependence and exploitation. An unconscious bargain is struck; this is the basis of most human relationships. Because the whole process is more or less unconscious, neither party to the bargain questions whether the need is valid, or whether it is an artificial and unhealthy need which it would be better not to encourage. In this situation, the relationship is likely either to terminate catastrophically or to settle down into an increasingly boring routine.

Does this mean that we should never look to another person to fulfil our needs? Do we not have some valid psychological needs? The answer to this question lies in this same verse from the *Dhammapada*. Yes, we do have valid needs – material needs, psychological needs, and spiritual needs – but we should fulfil them as the bee takes pollen from the flower, without exploiting the person who fulfils those needs.

There are two kinds of need. Under the influence of one kind, we unconsciously negotiate a situation of mutual exploitation. The other kind of need is one of which we are more conscious, more aware. It is not bargain-hunting, but an ever-deepening spirit of mutual giving, without any thought of return. It happens between parents and children at their best. The parents give freely to the children without thinking that the children are going to reward them later for their efforts. The children, likewise, give what they can to their parents, not thinking about everything their parents have done for them, but simply giving to them because they love them.

This principle of non-exploitation and mutual generosity is the key to the Buddha's philosophy of personal relations, whether in political, religious, economic, or more intimate personal relationships. It is a principle the Buddha himself exemplified. He spent forty-five years going around north-eastern India on foot, teaching. All that he took from people was one meal a day, a few yards of yellow cloth, a little hut somewhere – perhaps in somebody's garden – which he borrowed from time to time, and occasional supplies of medicine.

What he took was infinitesimal. But what he gave was – is – incalculable: indeed its nature is that it cannot be measured out and bartered. The gifts he gave – compassion, understanding, sympathy, wisdom, guidance, love – by their very nature can only be given with no thought of return. His was the perfect example of his philosophy of personal relationships. He took only what he needed; he gave everything he had to give. Ranged against this philosophy is a sort of shopkeeper's mentality, which is the bane of the human race. And in all our relationships we can choose between these two attitudes.

19

GRATITUDE

Usually, influenced by books or even Buddhist scriptures, we think of the Buddha's Enlightenment as having taken place at a particular time, roughly 2,500 years ago – which, of course, in a sense, it did. We also tend to think of it as having taken place on a particular day, at a particular hour, even at a particular minute, at the instant when the Buddha broke through from the conditioned to the Unconditioned.

But a little reflection, and a little further study of the scriptures, will show us that it didn't happen quite like that. Here we can consider the distinction between the path of vision and the path of transformation – a distinction usually made in connection with the Noble Eightfold Path. On the path of vision one has an experience of the transcendental, a profound insight into the true nature of Reality which goes far beyond any merely intellectual understanding. This insight comes gradually to pervade and transform every aspect of one's being – one's body, speech, and mind, to use the traditional Buddhist classification. It transforms all our activities. It transforms one, in fact, into a very different kind of person – a wiser and more compassionate person. This process is known as the path of transformation.[101]

Something like this takes place in the spiritual life of each and every one of us. And we see the same sort of thing happening, on a much more exalted plane, in the case of the Buddha. The Buddha's vision is unlimited, absolute, and all-embracing, and his transformation of body, speech, and mind can therefore be described as total, even infinite. But all the same, it did take a little time for this final transformation to take place. Buddhist tradition speaks of the Buddha as spending seven – or nine – weeks (accounts vary) in the vicinity of the bodhi tree, the tree beneath which he attained Enlightenment. In the course of each of those weeks something of importance happened. We could say that the Buddha's experience of Enlightenment started percolating through his being, until by the end of the last week (whether the seventh or the ninth) the process of transformation was at last complete.

One week a great storm arose, and the Buddha was sheltered from the rain, so the story goes, by the serpent king Mucalinda, who spread his sevenfold hood over the Buddha's head as he meditated. Another week, Brahmā Sahampati, the ruler of a thousand worlds, requested the Buddha to teach the Dharma, saying that at least some of the beings in the world would be capable of understanding it, their eyes being covered with only a little dust. And the Buddha, out of compassion, agreed to teach.

But here I want to focus on another episode, one that occurred quite early in the period after the Buddha's attainment of Enlightenment – during the second week, according to one source. According to this tradition, the Buddha stood at a distance to the north-east of the bodhi tree and remained for one week gazing at the tree with unblinking eyes.[102]

Centuries later, a stupa was erected on that very spot, to mark the place where the Buddha had gazed at the bodhi tree. It was known as 'the stupa of unblinking eyes', and Hsüan Tsang, the great Chinese pilgrim, saw it when he visited India in the seventh century CE. In the memoirs he dictated to his disciples in his old age back in China, he described it thus: 'On the left side of the road, to the north of the place where the Buddha walked, is a large stone on the top of which, as it stands in a great vihara, is a figure of the Buddha with his eyes raised and looking up. Here in former times the Buddha sat [he says 'sat' but the source text says 'stood'] for seven days contemplating the bodhi tree.'[103]

Perhaps the Buddha didn't literally stand or sit there for a whole week, but we may take it that he gazed at the bodhi tree for a very long time. And the source text makes it clear why. He did it because he was grateful to the tree for having sheltered him at the time of his attainment of Enlightenment. According to the scriptures, the Buddha demonstrated gratitude in other ways too. After Brahmā Sahampati had made his request that the Buddha should teach the Dharma, and the Buddha had decided to do so, he then wondered to whom he should teach it. He thought first of his two old teachers, from whom he had learned to meditate not long after he left home. Finding their teaching insufficient, he had left them, but they had been helpful to him at a particular stage of his career, and after his Enlightenment he remembered that. It's as though he had a spiritual debt to them that he wanted to repay. But he quickly realized that his old teachers were dead.

He then thought of his five former companions. They too were people he knew from an earlier period of his spiritual quest, from the time of his experiments in asceticism. After leaving his first two teachers, he started practising extreme self-mortification, in the company of five friends who became disciples of his and admired him greatly because he had gone further in his self-mortification than anybody else at that time. But eventually the Buddha-to-be saw the futility of asceticism, realized that that was not the way to Enlightenment, and gave it up. When he started taking solid food again, just a few handfuls of rice to sustain himself, the five ascetics left him in disgust, saying, 'The śramaṇa Gautama has returned to luxurious living.' But this parting was not what remained in the Buddha's mind. Having realized that his two old teachers were dead, he reflected, 'The five ascetics were of great help to me when I was practising the penances. I would like to preach the Dharma to them.' So this is what he did. He went to them, he taught them, and eventually they too realized the Truth that he had realized. And he did this out of gratitude.

So the newly Enlightened Buddha was a *grateful* Buddha, an idea which is perhaps unfamiliar to us. We think of the all-wise Buddha, the compassionate Buddha, the resourceful Buddha, but we don't usually think of the grateful Buddha. But one of the very first things the Buddha did after his attainment of Enlightenment was to show his gratitude to those who had helped him. He was even grateful to a tree.

This incident alone gives us food for thought. The Buddhist scriptures contain a number of references that show that the Buddha and his disciples didn't regard trees and stones as inanimate dead matter. They regarded them as living things. They would even have a relationship with them; they would talk to a tree or a flower, or rather to the spirit – the devatā, as they called it – inhabiting it. It is surely much better to have this attitude, to be an animist, than to think that trees and flowers and rocks and stones are just dead matter. The Buddha certainly didn't think in that way, and it was therefore possible for him to be grateful even to a tree.

It is not surprising, given that this was the Buddha's attitude, that gratitude finds a place in his ethical and spiritual teaching. It is found, for example, in the *Maṅgala Sutta*, the 'Sutta of Blessings or Auspicious Signs'. This sutta, which is very short and is found in the Pāli Canon, is often regarded as summarizing the whole duty, as we may call it, of the serious-minded Buddhist, and it enumerates gratitude as one of the auspicious signs. According to the *Maṅgala Sutta*, it is a sign that you are making spiritual progress.[104]

But what is gratitude? What do we mean when we use this term? To find this out, we can turn to the dictionaries – and, of course, we should be very grateful to the makers of dictionaries. I am personally very grateful to Samuel Johnson. His historic dictionary is always at my elbow in my study, and when I am writing I sometimes consult it several times a day. Johnson defines gratitude as 'duty to benefactors' and as 'desire to return benefits'. Coming to more modern dictionaries the *Concise Oxford* says, 'being thankful; readiness to show appreciation for and to return kindness', and *Collins* has 'a feeling of thankfulness or appreciation, as for gifts or favours'.

Such are the definitions of the English word, and they do give us some understanding of what gratitude is. But from a Buddhist point of view we need to go further, and look at the Pāli word being translated as gratitude: *kataññutā*. *Kata* means that which has been done, especially that which has been done to oneself; and *aññutā* means knowing or recognizing; so *kataññutā* means knowing and recognizing what has been done to one for one's benefit. These definitions indicate that the connotation of the Pāli word is rather different from that of its English translation. The connotation of the English word gratitude is emotional – we speak of *feeling* grateful. But the connotation of *kataññutā* is rather more intellectual, more cognitive. It makes it clear that what we call gratitude involves an element of *knowledge*: knowledge of what has been done to us or for us for our benefit. If we do not know that something has benefited us, we will not feel grateful.

The Buddha knew that the bodhi tree had sheltered him, and he knew that his five former companions had been helpful to him, so he felt gratitude towards them. Not only that: he gave expression to that feeling. He acted upon it by spending a whole week simply gazing at the bodhi tree, and then by going in search of his five former companions so that he could communicate to them the truth that he had discovered. The important implication is that it is a perfectly natural thing to feel grateful for benefits we have received.

But the benefit has to be recognized as a benefit. If we don't feel that someone or something actually has benefited us, we won't feel grateful to them or to it. This suggests that we have to understand what is truly beneficial, what has really helped us to grow and develop as human beings. We also have to know who or what has benefited us, and remember that they have done so – otherwise no feeling of gratitude is possible.

In Buddhism there are traditionally three principal objects of gratitude: our parents, our teachers, and our spiritual friends. We have already considered some aspects of each of these relationships. Here I want to reflect a little on gratitude in relation to each of them.

I came back to England after spending twenty years uninterruptedly in the East studying, practising and teaching the Dharma. When I came back, I found that much had changed. Quite a few things struck me as unusual – I hadn't encountered them in India, or at least not to the same extent. One thing that definitely surprised me was finding out how many people, at least among those I knew, were on bad terms with their parents. Perhaps I noticed this especially because I was in contact with people who were concerned about their spiritual development, and wanted to straighten themselves out psychologically and emotionally.

If one is on bad terms with one's parents, something is quite seriously wrong. Perhaps it wouldn't even be an exaggeration to say that one's whole emotional life is likely to be affected, indirectly at least, by this state of affairs. I therefore used to encourage people to get back into positive contact with their parents, if it happened that they were estranged from them for any reason. I encouraged people to be more open with their parents and to develop positive feelings towards them. This was especially necessary in connection with the practice of the mettā bhāvanā, the development of loving kindness. People had to learn to develop mettā even towards their parents, and for those who had had difficult childhoods, or had even suffered at the hands of their parents in some way, this was not easy. But even so, it was necessary in the interests of their own emotional, psychological, and spiritual development to get over whatever feelings of bitterness or resentment they were harbouring.

Some people, I discovered, blamed their parents in all sorts of ways for all sorts of things – an attitude which is reflected in a well-known little poem by Philip Larkin called 'This Be The Verse'. In this poem,

Larkin gives expression in rather crude language to what he thinks your mum and dad have done to you, and he draws a rather depressing conclusion from that. The last verse of the poem reads:

Man hands on misery to man,
It deepens like a coastal shelf;
Get out as early as you can,
And don't have any kids yourself.

What a grim, nasty little poem! In 1995, however, it was voted one of Britain's favourite poems, coming in between Thomas Hood's 'I remember, I remember' and D.H. Lawrence's 'The Snake'. The fact that Larkin's poem should be so popular among intelligent poetry readers gives food for thought, suggesting as it does that negative attitudes towards parents are fairly widespread in our society.

The Buddha himself had quite a lot to say about our relation to our parents. In the *Sigālaka Sutta* he is represented as saying that there are five ways in which a son should minister to his mother and father as the eastern direction. He should think, 'Having been supported by them, I will support them, I will perform their duties for them. I will keep up the family tradition. I will be worthy of my heritage. After my parents' deaths I will distribute gifts on their behalf.'[105] The same applies, of course, to a daughter. She too should minister to her mother and father as the eastern direction, she too should think in this manner.

There is a lot that could be said about the five ways in which one should minister to one's parents. Here, though, I want to touch on something even more fundamental – so fundamental that in this sutta the Buddha seems to take it for granted. It is hinted at, however, in the imagery of the sutta. The Buddha explains to Sigāla that one pays homage to the east by ministering to one's parents in five ways. But why the east?

The reason is perhaps obvious. The sun rises in the east, it has its origin in the east, so to speak, and similarly we owe our origin to our parents – leaving aside questions of karma, of which perhaps parents are only instruments. If it were not for our parents, we would not be here now. They have given us life, they have given us a human body, and in Buddhism the human body is regarded as a very precious thing. It is precious because it is only in a human body (whether male or female) that one is able to attain Enlightenment. In giving us a human body, our parents are therefore giving us the possibility of attaining

Enlightenment and we should be intensely grateful to them for that, especially if we are actually practising the Dharma.

Not only do our parents give us a human body; despite Larkin, they bring us up as best they can. They enable us to survive, they educate us. They may not always be able to send us to university and all that, but they teach us to speak, and this is the basis of most of the things we subsequently learn. Usually it's our mother who teaches us our first words, and this gives us the expression 'mother tongue'. It is through our mother tongue that we have access to all the literature that has been written in the language we learn in our earliest days, and we can enjoy that literature fully because it is in our mother tongue, rather than in a language we learn in later life.

Not everybody cares to acknowledge their debt to their parents. The classic example in English literature is the character Mr Bounderby in Charles Dickens's *Hard Times*, which happens to be one of my favourite Dickens novels. Mr Bounderby is a successful industrialist, and he is very fond of telling everybody that he is a self-made man. He tells them this on every possible occasion and at great length. He describes in vivid detail how he was abandoned by his mother, how he was beaten by a drunken grandmother, how he lived in the gutter as a child and had to fend for himself, how nobody had ever helped him and how he had made his own way in the world and become a rich man entirely by his own efforts. In the course of the novel, however, it transpires that all this is completely false. In truth he had a loving mother who brought him up carefully and educated him and helped him as much as she possibly could. In fact, his mother is still alive, but he keeps her at a distance in the country somewhere and won't allow her to visit him. In other words, Mr Bounderby is a monster of ingratitude.

We will consider the question of why people are so ungrateful later on. First, though, let us turn to the second of the principal objects of gratitude in Buddhism: our teachers. By teachers here I mean not Dharma teachers, but all those from whom we derive our secular education and culture. Here our school teachers obviously have an important place. From them we derive the rudiments of such learning as we have, and we therefore have to be grateful to them. The fact is that we have found out very little of what we know, or what we think we know, as a result of our own efforts. Practically everything we know has been taught to us in one way or another. If we think of our knowledge of science or history, for example, few of us have even performed a single scientific experiment, or discovered a single historical fact, which no one else had performed, or discovered, before. All our work in this field has been done for us by others. We have benefited from their efforts, and our knowledge is little more than the echo of theirs.

As well as learning from living teachers, we also learn from people who have been dead for hundreds of years, from the writings they have left and the records of the words they spoke. It is not just a question of learning from them in a purely intellectual sense, acquiring information. Among those books are great works of the imagination – great poems, great novels, great dramas – and these works are a source of infinite enrichment, without which we would be immeasurably poorer. They help us deepen and enlarge our vision. We should therefore be grateful to the great men and women who have produced them. We should be grateful to Homer and Virgil, Dante and Milton, Aeschylus and Kālidāsa, Shakespeare and Goethe. We should be grateful to Murasaki Shikibu, Cervantes, Jane Austen, Dickens, Dostoyevsky, and hundreds of others, who have influenced us more than we can possibly realize. The American critic Harold Bloom has gone so far as to claim that Shakespeare is the creator of human nature as we know it, which is a very big claim indeed (though he gives his reasons for it).

Of course, our experience is also deepened, and our vision enlarged, by the visual arts and by music. The great painters, sculptors, and composers are also among our teachers. They too have enriched our lives, and to them too we should be grateful. I won't mention any names in this connection because there are simply too many to choose from – both ancient and modern, Eastern and Western – certainly not because I think that the great artists and composers are any less important than the great poets, novelists, and dramatists.

Thus by 'teachers' I mean all those who between them have created our collective cultural heritage, without which we would not be fully human. Remembering what we owe them, and feeling grateful to the great artists, poets, and composers, we should not only enjoy their work but also celebrate their memory and share our enthusiasm for them with our friends.

Before we go on to consider the third principal object of gratitude, our spiritual friends, I want to make the general point that we need not think of these three objects of gratitude as being completely separate and distinct from one another. There's a certain amount of overlap between the first and second, and between the second and third. Our parents are also our teachers to an extent. In Buddhist tradition parents are called *porāṇacariyas*, which means 'former (or ancient) teachers'. They are called this because they are the first teachers we ever had, even if they only taught us to speak a few words. We can be grateful to our parents not only for giving us life but also for giving us at least the rudiments of knowledge, and initiating us into the beginnings of our cultural heritage.

Similarly there is some overlap between teachers and spiritual friends. The very greatest poets, artists, and composers can inspire us with spiritual values, help us rise to spiritual heights. In the course of the last few hundred years, great changes have taken place, at least in the West. Previously, Christianity as represented by the Church was the great, even the sole, bearer of spiritual values. But now, having lost faith in Christianity, many people look elsewhere to find meaning and values, and they find them in great works of art: in the plays of Shakespeare, the poetry of Wordsworth, Baudelaire, and Rilke, the music of Bach, Beethoven, and Mozart, the great painters and sculptors of the Italian Renaissance. These great masters become, as it were, our spiritual friends, especially if we remain in contact with them and with their work over many years. Learning to admire and love them, we feel intensely grateful to them for what they have given us. They are among our spiritual friends in the broadest sense.

But now let us come to our spiritual friends 'proper'. Here, as with the word gratitude, we have to go back to the Sanskrit words behind the English equivalent. As we have already seen, the Sanskrit phrase translated as 'spiritual friend' is *kalyāṇa mitra*. *Mitra* comes from the word *maitri* (Pāli, *mettā*), and *maitrī* is strong, unselfish, active love, sharply distinguished in Buddhist tradition from *prema* (Pāli, *pema*), in the sense of sexual love or attachment. A mitra or friend is therefore one who feels a strong unselfish active love towards one. And *kalyāṇa* means firstly 'beautiful, charming,' and secondly 'auspicious, helpful, morally good'. Thus kalyāṇa mitra has a much richer connotation than the English phrase 'spiritual friend'.

Our spiritual friends are all those who are spiritually more experienced than we are. The Buddhas are our spiritual friends. The Arhants and the Bodhisattvas are our spiritual friends. The great Buddhist teachers of India and China, Tibet and Japan, are our spiritual friends. Those who teach us meditation are our spiritual friends. Those with whom we study the scriptures are our spiritual friends. Those who ordain us are our spiritual friends. And all these spiritual friends should be the objects of our intense, heartfelt gratitude. We should be even more grateful to them than we are to our teachers.

Why? Because from our spiritual friends we receive the Dharma. We have not discovered or invented the Dharma. We have received it as a free gift from our spiritual friends, from the Buddha downwards. In the *Dhammapada* the Buddha says, 'The greatest of all gifts is the gift of the Dharma.'[106] The greater the gift, the greater the gratitude we should feel. We should not only feel that gratitude in our hearts; we should give expression to it in words and deeds. We can do this in three ways: by singing the praises of our spiritual friends, by practising the Dharma they have given us, and by passing on that Dharma to others to the best of our ability.

The greatest of our spiritual friends is the Buddha Śākyamuni, who discovered – or *re*-discovered – the path that we as Buddhists follow today. It is to him that we go for Refuge, it is the Dharma he taught that we try to practise, and it is with the support of the Sangha he founded that we are able to practise the Dharma. We therefore have reason to be intensely grateful to him – more grateful, in principle, than we are to anyone else. Our parents have indeed given us life, but what is life without the gift of the Dharma? Our teachers have given us knowledge, education, and culture, but what value do even these things have without the Dharma? It is because they are so intensely grateful to the Buddha that Buddhists perform pujas in devotion to him, and celebrate his life in the context of the various Buddhist festivals.

But people don't always find it easy to be grateful to their parents, or their teachers, or even their spiritual friends. Why is this? It is important to understand the nature of the difficulty. After all, gratitude is an important spiritual quality, a virtue exemplified and taught by the Buddha and many others. Cicero, the great Roman orator and philosopher, said that gratitude is not just the greatest virtue, but the mother of all the rest. Ingratitude therefore represents a very serious defect. On one occasion the Buddha said that ingratitude was one of the four great offences which bring about *niraya* in the sense of rebirth in a state of suffering – a very serious and weighty statement.[107]

But why are we ungrateful to our parents, our teachers, our spiritual friends? One would have thought that as Buddhists we would be simply bubbling over with gratitude to all these people. A clue is to be found in the Pāli word which we render as gratitude, *kataññutā*. As we have seen, it means knowing or recognizing what has been done for one's benefit. Similarly, *akataññutā* (*a* being the negative prefix), ingratitude, means not knowing or recognizing what has been done for one's benefit.

There are a number of reasons for ingratitude. Firstly, one may fail to recognize a benefit as a benefit. There are some people who do not regard life itself as a benefit, and hence do not feel grateful to their parents for bringing them into the world. Sometimes people say things like, 'Well I didn't ask to be brought into this world.' If you believe in karma and rebirth, of course, this isn't quite true – but anyway, it is what people say. In a few cases, they may not regard life as a benefit because they experience it as painful, even predominantly painful, and therefore don't appreciate its value, don't realize the immense potential of human life. In Buddhist terms, they don't realize that it is possible for a human being, and only for a human being, to attain Enlightenment, or at least to make some progress in that direction.

Similarly, there are people who don't regard knowledge or education or culture as benefits. They feel no gratitude towards their teachers, or towards those who at least try to teach them something. They may even feel resentment. They may feel that education or culture is being imposed upon them. Such people are unlikely to come into contact with spiritual values, with the Dharma, or with spiritual friends, and even if they do, such contact will be external and superficial. They will not be able to recognize it for what it is. They may even see those who try to be their spiritual friends as enemies, and therefore the question of gratitude will not arise.

This was true of some people's responses to the Buddha himself. Not all those who heard him speak or teach felt grateful to him, by any means. There were many people in his day who saw him as a rather eccentric, unorthodox teacher. They certainly didn't feel any gratitude towards him for the gift of the Dharma. Sometimes people slandered him, and some people even tried to kill him.

On the other hand, we may recognize benefits as benefits, and even recognize that they have been given to us by other people, but we may take those benefits for granted. Not realizing that they are a free gift, we may think that they are owed to us, that we have a right to them, and that therefore in a sense they belong to us already, so that we have no need to be grateful for them.

This attitude is widespread in society today. People tend to think that everything is due to them, that they have a right to everything. Parents, teachers, or the state have a duty to provide them with whatever they want. Even spiritual friends, they may think, have a duty to provide them with what they want. If they don't get what they want from one spiritual friend, or teacher, or guru, and get it quickly, in the way they want it, off they will go, to try to get it from someone else. Once again, the question of gratitude doesn't arise. Of course, parents, teachers, and friends have a duty to bestow benefits to the best of their ability. But it should be recognized that those benefits have been *given*, and that the response to them should therefore be one of gratitude.

Another reason for ingratitude is egoism. Egoism takes many forms, and has many aspects. Here I mean by it an attitude of chronic individualism: the belief that one is separate from others, not dependent on others in any way, and that one therefore does not owe anything to others. One feels that one is not obliged to them, because one can do everything oneself. Dickens's Mr Bounderby is a good example of this sort of attitude, but there are other examples in literature, like Satan in Milton's *Paradise Lost*, and 'Black Salvation' in *The Life and Liberation of Padmasambhava*. The person who is egoistical in this sense is incapable of feeling gratitude, and cannot admit that they have been benefited by others. They may not actually say so in the way Mr Bounderby does, but this is their underlying attitude.

This attitude sometimes finds expression in the sphere of the arts. Some writers and artists don't like to think that they owe anything to their predecessors. Wanting to be original, to strike out on a completely new path, they don't like to think that there is such a thing as cultural heritage, or a literary canon. In some circles this attitude has taken an extreme, even a virulent form, and has resulted in an attempt to repudiate the greater part of our literary and artistic heritage on ideological grounds. This is an extremely unfortunate, even potentially disastrous development, and it is to be resisted wherever possible. Egoism in the sense in which I am using the word also finds expression in the sphere of religion. It happens when we don't acknowledge the sources of our inspiration, or when we try to pass off as our own a teaching or practice that we have in fact learned from our spiritual friends.

The fourth and last reason for ingratitude that I want to mention here is forgetfulness. There are two main reasons for forgetfulness of benefits received. First, there is simply the passage of time. Perhaps the benefits were given to us a long time ago – so long ago that we have no distinct recollection of them, and no longer feel grateful to whoever bestowed them upon us, even if we did originally feel grateful. This is perhaps the principal reason for our not feeling actively grateful towards our parents. Over the years so much has happened in our life: early memories have been overlaid by later ones, other relationships have assumed importance, and perhaps we have moved away from our parents, geographically, socially, or culturally. And the result is that – practically speaking – we forget them. We forget the numerous ways in which they benefited us when we were young, and we cease therefore to feel grateful. The other possible reason for our 'forgetting' to be grateful is that we did not feel the positive effects of the benefits very strongly in the first place, and therefore did not feel much gratitude. In such circumstances, it is easy for the gratitude to fade away and be forgotten altogether.

These, then, are the four most important general reasons for ingratitude: failure to recognize a benefit as a benefit, taking benefits for granted, egoism, and forgetfulness. Ingratitude is, unfortunately, liable to crop up in various ways in the context of the life of a practising Buddhist. Beyond a certain point of spiritual progress, it is simply impossible to feel ungrateful. A Stream-entrant is incapable of it, and in fact will be overflowing with gratitude to parents, teachers, and spiritual friends. But until we have reached that point, we are in danger of forgetting to be grateful.

Over the years – more than thirty, at the time of writing – since I myself founded a Buddhist movement, I have received many, many letters, perhaps thousands, from people who have recently discovered the Dharma through one of the centres of the movement I founded, or through contact with individual members of the order. Every year I receive more and more of these letters. They come from young people and old people, from people in many different walks of life, from many different cultural backgrounds and nationalities. And all these letters say, among other things, one and the same thing. They say how glad the writers are to have discovered the Dharma. Not only that, the writers of the letters want to express their gratitude to the Three Jewels and to the Buddhist movement, and to me personally for having founded it. Some people express their feeling of gratitude very strongly indeed. They say that the Dharma has changed their lives, given their lives meaning, saved them from despair, even saved them from suicide.

Such letters of gratitude reach me nearly every week, and they make me think that I have not altogether wasted my time all these years. But over the years I've also noticed that while some people, perhaps the majority, stay grateful, and even become more and more grateful, in the cases of a few people, unfortunately, the feeling of gratitude weakens. They start forgetting the benefits they have received, and even start questioning whether they really were benefits at all. No longer knowing or recognizing what has been done for them, they become ungrateful. Feeling ungrateful to their spiritual friends, they may even start finding fault with them. This is a very sad state of affairs indeed, and in recent years I have given some thought to it and have come to certain conclusions about how it happens.

It seems to me that people forget the benefits they have received because they no longer actually feel them. And they no longer feel them because for one reason or another they have put themselves in a position where they cannot receive them. Let me give a concrete example. Suppose you have started attending a meditation class. You learn to meditate, and you achieve some success. You start practising at home. But one day, for one reason or another, you stop attending the class and then you gradually stop practising at home. You cease to meditate. Eventually you forget what meditative experience was like. You forget the peace and the joy you felt. You forget the benefits of meditation. So you cease to feel grateful to those who introduced you to the practice. The same thing can happen with regard to retreats, Dharma study, spending time with spiritual friends, taking part in pujas, and attending Buddhist celebrations. People can get out of touch. They can forget how much they did, once upon a time, benefit from those activities, and therefore they can cease to feel grateful to those who made the activities possible.

Sometimes people reconnect after a while; they start attending the meditation class again, or go on retreat again, perhaps after many years. I have known people who have re-established contact after anything up to twenty-two years – rather a long time in anybody's life. When this happens, they nearly always say the same thing: 'I had forgotten how good it was.' And therefore they feel renewed gratitude.

This is entirely appropriate. It is appropriate that we should be grateful, that we should recognize the benefits we have received. It is appropriate that we should be grateful to our parents, with all their admitted imperfections – parents are not perfect any more than children are. It is appropriate that we should be grateful to our teachers, to our spiritual friends, and to the Buddhist tradition. Above all, it is appropriate that we should be grateful to the Buddha, who, as we have seen, was himself utterly and instinctively full of gratitude.

CONCLUSIONS

Can the Spiritual Community Save the World?

20

A BUDDHIST VIEW OF
CURRENT WORLD PROBLEMS

IN 1943 I WAS POSTED to India as a signals operator, and after the war I stayed on to spend the next twenty years in the East, seventeen of them as a Buddhist monk. During this time I had the opportunity – I might say I was under the obligation – of attending a large number of public meetings. It is probably fair to say that Indians have a positive weakness for public meetings. Very often these are open air meetings held late at night under the glare of arc-lights, and they go on and on. In fact, the bigger they are, and the longer they go on, the better. To be called a success a meeting needs to be distinguished by a long line of speakers, each speaking for at least an hour. I can remember on one of these occasions being enjoined, in an authoritative whisper from behind me as I rose to my feet, to 'speak for at least two hours'.

People in India can be very generous with their time (and, it must be said, with other people's time as well), so I used to hear a lot of speeches. Some of the topics – and even their treatment – became very familiar to me indeed. For example, I got used to the idea that at some point during an evening of talks on Buddhist subjects you had a reasonable expectation of hearing a talk on Buddhism and world peace. This subject would come round regularly, and it didn't matter who was giving it, it was practically always the same talk.

First of all you would be treated to a graphic description of the terrible plight of mankind in the modern world, and the usual suspects would be rounded up. You would be reminded of the prevalence of flood, fire, pestilence, and war; then you would be led through the various incontrovertible signs of a universal and unprecedented breakdown of moral and spiritual values, focusing in particular on the behaviour and attitudes of young people today. Then, when you were judged to be fully reconciled to an altogether bleak prospect culminating in nuclear holocaust and no solution in sight, Buddhism would be brought in to save the day. Buddhism, you would be told, teaches non-violence; it teaches peace, love, and compassion. If everybody in the world followed the teachings of the Buddha you would have world peace, and all our problems would be solved automatically. And that would be it – end of talk. Spontaneous applause would break out, the speaker would sit down, beaming with satisfaction, the audience would clap away, happy in the knowledge that there was hope for the world after all. And, of course, the world would go on just as before.

The problem with this sort of analysis of our situation is not that it isn't true. If everybody in the world meditated every day and tried to develop kindness and love and compassion and joy, and worked at the precepts and followed the Noble Eightfold Path, then – well, we wouldn't just have peace, we'd have heaven on earth. No, the problem with this line of argument is that it's an over-simplification of both problem and solution. In the abstract, it's beautiful, but that is where it remains: in the abstract.

Another big difficulty with talking about Buddhism and world peace is that Buddhists are not the only people with values that support world peace. If everyone in the world followed the teachings of Jainism, or Taoism, or certain forms of Hinduism, you would still get world peace, without any need to mention Buddhism. There's no need, in fact, to bring in any religion at all – religions don't have a monopoly on peaceful values. If everybody followed the teachings of Plato, or even Bertrand Russell, you would have world peace on the spot.

So if one is not simply going to offer Buddhism as a universal panacea for the world's ills, what *does* it offer? One cannot talk about *the* Buddhist view of world problems because there isn't an official Buddhist party line on these or any other issues. All one is left with is *a* Buddhist view of world problems. One can talk about world problems only from one's individual standpoint. And as a Buddhist standpoint, its validity can only be measured by how deeply one has been influenced by Buddhist teachings.

There is still, however, the question of what an individual Buddhist can have to say that is truly relevant to world problems. All I can say for myself is that the work I have engaged in as a Buddhist has arisen, to some considerable extent, out of the view I take of current world problems. This topic is not of academic or peripheral interest to me. In approaching it I am in some sense trying to make clear the *raison d'être* of my own existence as a practical working Buddhist; that is, as a Buddhist not just inwardly, in faith and conviction, but also as far as outward activities are concerned. My view of current world problems constitutes a sort of philosophical autobiography, even a confession of faith. It will, I hope, show where I stand and perhaps, to some extent, why I stand there.

We can probably all make our own list of world problems, and we hardly need reminding of them: most of them have been with us since the dawn of history, and the news industry keeps us abreast of those that are of more recent provenance. What is new about the problems of today is the very fact that we hear about them. They are global in character, world-scale problems. It really is as though we live in a global village, and although this is a matter of common knowledge, even a truism, it perhaps does not sink as decisively and deeply into our awareness as it should.

The result of 'globalization' is that all world problems affect all of us in some way, either directly or indirectly, either potentially or in actuality. Not very long ago, the vast majority of people knew absolutely nothing about the problems of people who lived just a few valleys away, let alone people on the other side of the world. Catastrophic events hardly impinged at all on the lives of those who were not directly and immediately involved. Even in a country ravaged by years of terrible warfare there would be peasants within its borders going about their everyday lives knowing nothing whatsoever about it.

But not any more. We have the world's problems at our fingertips. The real problem for us is how to respond to them personally. How do we ensure that every individual citizen in the world grows up healthy and sound in body and mind? What can be done about the apparently increasing incidence of mental illness in the West? What is the role of women – and what is the role of men – in modern society? How do people with jobs avoid making themselves ill through overwork? How do people without work make the best use of their enforced leisure? How do we ensure that people are not discriminated against or abused on account of their racial origin? How do we reconcile the claims of law and order with those of individual freedom? How do we reconcile the conflicting interests of sovereign nation states? How can we all get along with one another?

Fresh outbreaks of hostilities between rival factions in some former European colony, food shortages and unrest in some ex-communist state, inner-city deprivation and crime, drug dependency and alcoholism, child labour, racial violence, industrial pollution, nuclear accidents, disease, drought, famine, starvation, 'ethnic cleansing' – these are just a few of the problems and crises that confront us, or at least pluck at our sleeves every now and then, and are recorded for us on the television and analysed for us in the newspapers. No doubt there are many others, equally pressing, which I have failed to mention. We all have our own pet world problems which seem more crucial than others. But the central problem for all of us is: how do we ourselves, individually, react to whatever we perceive to be the world's problems?

Sometimes our initial reaction will be very strong. For a while we may get quite carried away by our indignation: we are outraged; this should never be allowed to happen; something must be done; those responsible – if particular perpetrators can be identified – should be brought to justice; and so on. And we may be anxious on our own account, if the problem seems likely to affect us directly at some point. In the end, however, when that initial reaction has exhausted itself, we are overtaken – overpowered – by a different kind of reaction: helplessness. The problem is too big, too involved, for us to do anything about it. So we try to forget about it and get on with our own personal lives, and deal with our own personal problems. We are very sorry that others suffer, but at least we can try to enjoy our own lives.

This is, I suspect, how many people react to world problems. However, my own view is that such an attitude of withdrawal from public concerns into purely personal ones is one that is not worthy of a human being – not worthy, at least, of someone who is trying to be a human being in the full sense of the term. It represents an abdication of responsibility. So, given that one is helpless to effect any kind of solution to these large issues, and given too that one can't turn aside and ignore them either, what is one to do?

World problems, by their very nature, are essentially group problems, as they always have been. What is new today is the size of the groups involved and the destructive power available to them. But whatever their size, the problems arising from these groups cannot be solved on the group level. All that can be achieved on the level of the group is a precarious balance of power between conflicting interests. And that balance, as we know only too well, can be disturbed at any moment.

The only hope for humanity is therefore necessarily a long-term solution, involving more people becoming clearer about how they need to develop as individuals and co-operating in the context of spiritual communities in order to make, in their various ways, a significant impact on the world, or on 'the group'. The alternatives before us are, in my opinion, evolution – that is, the higher evolution of the individual – or extinction. That would be my overall diagnosis of the situation facing us. As for practical ways to effect a remedy, I would prescribe four courses of action for the individual to undertake.

1. SELF-DEVELOPMENT

This means essentially the development of the mind, the raising of consciousness to ever higher levels of awareness. Human development essentially consists in this, and for most people the route to achieving it is through meditation. The practice of meditation essentially involves three things. Firstly, it involves concentration, the integration of all our energies, conscious and unconscious. Secondly, it involves the raising of consciousness to supra-personal states, leaving the ego-realm for higher, wider, even cosmic dimensions. And thirdly, it involves contemplation: the direct insight of the uncluttered mind – the mind in a state of higher consciousness – into the ultimate depths of existence, the seeing of reality face to face. Meditation is concerned with achieving all this. There are many different methods; you just need to find a teacher who will introduce you to one or two of them. After that, you stick with the methods and practise them regularly. That's all there is to it, really.

The more demanding aspect of self-development consists in what one does with the rest of one's life in order to support one's meditation practice. One will look after one's health. One will simplify one's life as far as possible, dropping all those activities, interests, and social contacts which one knows to be a waste of time. One will try to base one's life, and in particular one's livelihood, on ethical principles. One will make time – perhaps by working part-time – for study; for study of the Dharma, of course, but also for study of other subjects of general human interest: philosophy, history, science, comparative religion. Finally, one will find opportunities to refine and develop one's emotions, especially through the fine arts.

Self-development always comes first. However active you might be in all sorts of external areas – political, social, educational, or whatever – if you are not trying to develop yourself, you are not going to be able to make any truly positive contribution to anything or anyone.

2. JOIN A SPIRITUAL COMMUNITY

This does not necessarily mean joining some kind of organized body or living under the same roof as other aspiring individuals. It simply means being in personal, regular, and substantial contact with others who are trying to develop as individuals. It means being able to enjoy, and seeking out, not just the psychological warmth of the herd, but the challenge of real communication, genuine spiritual exchange.

3. WITHDRAW SUPPORT FROM ALL GROUPS OR AGENCIES THAT ACTUALLY DISCOURAGE, DIRECTLY OR INDIRECTLY, THE DEVELOPMENT OF THE INDIVIDUAL

Groups derive their strength from their members, so it is a basic first step to weaken the power of the group by removing yourself from among its contributing members. Otherwise you are pulling in two directions at once: on the one hand trying to be an individual, and on the other lending your support to the very forces that hinder this process. If you wanted to take this principle to its ultimate conclusion you would withdraw support from the state, as the ultimate group of groups, though this would clearly be extremely difficult, however desirable.

4. ENCOURAGE THE DEVELOPMENT OF INDIVIDUALITY WITHIN ALL THE GROUPS TO WHICH ONE UNAVOIDABLY BELONGS

It may be that one cannot help having a circle of friends or acquaintances, whether at home or at work, who are not interested in any kind of self-development. One may have to remain very nominally a member of a group. Still, one can stand up for what one believes in, and speak up whenever it is appropriate to do so. It is always possible to act in accordance with one's ideals even when others cannot – or do not appear to – understand what one is doing. The way to disrupt a group is simply to encourage people within it to think for themselves, develop minds of their own. So in the context of the group one can still work to undermine it. Even in the enemy camp, so to speak, one need not surrender one's individuality.

These, then, are the four strategies to get under way in order to begin to make a meaningful impact on world problems. A network of spiritual communities of all kinds, many of whose members would be in contact with one another, could exert a significant degree of influence, such as might – just possibly – shift the centre of gravity in world affairs. Spiritual communities have had a crucial impact in the past, and they may, with sufficient vitality, do so again.

It doesn't matter how humble a level we are operating at, or how undramatic our work may be. The true individual is not so much the king of the jungle as the indefatigable earthworm. If enough earthworms burrow away under the foundations of even the most substantial building, the soil begins to loosen, it starts to crumble away, the foundations subside, and the whole building is liable to crack and collapse. Likewise, however powerful the existing order may seem, it is not invulnerable to the undermining influence of enough individuals working – whether directly or indirectly – in co-operation.

A spiritual community is necessarily small, so the best we can hope for is a multiplicity of spiritual communities, forming a sort of network through personal contact between their members. A silent, unseen influence is exerted in this way, which we must hope will be able, at some point, to shift the centre of gravity in world affairs from the conflict of groups to the co-operation of communities. If this were achieved, if the influence of the spiritual community were to outweigh that of the group, then humanity as a whole would have passed into a new, higher stage of development, a kind of higher evolution as I like to call it – into what we might even describe as a fifth period of human history.

Such a shift in the governing values of the world is probably all that can save us from extinction as a species in the not very distant future. There are certainly signs of hope, but there is also perhaps little time left. In this situation it becomes the duty of every thinking human being to take stock of his or her position, and the responsibilities that it throws up. We have to appreciate that it is, without exception, the most important issue we shall ever face, either individually or collectively. It is certainly more important than any merely religious question, anything that concerns Buddhism in the sense of a formal or established religion. It concerns both the purpose and the very survival of human life.

21

BUDDHISM AND WESTERN SOCIETY

THIS IS A BOLD TITLE for such a short chapter, and I don't intend to deal with the subject systematically. Instead I shall take an altogether subjective approach, basing myself on my own experience of attempting to introduce Buddhism into Western culture.

During my time in India I became used to leading a simple life within the context of a traditional culture. Returning in 1964 to an England of postwar prosperity I found a culture that was quite different not only from the one I had become used to, but also from the one I had left twenty years previously. People spoke differently, they dressed differently, they behaved differently. Manners and morals had changed – to be frank, not always for the better.

There was already a Buddhist presence in that society. Indeed, I first returned to England in order to take up the position of resident monk in the Hampstead Buddhist Vihara. However, when in 1967 I founded a new Buddhist movement, I did so with few preconceived ideas of how Buddhism might be introduced most effectively into this – as it seemed to me then – quite strange society.

My initial point of interaction was meditation. I started conducting weekly meditation classes in a tiny basement room in central London. This setting was, I feel now, quite appropriate for my earliest forays into alien territory, into a culture devoted to values that are largely inimical to my own. In some sense one had to work below the surface, as an underground movement, rather like the early Christians in Rome who are supposed to have met in the Catacombs to take refuge from persecution. We are very fortunate in the West that we are not subject to overt persecution; but modern values which are antipathetic to religious faith of any kind – like materialism, consumerism, and relativism – are enforced in subtle but pervasive ways that make them all the more difficult to resist.

In these 'underground' meditation classes, I taught two methods of meditation: the mindfulness of breathing, known in Pāli as *ānāpānasati*,[108] and the cultivation of universal loving kindness, the *mettā bhāvanā*. Quite soon, people attending these classes regularly were becoming noticeably calmer, clearer, and happier – as was only to be expected. There are many ways of defining meditation, but in very simple terms we can say that it enables the mind to work directly on itself in order to refine the quality of one's conscious experience, and in this way to raise one's whole level of consciousness. This process may be augmented by various indirect methods of raising consciousness, such as hatha yoga, t'ai chi ch'uan, and similar physical disciplines, together with the practice and appreciation of the arts. Thus the integration of Buddhism into Western society begins with at least some members of that society raising their levels of consciousness both directly through meditation, and indirectly through various other disciplines.

After a few months, we held our first retreat in the countryside, for just one week. It was attended by fifteen or twenty people who had been coming along regularly to these weekly meditation classes. On this retreat we meditated together, engaged in various devotional practices together, and discussed the Dharma together. Some of the retreatants were there to deepen their experience of meditation, and this they were able to do. But all of them discovered that simply being away from the city, away from the daily grind of work and home life, and being in the company of other Buddhists, with nothing to think about except the Dharma, was sufficient to raise their level of consciousness. So here was another point of interaction: changing the environment, changing the conditions in which people lived. That is, consciousness can be raised, at least to some extent, by changing society.

The integration of Buddhism into Western society therefore involves changing Western society. Inasmuch as our level of consciousness is affected by external conditions, it is not enough for us to work directly on the mind itself through meditation. We cannot isolate ourselves from society or ignore the conditions in which we and others live. We must make it easier for anyone within that society who wants to live a life dedicated to the Dharma to do so. To the extent that Western society has not been changed by Buddhism, to that extent Buddhism has not been integrated into Western society. In order to change Western society it is necessary to create Western Buddhist institutions and Western Buddhist lifestyles.

Thus, after a few retreats had been held, some of the people who had taken part in them decided to do what they could to prolong that experience. They set up residential spiritual communities so that they could live with other Buddhists, and have more time and space for their practice of the Dharma, and for support and encouragement. Some of our communities today comprise just two or three people living together; others consist of anything up to thirty people. Some members of communities have ordinary jobs like anyone else; others work full-time within Buddhist institutions and businesses. The most successful and typical kind of community is the single-sex community. Communities of men and women living together, sometimes with children, have been tried out, but rarely with great success. Clearly, such an arrangement is always going to involve additional complications.

Perhaps the most characteristic Western Buddhist institution is what we call the team-based right-livelihood business or project. However, the way one earns one's living is a matter to which all Buddhists attach a great deal of importance. 'Right means of livelihood' is, as we have seen, the fifth step of the Buddha's Noble Eightfold Path. So here the interaction with Western society is economic.

The way it happened in our case was that some of the people living in communities felt they would be happier if they could work with other Buddhists as well as living with them. This team-based aspect of work became an important principle of our businesses. But the fundamental principle of Buddhist work is that it should be ethical, and when a number of people found their ordinary jobs not ethical enough, they resolved to create enterprises that were, and which could therefore be called 'right-livelihood projects'. The third factor that went into establishing the founding principles of businesses came out during the creation of the complex of Buddhist centre and community in Bethnal Green in East London. The large sums of money required to complete the work were raised not simply by appealing for funds to generous patrons, welcome as such donations always are, but also by setting up co-operative right-livelihood businesses – as they were then called – which donated their profits towards the creation of the Buddhist centre.

As they became established, right-livelihood businesses came to do four things. They provided those working in them with material support, they enabled Buddhists to work with one another, they conducted themselves in accordance with Buddhist ethical principles, and they gave financial support to Buddhist and humanitarian activities.

In general, this Buddhist movement tries to create conditions that are conducive to human development. It does this in three main ways corresponding to three central aspects of ordinary human life which on balance are not conducive to spiritual development – the conventional nuclear family, work, and leisure activities. The idea is to open up and revolutionize these keystones of modern life, and where appropriate offer a more positive alternative to them.

Firstly, residential communities are meant to offer an alternative to stagnant relationships, particularly those of the tightly-knit family unit – or rather, the claustrophobic and neurotic closed system of a couple who no longer communicate with each other, orbited by one or two children, two cars, three television sets, a dog, a cat, and a budgerigar. Secondly, team-based right-livelihood projects are meant to offer an alternative to earning money in ways which are harmful to one's own development and which exploit others. And thirdly, the various activities provided and promoted by the spiritual community, both those which are directly Dharmic and those which are more indirectly helpful to spiritual growth, give us something positive to do with our free time. They give us an alternative to activities which merely enable us to pass the time, to forget about the stresses of work or family life, and all too often to forget about our own selves. These three things between them constitute the nucleus of the new society; they represent the transformation of conditions that tend to be unconducive to spiritual development into conditions that are conducive.

How each project goes about this work is up to the individuals concerned. Every one of these institutions is meant to function autonomously. Those who run it have to make their own decisions and take responsibility for them. At the same time, as an aspect of the development of this sangha, people with similar responsibilities for similar institutions make sure that they meet regularly to swap notes, and support and advise each other.

During the first few years of this movement's existence I was also delivering public lectures in which I sought to communicate the fundamental concepts of Buddhism in a way that was both intelligible to a Western audience and faithful to the Buddhist tradition. This was yet another point of interaction with Western society: the introduction of Buddhist ideas into Western intellectual discourse. By Buddhist ideas I do not mean doctrinal refinements or philosophical subtleties. I mean ideas so fundamental that Buddhists themselves often take them for granted, and fail to realize their full significance. Such, for example, is the idea that religion does not necessarily involve belief in the existence of God, of a creator and ruler of the universe. Another, related, idea is that it is possible for us to lead an ethical life, to raise the level of our consciousness, and to realize a transcendent reality, without invoking the aid of any outside supernatural power. If Buddhism is to be integrated into Western society, ideas of this fundamental kind will have to become familiar to all educated Westerners.

However, the most important kind of integration – without which the other kinds cannot exist – is the integration of the individual Buddhist into Western society. It is, after all, the individual Buddhist who meditates – meditation does not exist in the abstract. Likewise, it is the individual Buddhist who goes on retreat, who works in a right-livelihood business, who communicates the fundamental ideas of Buddhism. Without the individual Buddhist there can be no integration of Buddhism into Western society.

The individual Buddhist is, as we have seen, someone who goes for Refuge to the Three Jewels. He or she does so not in isolation but in the company of other individuals who are also Going for Refuge. That is, he or she belongs to the sangha or spiritual community in the widest sense. It is this sangha rather than the individual Buddhist which will raise the level of consciousness of people living in Western society, which will change that society by creating Buddhist social and economic institutions, and which will introduce fundamental Buddhist ideas into Western intellectual discourse. It is this wider spiritual community that will effect the psychological, social, economic, and intellectual integration of Buddhism into Western society. This is what the sangha is really for; this is what the sangha really is.

NOTES AND REFERENCES

1   For more about these experiences, see Sangharakshita, *The Rainbow Road*, Windhorse, Birmingham 1997, pp.80ff.

2   For more on these definitions, see Sangharakshita, *What is the Dharma?*, Windhorse, Birmingham 1998, pp.6–8.

3   Canonical references are to be found in *Vinaya Cullavagga* 10:5 and *Aṅguttara-Nikāya* 8:53. See also Bhikkhu Ñāṇamoli, *The Life of the Buddha*, Buddhist Publication Society, Kandy 1992, pp.107–8.

4   *Alagaddūpama Sutta* (*Majjhima-Nikāya* 22).

5   *Adhyāśayasaṁcodana Sūtra*. Quoted by Śāntideva. See *Śikṣā-samuccaya*, trans. Cecil Bendall and W.H.D. Rouse, Motilal Banarsidass, Delhi 1971, p.17.

6   See *Dakkhiṇāvibhaṅga Sutta*, *Majjhima-Nikāya* 142, verses 1–2.

7   The story of the Buddha's first discourse is told in the *Mahāvagga* of the Vinaya Piṭaka. It is quoted in, for example, Bhikkhu Ñāṇamoli, *The Life of the Buddha*, Buddhist Publication Society, Kandy 1992, pp.41–7.

8   See Stephen Batchelor, *The Awakening of the West*, Thorsons, London 1995, pp.232ff.

9   The language of refuge has been used in Buddhism since the earliest

times. According to the Vinaya Piṭaka, the first two people to encounter the Buddha after his Enlightenment (they were two merchants called Tapussa and Bhalluka) declared: 'We go for refuge to the Blessed One, and to the Dhamma.' See Ñāṇamoli, op.cit., p.34. Also see *Dhammapada* 188–92.

10 For more on this way of seeing Going for Refuge, see Sangharakshita, *The Meaning of Conversion in Buddhism*, Windhorse, Birmingham 1994, chapter 1.

11 One may have heard, for example, that faith in Buddhism is not 'blind', but traditionally based on three things: intuition, reason, and experience.

12 *Dīgha-Nikāya* 16. Quoted in Ñāṇamoli, op. cit., pp.286–9.

13 *Saṁyutta-Nikāya* iii.18.

14 For an account of pratyekabuddhas, see Reginald Ray, *Buddhist Saints in India*, Oxford University Press, Oxford and New York 1994, chapter 7.

15 'Suppose, monks, an ass follows close behind a herd of kine, thinking: I'm a cow too! I'm a cow too! But he is not like cows in colour, voice or hoof. He just follows close behind a herd of kine thinking: I'm a cow too! I'm a cow too! Just in the same way, monks, we have some monk who follows close behind the Order of Monks thinking: I'm a monk too! I'm a monk too! But he has not the desire to undertake the training in the higher morality which the other monks possess, nor in the higher thought, nor that in the higher insight which other monks possess. He just follows close behind thinking: I'm a monk too! I'm a monk too!' *Saṁyutta-Nikāya* iii.9.81 in *The Book of Gradual Sayings vol.1* trans. F.L. Woodward, Pali Text Society, Oxford 1995, p.209.

16 *Dhammapada* 194.

17 These rules comprise the *prātimokṣa*, the set of training rules recorded in the Vinaya Piṭaka as originating from the Buddha. The versions followed by different Buddhist traditions vary slightly. See Sangharakshita, *The Three Jewels*, Windhorse, Birmingham 1998, pp.185–7.

18 See *Saṁyutta-Nikāya* chapter xxviii, section 1. (*The Book of the Kindred Sayings* Part III, trans. F.L. Woodward and Mrs Rhys Davids, Pali Text Society, Oxford, p.186.)

19 For more about Ananda Maitreya, see Stephen Batchelor, *The Awakening of the West*, Thorsons, London 1995, pp.40–1.

20 The Buddha often described the path to Enlightenment in these terms and according to the Pāli Canon he did so many times in the last days of his life. See *Dīgha-Nikāya* 16, and also Ñāṇamoli, op.cit., p.291. For an exposition of the threefold path, see Sangharakshita, *What is the Dharma?*, Windhorse, Birmingham 1998, chapters 10–12.

21 For a canonical reference to the three levels of wisdom, see *Dīgha-Nikāya* 33, and for an exposition, see Sangharakshita, *What is the Dharma?*, op.cit., pp.148–50.

22 The Buddha is recorded as making this fourfold classification on many occasions; see, for example, *Dīgha-Nikāya* ii.252; see also Ñāṇamoli, op. cit., p.162.

23 See Ñāṇamoli, op. cit., p.162.

24 For an account of the origin of the Pāli Canon and the way it is organized, see Sangharakshita, *The Eternal Legacy*, Tharpa, London 1985, chapters 1–7.

25 See Sangharakshita, *The Bodhisattva Ideal*, Windhorse, Birmingham 1999, pp.180–5.

26 Canonical references can be found at *Majjhima-Nikāya* i.243–5 and *Dīgha-Nikāya* iii.234.

27 'In Memoriam A.H.H.' canto 96.

28 *Richard the Second*, act 5, scene 5.

29 Mark 2:27.

30 For more on the three fetters, see Sangharakshita, *The Taste of Freedom*, Windhorse, Birmingham 1997, chapter 1, in which the three fetters are described as habit, superficiality, and vagueness.

31 This meditation was taught by the Buddha himself, and is practised by Buddhists of most schools. For a brief account, see Sangharakshita, *What is the Dharma?*, op.cit., pp.190–2.

32 See Georg Wilhelm Friedrich Hegel, *The Philosophy of History*, Dover Publications, New York 1956.

33 See Arnold J. Toynbee, *A Study of History: The Geneses of Civilizations*, Oxford University Press, New York 1962.

34 See Francis Fukuyama, *The End of History and the Last Man*, Avon Books, 1997.

35 See Karl Jaspers, *The Origin and Goal of History*, Routledge and Kegan Paul, London 1953.

36 *The Philosophy of History*, op. cit., p.319.

37 'The safest characterization of the European philosophical tradition is that it consists of a series of footnotes to Plato.' A.N. Whitehead, *Process and Reality*, 1929, part 2, chapter 1.

38 *The Philosophy of History*, op.cit. pp.2–3.

39 The school Nichiren (1222–82) founded bases its teaching on the *White Lotus Sūtra*. The best known and most widespread contemporary school based on Nichiren Buddhism is Soka Gakkai.

40 See Sangharakshita, *The Bodhisattva Ideal*, Windhorse, Birmingham 1999, chapter 2: 'The Awakening of the Bodhi Heart'.

41 See *Amitāyur-Dhyāna-Sūtra* in *Buddhist Mahāyāna Texts*, ed. E.B. Cowell et al., Motilal Banarsidass, Delhi 1997, pp.161–201.

42 Traditional accounts vary. In the *Majjhima-Nikāya* (sutta 26) the Buddha simply says that 'though my mother and father wished otherwise and wept with tearful faces', he shaved his hair and beard, put on the robes of a wanderer, and left home. But other biographies, notably those of the Mahāyāna, describe in great detail, as suggested here, the Buddha's sorrowful leave-taking. It is this latter version of the story that Sir Edwin Arnold used in his epic poem about the Buddha's life, *The Light of Asia*.

43 This is what the Buddha (in *Dīgha-Nikāya* 11) calls 'the miracle of instruction'.

44 For more on this way of classifying awareness, see Sangharakshita, *Vision and Transformation*, Windhorse, Birmingham 1999, chapter 7, 'Levels of Awareness'.

45 See Dwight Goddard, *A Buddhist Bible*, Beacon Press, Boston 1970, p.612.

46 Jack Hirschman (ed.), *Antonin Artaud Anthology*, City Light Books, San Francisco 1965, p.222.

47 *Majjhima-Nikāya* 36; see also Ñāṇamoli op. cit., p.21.

48 Vladimir Nabokov in conversation with James Mossman, *The Listener*, 23 October 1969.

49 For more on the levels of consciousness, see Robin Cooper, *The Evolving Mind*, Windhorse, Birmingham 1996, chapter 6.

50 There is clearly scope here for wondering whether this conception of a 'transcendental awareness' is not more or less the same thing as a conception of an absolute being. For more reflection on this theme, see

Sangharakshita, *The Bodhisattva Ideal*, op.cit., p.38.

51 *Bhagavad Gītā* chapter 7, verse 3.

52 *Dhammapada* 182.

53 *Analects* 13.3.

54 (Untraced at time of going to press.)

55 His exposition of *anattā* was, according to the Pāli records, an aspect of the Buddha's teaching to his first five disciples; see Ñāṇamoli p.46. The essence of the teaching is that one cannot identify any aspect of one's being – whether material form, feeling, perception, volitions, or consciousness – as being one's self. At the same time, one's being is made up solely of these elements (traditionally called the five *skandhas* or 'heaps'); there is no 'true self' or soul as it were standing behind them – no unchanging essence – and therefore, in a sense, no 'self' to be reborn. One's existence is simply an ever-changing combination of these five elements. It is therefore perhaps most useful to think in terms of there being no *fixed* self.

56 'The will to a *system*: in a philosopher, morally speaking, a subtle corruption, a disease of the character; amorally speaking, his will to appear more stupid than he is....' See Walter Kaufmann, *Nietzsche: Philosopher, Psychologist, Antichrist*, Princeton University Press, 1975, p.80.

57 Ibid.

58 Friedrich Nietzsche, *Thus Spoke Zarathustra*, Penguin, London 1961, p.41.

59 Ibid., p.43.

60 Kaufmann, op. cit., p.151.

61 '"Giving style" to one's character – a great and rare art! It is exercised by those who see all the strengths and weaknesses of their own nature and then comprehend them in an artistic plan until everything appears as art and reason.' quoted Kaufmann op.cit., p.251.

62 See Kaufmann, op. cit., chapter 6.

63 *Dhammapada* 103.

64 For more on the bodhicitta, see Sangharakshita, *The Bodhisattva Ideal*, Windhorse, Birmingham 1999, chapter 2: 'The awakening of the bodhi heart'.

65 See 'Some Notes on my own Poetry' in *Collected Poems*, Macmillan, London 1957, pp.xv–xlvi.

66 These engravings are to be seen in the British Museum.

67 Sangharakshita, *The Religion of Art*, Windhorse, Glasgow 1988, pp.84–5.

68 Just as the eye observes forms, the ear hears sounds, and so on, the mind contacts mental objects: ideas, memories, and so on. The mind is thus classified as a sense organ in the same sense as the organs associated with the five physical senses.

69 Vladimir Nabokov in conversation with James Mossman, *The Listener*, 23 October 1969.

70 For a description of how visualization practices work, see Vessantara, *Meeting the Buddhas*, Windhorse, Birmingham 1993, chapter 2: 'The Development of Buddhist Visualization'.

71 See *Puja*, Windhorse, Birmingham 1999, p.37.

72 *Dīgha-Nikāya* 31.

73 See Plato, *The Last Days of Socrates*, Penguin, Harmondsworth 1969.

74 cf. *Udāna* ii.3 and v.4.

75 Maurice Walshe (trans.), *The Long Discourses of the Buddha*, Wisdom Publications, Boston 1995, pp.67–8.

76 *Majjhima-Nikāya* 72.

77 Subhūti, what do you think? Has the Tathāgata attained the consummation of incomparable enlightenment? Has the Tathāgata a teaching to enunciate?

Subhūti answered: As I understand Buddha's meaning there is no formulation of truth called consummation of incomparable enlightenment. Moreover, the Tathāgata has no formulated teaching to enunciate. Wherefore? Because the Tathāgata has said that truth is uncontainable and inexpressible. It neither is nor is not.

A.F. Price (trans.), *The Diamond Sūtra*, Shambhala, Boston 1990, p.24.

78 See *The Lankavatara Scripture* in *A Buddhist Bible*, Beacon Press, Boston 1970, p.348.

79 An account of Sangharakshita's meeting with Anandamayi, 'the blissful mother', is to be found in *The Rainbow Road*, Windhorse, Birmingham 1997, chapter 20.

80 This story is told in the *Mahāvagga* of the Vinaya Piṭaka, and recounted in Ñāṇamoli, op. cit., p.77.

81 Porphyry, in *Plotinus*, trans. A.H. Armstrong, Heinemann, London 1966. vol.1, p.3 *et seq.*

82　*Dīgha-Nikāya* 25, section 22.

83　*Hamlet* act 1, scene 4.

84　The language of near and far enemies is derived from the *Visuddhimagga*, in which Buddhaghosa identifies the near and far enemies of emotions such as loving kindness and compassion. A far enemy is clearly opposite and inimical to the positive quality one wishes to cultivate: thus, ill will is the far enemy of loving kindness. A near enemy, by contrast, is sufficiently like the desired quality to be mistaken for it: thus, sticky or needy affection (*pema*) is said to be the near enemy of loving kindness. See Buddhaghosa, *The Path of Purification (Visuddhimagga)*, trans. Bhikkhu Ñāṇamoli, Buddhist Publication Society, Kandy 1991, p.311.

85　*Paradise Lost*, Book Five, 896–907.

86　See Note 41 above.

87　*Dīgha-Nikāya* iii.190.

88　Śāntideva, *The Bodhicaryāvatāra*, trans. Kate Crosby and Andrew Skilton, Oxford University Press, Oxford 1995, chapter 8, verses 112ff.

89　*Dīgha-Nikāya* iii.190.

90　See Sangharakshita, *The Inconceivable Emancipation*, Windhorse, Birmingham 1995, pp.51–4.

91　'Are not religion and politics the same thing? Brotherhood is religion,/ O demonstrations of reason, dividing families in cruelty and pride!' William Blake, *Jerusalem*, plate 57, lines 10–11.

92　For more on the love mode and the power mode, see Sangharakshita, *The Ten Pillars of Buddhism*, Windhorse, Birmingham 1996, pp.58–9.

93　Quoted in Ñāṇamoli, op. cit., pp.130–2.

94　See Sangharakshita, *The Ten Pillars of Buddhism*, Windhorse, Birmingham 1996, p.68.

95　*Dīgha-Nikāya* 19.

96　See Sangharakshita, *The Ten Pillars of Buddhism*, Windhorse, Birmingham 1996, pp.60–6.

97　For more on right livelihood as a limb of the Noble Eightfold Path, see Sangharakshita, *Vision and Transformation*, Windhorse, Birmingham 1999, chapter 5: 'The ideal society'.

98　This list is to be found in the *Aṅguttara-Nikāya* (v.177), and is quoted in

Ñāṇamoli, op. cit., p.239.

99 *Dīgha-Nikāya* 31, section 32.

100 *Dhammapada* 49.

101 For more on the path of vision and the path of transformation, see Sangharakshita, *Vision and Transformation*, Windhorse, Birmingham 1999, pp.12–15.

102 See, for example, the *Lalitavistara* in *The Voice of the Buddha*, trans. Gwendolyn Bays, Dharma Publishing, Berkeley 1983, vol.ii, p.570; or the *Abhiniṣkramaṇa Sūtra* in *The Romantic Legend of Śākya Buddha*, trans. Samuel Beal, Motilal Banarsidass, Delhi 1985 (first published 1875), p.237.

103 Huien Tsiang, in *Buddhist Records of the Western World*, trans. Samuel Beal, Motilal Banarsidass, Delhi 1981 (first published 1884), part ii, p.123.

104 'Reverence, humility, contentment, gratitude and timely hearing of the Dhamma; this is the most auspicious performance.' *Mahāmaṅgala Sutta* in *Sutta-Nipāta* verse 265. This translation by H. Saddhatissa, Curzon Press, London 1985, p.29.

105 from *Sigālaka Sutta* (also known as the *Sigālovāda Sutta*), *Dīgha-Nikāya* iii.188. This translation from *The Long Discourses of the Buddha*, trans. Maurice Walshe, Wisdom Publications, Boston 1995, p.467.

106 *Dhammapada* 354.

107 *Aṅguttara-Nikāya* IV.xxii.213.

108 The Buddha's description of this practice is found in the *Mahāsatipaṭṭhāna Sutta*, *Dīgha-Nikāya* ii.291.

FURTHER READING

Part One

ON THE TRADITIONAL SANGHA
S. Dutt, *The Buddha and Five After-Centuries*, Sahitya Samsad, Calcutta 1978
Reginald Ray, *Buddhist Saints in India*, Oxford University Press, Oxford and New York 1994
Sangharakshita, *The Three Jewels*, Windhorse, Birmingham 1998, part three: 'The Sangha.'

ON THE HISTORY OF SPIRITUAL COMMUNITIES
Sangharakshita, *Alternative Traditions*, Windhorse, Glasgow 1986, 'Alternative Traditions' and 'D.H. Lawrence and the Spiritual Community'

ON THE INDIVIDUAL AND THE SPIRITUAL COMMUNITY
Sangharakshita, *New Currents in Western Buddhism*, Windhorse, Glasgow 1990

ON STREAM-ENTRY AND THE FETTERS
Sangharakshita, *The Taste of Freedom*, Windhorse, Birmingham 1997
Sangharakshita, *What is the Dharma?*, Windhorse, Birmingham 1998, chapter 6: 'The Gravitational Pull and the Point of No Return.'

Part Two

ON EVOLUTION
Robin Cooper, *The Evolving Mind*, Windhorse, Birmingham 1996

Karl Jaspers, *The Origin and Goal of History*, Routledge & Kegan Paul, London 1953

P.D. Ryan, *Buddhism and the Natural World*, Windhorse, Birmingham 1998

ON NIETZSCHE

Friedrich Nietzsche, *Thus Spoke Zarathustra*, trans. R.J. Hollingdale, Penguin, Harmondsworth 1961

Walter Kaufmann, *Nietzsche: Philosopher, Psychologist, Antichrist*, Princeton University Press 1975

ON ART

Sangharakshita, *The Religion of Art*, Windhorse, Glasgow 1988

Sangharakshita, *In the Realm of the Lotus*, Windhorse, Birmingham 1995

Roger Lipsey, *An Art of Our Own: The Spiritual in Twentieth-Century Art*, Shambhala, Boston, 1988.

Part Three

ON ETHICS

Damien Keown, *The Nature of Buddhist Ethics*, Macmillan, London 1992

H. Saddhatissa, *Buddhist Ethics*, Wisdom Publications, Boston 1997

Sangharakshita, *The Ten Pillars of Buddhism*, Windhorse, Birmingham 1996

ON SPIRITUAL TEACHERS

Alex Berzin, *Relating to a Spiritual Teacher: Building a Healthy Relationship*, Snow Lion, Ithaca 2000

Kulananda, *Teachers of Enlightenment*, Windhorse, Birmingham 2000

INDEX

A
Abdiel 193
acts of God 66
ādikārmika-bodhisattva 33
Aeschylus 45, 226
Aesop 45
Age of Divine Kingship 44
Age of Prometheus 43
agriculture 44
Ajātasatru 72, 195
Al-Ghazālī 47
alienated awareness 108ff, 112
almsround 213
aloneness 92
Alpert, R. 183
Amitābha 72, 74, 75
Amitāyur-Dhyāna Sūtra 72, 195
Amitāyus 72, 73, 195
Amos 45, 123
anāgāmin 32
Analects, The 45

Ānanda 19, 73, 195, 202
Ananda Maitreya 30
Anandamayi 254
anattā 109, 113, 253
Anaximander 45
anger 39
animist 221
anxiety 44
Apollonius of Tyana 182
apprenticeship 147
Archimedes 45
arhant 32, 216
Aristophanes 45
Aristotle 45, 99
art 132ff, 136ff
Artaud, A. 91
artist 128ff
ārya 30, 35, 40
  pudgala 32
  -sangha 30ff
Aśoka 14

attachment 191
Austen, J. 226
authority 63ff, 159
Avalokiteśvara 74
awareness 88ff, 97ff, 100, 108, 109, 252
　alienated 108ff, 112
　of artist 129ff
　of self 89
　transcendental 252
Axial Age 42, 44

B
Bach, J.S. 131, 227
Baudelaire, C.P. 227
beauty 49
Beethoven 193, 227
Bell, C. 132
Benedict, St 48
Benedictine order 48
Bennett, A. 30
Bertolucci, B. 1
Bhagavad Gītā 104
Bhalluka 250
bhāvanā-mayī-prajñā 31
bhikṣu 216
bhikṣuṇī 28
　ordination 28
bhikṣu-bhikṣuṇī sangha 27ff
bhūmis 33
Bimbisāra 72, 195
Birth of Tragedy 116
Blake, W. 117, 199
Bloom, H. 226
bodhi tree 220
Bodhicaryāvatāra 198
bodhicitta 69, 71, 125, 253
Bodhisattva 196
　ādikārmika- 33
　of the dharmakāya 34
　hierarchy 33

Hīnayāna 34
　ideal 33
　irreversible 33
　novice 33
　of the Path 33
body 99, 224
bonds 52
Bounderby, Mr 225, 230
brahma 203
brahmacariya 203
brahmaloka 203
Brahmā Sahampati 220, 221
Buddha 73, 91, 98, 168, 171, 216, 218, 228
　disciples of 15
　Enlightenment 219
　going forth 80
　as ideal 21
　Jayanti 23
　Jewel 13
Buddhaghosa 256
buddhavacana 14
Buddhism 98, 125, 235ff
Buddhist centre 75, 82
Buddhist festivals 23, 161
Buddhist movement 76
Buddhist Society 16
butcher 207

C
Calcutta 186
cariya 203
caste 81, 186
Cervantes 226
Chandramani, U 3
character 122, 253,
　see also personality
Charlemagne 48
Chekhov, A. 136
child 101, 145, 153ff

China 145
Christ (Jesus) 38, 44, 45, 47, 67
Christian movements 48
Christianity 48, 67, 137, 172, 182, 227,
    see also God, religion
Chuang Tzu 45
Church, the 67ff,
    see also Christianity, religion
Cicero 228
cintā-mayī-prajñā 31
clarity 88,
    see also awareness, mindfulness
class 58
coersion 65
Coleridge, S.T. 117
commitment 16, 23, 37, 93, 148
communication 20, 56, 136, 143, 157,
    161, 176, 178, 199
    horizontal 176
    spiritual 176
    vertical 176ff
compassion 69, 71, see also mettā
conditioning 55, 88
Confucius 45, 91, 92, 110, 111
Confucianism 145
consciousness 99ff, 133, 137
    absolute 101
    development of human 42ff
    four levels 100, 252
    reflexive 189
    self- 88, 97ff, 189
    simple 100
    transcendental 100, 104, 134
    universal 101
consistency 189
control 65
Conversations with Eckermann 91
Conze, E. 30
coolies 209
Creation, The 135

creativity 91, 131, 138
criticism 169
Croce, B. 132
crow 164
culture 137

D
Dante 226
Darwin, C. 95
death 39, 192
dependence on rules 38
desire 39
Devadatta 73
Dhammapada 22, 104, 124, 213, 218, 228
Dharma
    Day 23
    Jewel 13
    as ideal 21
    as raft 14
dharmadhātu 22
Dharmarakshita 3
Diamond Sūtra 9, 171
Dickens, C. 147, 225, 226
dictionary 222
diet 159, see also food
difficulty 173
disciple 24, 167ff, 177, 178, 214ff
    of Buddha 15
dissatisfaction 82ff
distraction 190
diṭṭhi see view
Dostoyevsky, F.M. 226
doubt 37
dṛṣṭi see view
drugs 207
duty 29, 148, 153, 158, 197, 209, 222, 229
    of employee 211
    of employer 209
    of monk 29
    of nun 29

E

education 156, 225, *see also* teachers
effort 60, 102
ego 112, *see also* self
egoism 230
Eliot, G. 130
emotion, positive 69, 92,
    see also mettā
emotional maturity 171
empathy 163
employee, duties of 211
employer, duties of 209
enemy 255
energy 92
Enlightenment 13, 23, 219, 220
environment 163
ethics 38, 108, 145, 206
ethnic religion 60
Euclid 45
Euripides 45
evolution 95ff, 120
    higher 98, 102
    lower 98

F

faith 250
family 58
    nuclear 162
    see also parents
far enemy 255
father 172, *see also* parents
Fernando 194
festivals, Buddhist 23, 161
fetters 36ff, 251
feudal system 146
Fidelio 193
fidelity 186ff
filial piety 145
Floristan 194
Foh 16

food 214, *see also* diet
forgetfulness 230, 232
forgiveness 25
fortune-telling 207
four requisites 214
'Four Stages of Cruelty' 164
freedom 91
Freud, S. 171
friendliness 69
friends 149, 199
friendship 56, 146, 197
    spiritual 227ff
Fukuyama, F. 42
Fuller, B. 183

G

Gandhi, M.K. 172
Ganges 144
generosity 205, 218, 230
genius 135
gestation 101
Ginsberg, A. 183
globalization 237
God 66ff, 119, 171, 180, 193,
    see also Christianity, religion
Goethe 91, 122, 131, 226
Going for Refuge 16ff, 72, 77
going forth 79ff, 150
Govinda, Lama 196
gratitude 219ff
group 50, 51ff, 168ff, 238, 240
    characteristics 53
    development of 52
    instinct 53
    leaving 79
    relationship to spiritual
        community 57ff
    religious 168
    symbols 53
guilt 164

guru 4, 167ff
　academic 182
　see also lama, teachers

H
Hamlet 187
Handel, G.F. 131
Hard Times 225
Haydn, J. 131, 135
Hegel, G. 42, 44
Herodotus 45
Hīnayāna 33
Hinduism 80
Hippocrates 45
history 41
　of mankind 42ff
Hitler 67
Hochhuth, R. 67
Hogarth, W. 130, 164
home 155
Homer 45, 135, 226
homosexuality 149
Hood, T. 224
Hsüan Tsang 220
human being 99, 104
human body 99, 224
human realm 100, 121
humanity 97, 121

I
ideal 56, 188
　Bodhisattva 33
　Buddha 21
　Dharma 21
　romantic 186
Iliad 135
imagination 158
independence 90ff, 131
India 209, 213, 235

individual (true) 4, 35, 40, 46, 55, 64, 87ff, 108, 112, 127, 187, 189
individualism 230
individuality 112, 240
indoctrination 154
infidelity 191
ingratitude 228ff
Inquisition 68
insight 31ff, 101, 219
instinct 53
integration 37, 108, 112, 134, 247
intelligence 88
Isaiah 45, 123
isolation 192

J
Jambudvīpa 73
James, H. 136
Japan 28, 59ff
Jaspers, K. 42, 44, 95
Jeremiah 45, 123
Jesus (Christ) 38, 44, 45, 47, 67
Johnson, S. 222
Joyce, J. 136
Jung, C.G. 112

K
kaṭhinacīvaradāna 25
Kālidāsa 226
Kalimpong 185
kalyāṇa 19, 227
kalyāṇa mitra(tā) 4, 19, 56, 57, 227
kāma-rāga 39
karma 165
kārttikapūrṇimā 26
kataññutā 222
Kaufmann, W. 118, 121
Kean, C. 117
knowledge 222
Krishna 104

L

Laertes 187
lama 27, 172, *see also* guru, teachers
Laṅkāvatāra Sūtra 171
Lao-tzu 45
Larkin, P. 223
Last Man 120
Lawrence, D.H. 224
lay-disciples 24, 214ff
Leary, T. 183
Leonora 193
Life and Liberation of Padmasambhava 230
literature 226
livelihood 207, 245
London Buddhist Centre 74
Lope de Vega 131
Lotus Sūtra 59
love 68, 200, 227
    mode 255
loyalty 53, 59, 146, 148, 193
Lucifer 193

M

madhukari bhikṣā 214
Mahāgovinda Sutta 203
mahākaruṇā 69
mahāmaitrī 69
Mahāmaudgalyāyana 73, 195, *see also* Moggallana
Mahāprajāpati 14
mahā-sangha 27
Mahāvīra 45
Mahāyāna 33
maitrī *see* mettā
Man and Superman 118
Maṅgala Sutta 222
mango grove 201
Mani 47, 49
Manicheism 49

manipulation 201
Mañjuśrī 74
manners 160
Manusmriti 161
marriage 149, 171, 186
Marx, K. 42
Mataji 172
Maudgalyāyana *see* Mahāmaudgalyāyana
Maugham, W.S. 136
mauna 216
Maupassant, G. de 136
medicine 214
meditation 31, 40, 108, 138, 191, 200, 239, 243
Meghiya 201
Meiji 59
Mencius 45
mendicant 80
mental state 158
mettā 69, 200, 227
mettā bhāvanā 40, 200
Milton, J. 135, 136, 193, 226, 230
mind 99, 254
mindfulness 108, *see also* awareness, clarity
miracle 83
mitra 200
mitratā 19
Moggallana 29, *see also* Mahāmaudgalyāyana
monasteries, Christian 48
monasteries, origin 26
monastic order 27
monk 24, 27, 82, 207, 214ff
    duties of 29
morality 38, *see also* ethics
More, T. 110
mother 172, 188, *see also* parents
Mozart, W.A. 131, 227

Mucalinda 220
muni 216
Murasaki Shikibu 226
muse 135
mystic 135, 139
myth 46

N
Nabokov, V. 98, 136
Nanda 179
Napoleon 123
nation state 58
near enemy 255
needs 217
new society 75ff, 84
Nichiren 59, 252
Nietzsche, F. 115ff
non-exploitation 205ff, 213
non-returner 32, 39
nun 24, 27
    duties of 29

O
Odyssey 135
once-returner 32, 39
order 76
ordination 82
overman 118, 120, 123ff
Oxford Movement 38

P
pabbajjā 82
Padmasambhava 49
Pāli Canon 33, 164
Paradise Lost 135, 193, 230
pārājika 28
parents 153ff, 223ff
parent-teacher organization 156
parivrājaka 80f
path of transformation 219, 256

path of vision 219, 256
pema 200, 227
personality 112, *see also* character
personality-belief 36
Phidias 45
Philosophy of History 44
philosophy, schools of 46
    Western 125
Pickwick Papers 147
Pickwick, Mr 147
Pindar 45
Pizzaro 194
Plato 45, 110, 121, 145, 182, 236
poison 207
Polonius 187
pope 68
Pope Innocent X 130
Pope Pius XII 67
porāṇacariyas 227
possessiveness 160
potential 52
power 55, 63ff, 71, 200
    mode 200, 255
prajñā 31
prātimokṣa 250
pratyekabuddhas 21
pravāraṇā 25
Praxiteles 45
precepts 28
Precepts of the Gurus 90
primitive man 42
problems 173ff
    world 235
Prometheus 43
promiscuity 190
promises 189, 198
'Proverbs of Hell, The' 117
pṛthagjanas 51
psychic powers 208
public meetings 235

punctuality 211
Pure Land 72, 74, 75
purisapuggala 35
Pushkin, A.S. 136
Pythagoras 45, 46, 182

R
raft 14
Rainbow Road, The 3
rainy season 25
Rājagṛha 195
Ram Dass 183
Ramdas (Swami) 18
Rampa, Lobsang 208
Read, H. 132
reality 9, 31, 89, 100, 130, 219
reason 17, 183
rebirth 32, 228
receptivity 88
refuge 17, 249,
　see also Three Refuges
relationships 20, 143ff
　in business 205
　continuity of 190
　employer and employee 209
　friendship 56, 69, 146, 149, 197,
　　199, 227ff
　group and spiritual community 57ff
　husband and wife 187
　master and servant 146, 147
　monk and laity 214ff
　parent and child 145, 153ff, 223ff
　romantic/sexual 146, 149, 171, 190
　teacher and disciple 167ff
　teacher and pupil 148
religion 137
　ethnic 60
　theistic 66
　universal 98, 103
　see also Christianity, God

Religion of Art 133
religious group 168
Rembrandt 131
renunciation 79, 81
representation 63ff
　of God 66
Representative, The 67
reputation 38
requisites, four 214
responsibility 93
Richard II 37
rickshaw pullers 209
rights 229
right livelihood 206, 255
　business 245
Rilke, R.M. 227
Ritschl, F.W. 116
ritual 38, 144
ritualist controversy 38
robes 25
Rocco 194
rock edicts 14
Roman Catholic Church 67, 68
romantic ideal 186
romantic/sexual relationship 146,
　149, 171, 190
Rubens 131
rules 38, 250
rūpadhātu 32
Russell, B. 236

S
Sabbath 38
sacred thread 81
saint 182
sakṛdāgāmin 32
Śākyamuni 73, 216, 228,
　see also Buddha
samānārthatā 199
Samayatārā 196

saṁgrahavastu 199
sangha 15
    ārya- 30ff
    bhikṣu-bhikṣuṇī 27ff
    entry into 81
    mahā- 27
    traditional categories 27ff
Sangha Day 24, 26
Sangharakshita 3
Śāntideva 198
śaraṇa 17
Sāriputta 29
Sarvāstivāda 27
Satan 230
satkāya-dṛṣṭi 36
scepticism 37
Schopenhauer, A. 116
Schubert 131
science 44
self 29, 36, 96, 107, 109, 110ff, 112ff, 253
    -awareness 189, 192
    -confidence 163
    -consciousness 88, 97ff, 189
    -determination 91
    -development 103, 150, 239
    -knowledge 20
    -worth 217
selfishness 203
separation 192ff
servant 147
service 148
sexual fidelity 189
sexual/romantic relationship 146, 149, 171, 190
sexuality 190
Shakespeare, W. 37, 131, 136, 187, 226, 227
Shangri-la 168
sharing 197
Shaw, G.B. 118

Shelley, P.B. 134
sibling 149
Sigālaka 144, 153
Sigālaka (Sigālovāda) Sutta 144, 187, 198, 209, 224
śīla 38
śīlavrata-parāmarśa 38
silence 216
Sitwell, O. 128
skilful means 199
slave 188, 200
slavery 206
smoking 159
society 75, 243ff
Socrates 45, 91, 92, 146
Sophocles 45
speech 161, 197,
    see also communication
spiritual attainment 28
spiritual community 76, 240
    characteristics of 55ff
    Christian 48
    history of 46
    Mahāyāna 47
    residential 245
    Sufi 47
    Theravāda 47
spiritual development 150, 178
spiritual friendship 227ff,
    see also kalyāṇa mitratā
spiritual life 203
śrotapanna 32
śruta-mayī-prajñā 31
Stalin 92
status 38
Stream-entrant 32, 34, 36, 39, 104, 231
stupa 220
Sufism 47
Sukhāvati 72, 74, 75
Sundarananda 179

superman 118
Sūtra of Wei Lang 9
Swami Ramdas 18

T
Tao-te Ching 45
tapo 22
Tapussa 250
Tārā 196
teachers 148, 167ff, 170, 225ff
television 158
Tennyson, A. 37
Thales 45
theistic religion 66
Theravāda 27, 33
Third Eye, The 208
thought 189
Three Jewels/Refuges 13ff, 15, 16, 196
Thucydides 45
Thus Spoke Zarathustra 115, 116
tiki 81
Tiratana Vandanā 32, 35
Titian 131
Tolstoy, L. 136
Toynbee, A. 42
transcendental consciousness 100, 104, 134
transformation 136
triratna *see* Three Jewels
triśaraṇa *see* Three Refuges
true individual 4, 35, 40, 46, 55, 64, 87ff, 108, 112, 127, 187, 189
Turgenev, I.S. 136

U
Übermensch 118
Udāna 201
universal consciousness 101
universal religion 98, 103
unpopularity 91, 132

Upanishads 45
upasampadā 28, 82
upāyapāramitā 199

V
Vaidehī 72, 195
Vaiśālī 18
Vajjians 18
Varanasi 144
varṣāvāsa 25
Velásquez 130
vicikitsā 37
view 36, 171
violence 158, 164
Virgil 226
Visākha 23
visualization 138, 254
Visuddhimagga 255
vyāpāda 39

W
Wagner 116
weapons 207
Weller, Sam 147
Wesak 23
Western Buddhist Order 74
What is the Dharma? 2
Whitehead, A.N. 45
Who is the Buddha? 1
Will to Enlightenment 69, 71, 125
Will to Power 123, 125
wisdom 71, 216
  levels of 30, 251
Wordsworth, W. 227
work 245
worship 145

Z
Zarathustra (Zoroaster) 45, 118ff

The Windhorse symbolizes the energy of the enlightened mind carrying the Three Jewels – the Buddha, the Dharma, and the Sangha – to all sentient beings.

Buddhism is one of the fastest-growing spiritual traditions in the Western world. Throughout its 2,500-year history, it has always succeeded in adapting its mode of expression to suit whatever culture it has encountered.

Windhorse Publications aims to continue this tradition as Buddhism comes to the West. Today's Westerners are heirs to the entire Buddhist tradition, free to draw instruction and inspiration from all the many schools and branches. Windhorse publishes works by authors who not only understand the Buddhist tradition but are also familiar with Western culture and the Western mind.

Manuscripts welcome. For orders and catalogues contact

WINDHORSE PUBLICATIONS	WINDHORSE BOOKS	WEATHERHILL INC
11 PARK ROAD	PO BOX 574	41 MONROE TURNPIKE
BIRMINGHAM	NEWTOWN	TRUMBULL
B13 8AB	NSW 2042	CT 06611
UK	AUSTRALIA	USA

Windhorse Publications is an arm of the Friends of the Western Buddhist Order, which has more than sixty centres on five continents. Through these centres, members of the Western Buddhist Order offer regular programmes of events for the general public and for more experienced students. These include meditation classes, public talks, study on Buddhist themes and texts, and 'bodywork' classes such as t'ai chi, yoga, and massage. The FWBO also runs several retreat centres and the Karuna Trust, a fund-raising charity that supports social welfare projects in the slums and villages of India.

Many FWBO centres have residential spiritual communities and ethical businesses associated with them. Arts activities are encouraged too, as is the development of strong bonds of friendship between people who share the same ideals. In this way the FWBO is developing a unique approach to Buddhism, not simply as a set of techniques, less still as an exotic cultural interest, but as a creatively directed way of life for people living in the modern world.

If you would like more information about the FWBO visit the website at www.fwbo.org or write to

LONDON BUDDHIST CENTRE	ARYALOKA
51 ROMAN ROAD	HEARTWOOD CIRCLE
LONDON	NEWMARKET
E2 0HU	NH 03857
UK	USA

ALSO FROM WINDHORSE

KULANANDA

TEACHERS OF ENLIGHTENMENT:

THE REFUGE TREE OF THE WESTERN BUDDHIST ORDER

Out of the depths of a clear blue sky emerges a beautiful tree of white lotus flowers. On the tree are many figures – historical, mythical, and transcendental – each a teacher of Enlightenment. This is the Refuge Tree: a compelling image which, in its many different forms, has inspired Buddhists for centuries.

Here, Kulananda explains the significance of the figures on the Refuge Tree of the Western Buddhist Order. These teachers, each in their own way, have all changed the world for the better, playing a part in the creation of the rich Buddhist tradition we know today.

304 pages, with illustrations and b&w photos
ISBN 1 899579 25 7
£12.99/$25.95

VESSANTARA

TALES OF FREEDOM: WISDOM FROM THE BUDDHIST TRADITION

Stories have the power to transform us as we enter their world. Drawn from the rich variety of the Buddhist tradition, these beautifully-told stories convey a sense of inner freedom. We see ordinary people liberate themselves from anger and grief, and great teachers remain free even in the face of death. Vessantara's commentary shows us how we can move towards that freedom in our own lives.

216 pages
ISBN 1 899579 27 3
£9.99/$19.95

SANGHARAKSHITA
WHO IS THE BUDDHA?

Who is the Buddha? What does it mean to be a Buddhist? Here a leading Western Buddhist looks at these questions from several angles. We see the Buddha in historical context, as the Indian warrior prince who went forth in search of the truth. We see him in the context of the evolution of the human race, in the context of karma and rebirth, in the context of time and in the context of eternity.

Above all, we meet the Buddha as a man who struggled to understand the mysteries of life, suffering, and death. He won that understanding by transcending human life altogether and becoming a Buddha – 'one who knows, who is awake'. For thousands of years people in the East have been following his path. Now it is the turn of the West.

184 pages, illustrated
ISBN 0 904766 24 1
£6.99/$11.95

SANGHARAKSHITA
WHAT IS THE DHARMA?
THE ESSENTIAL TEACHINGS OF THE BUDDHA

Guided by a lifetime's experience of Buddhist practice, Sangharakshita tackles the question 'What is the Dharma?' from many different angles. The result is a basic starter kit of teachings and practices, which emphasizes the fundamentally practical nature of Buddhism.

In turn refreshing, unsettling, and inspiring, this book lays before us the essential Dharma, timeless and universal: the Truth that addresses the deepest questions of our hearts and minds and the Path that shows us how we can renew our lives.

272 pages, illustrated
ISBN 1 899579 01 x
£9.99/$19.95

SANGHARAKSHITA

THE THREE JEWELS: THE CENTRAL IDEALS OF BUDDHISM

The Three Jewels are living symbols, supreme objects of commitment and devotion in the life of every Buddhist.

This authoritative book, by an outstanding Western Buddhist teacher, explains the pivotal importance of the Three Jewels. To understand the Three Jewels is to understand the central ideal and principles of Buddhism. To have some insight into them is to touch its very heart.

264 pages
ISBN 1 899579 06 0
£11.99/$23.95

SANGHARAKSHITA

BUDDHISM FOR TODAY – AND TOMORROW

To lead a Buddhist life we need, above all, four things: a vision of the kind of person we could become; practical methods to help us transform ourselves in the light of that vision; friendship to support and encourage us on the path; and a society or culture that supports us in our aspirations.

This book is a succinct introduction to a Buddhist movement that exists precisely to make these things available. The author, Sangharakshita, brought the experience of twenty years' practice of Buddhism in India back to his native Britain, to found the Friends of the Western Buddhist Order in 1967.

This heartfelt statement of his vision is recommended reading for anyone who aspires to live a Buddhist life in the world today – and tomorrow.

64 pages
ISBN 0 904766 83 7
£4.99/$8.95

TEJANANDA

THE BUDDHIST PATH TO AWAKENING

The word Buddha means 'one who is awake'. In this accessible introduction, Tejananda alerts us to the Buddha's wake-up call, illustrating how the Buddhist path can help us develop a clearer mind and a more compassionate heart.

Drawing on over twenty years of Buddhist meditation and study, Tejananda gives us a straightforward and encouraging description of the path of the Buddha and his followers – the path that leads ultimately to our own 'awakening'.

224 pages, with diagrams
ISBN 1 899579 02 8
£8.99/$17.95

KAMALASHILA

MEDITATION: THE BUDDHIST WAY OF TRANQUILLITY AND INSIGHT

A comprehensive guide to the methods and theory of Buddhist meditation, written in an informal style. It provides a complete introduction to the basic techniques, as well as detailed advice for more experienced meditators seeking to deepen their practice.

The author is a long-standing member of the Western Buddhist Order, and has been teaching meditation since 1976. In 1979 he helped to establish a semi-monastic community in North Wales, which has now grown into a public retreat centre. For more than a decade he and his colleagues developed approaches to meditation that are firmly grounded in Buddhist tradition but readily accessible to people with a modern Western background. Their experience – as meditators, as students of the traditional texts, and as teachers – is distilled in this book.

304 pages, with charts and illustrations
ISBN 1 899579 05 2
£13.99/$27.95

SANGHARAKSHITA

THE HISTORY OF MY GOING FOR REFUGE

The founder of the Western Buddhist Order traces the 'erratic process of discovery' that has led him to conclude that the monastic life-style and spiritual life are not identical, that it is possible to be a good monk or nun and at the same time a bad Buddhist, and that Going for Refuge – the act of commitment to Buddhist spiritual ideals – is the central and definitive act of the Buddhist life, and the fundamental basis of unity among Buddhists.

For anyone concerned with the spiritual vitality of the Buddhist tradition – and with its transmission in the modern world – this meticulously plotted 'history' makes indispensable reading.

132 pages
ISBN 0 904766 33 0
£4.95/$9.95

SANGHARAKSHITA

HUMAN ENLIGHTENMENT

We often hear about the 'ideal home', the 'ideal car', the 'ideal holiday' ... but is there such a thing as an ideal man or woman?

According to Buddhism there is. A Buddha is a fully perfected human being, one who has developed the qualities of awareness, love, and energy – germinal in us all – to a peak of excellence. According to Buddhism, Enlightenment is the natural ideal for humankind.

   The Ideal of Human Enlightenment
   What Meditation Really Is
   The Meaning of Spiritual Community

Under these three headings, Sangharakshita – an outstanding figure in the Western Buddhist world – leads us into a straightforward and practical encounter with the ideals and methods of Buddhism.

80 pages
ISBN 0 904766 57 8
£3.99/$6.95

SANGHARAKSHITA
FORTY-THREE YEARS AGO:
REFLECTIONS ON MY BHIKKHU ORDINATION

Here we are given a frank chronicle of the events and reflections which led Sangharakshita to question his own bhikkhu ordination and to reassess the effect of formal, monastic ordination on the Buddhist experience. Vividly documented and clearly argued, this book deserves to be read by all who are concerned with the future of Buddhism – whether in the East or in the West.

64 pages
ISBN 0 904766 64 0
£3.50/$6.50

SANGHARAKSHITA
WAS THE BUDDHA A BHIKKHU?

The reflections sparked by Sangharakshita's discovery that his bhikkhu ordination was technically invalid have decisively influenced his vision of the Buddhist spiritual life. They underlie many features of the Western Buddhist Order and the Friends of the Western Buddhist Order, which he founded.

If, as Sangharakshita argues, the Theravada ordination tradition no longer meets its own stipulations, then a number of issues present themselves for re-examination. Is it not possible that a 'bad' monk might be a better Buddhist than a good one? What does it really mean to venerate the 'robe'? How does the laity's reverence affect the spiritual health of a bhikkhu? Do women need to resurrect the bhikkhuni sangha in order to live spiritual lives?

64 pages
ISBN 0 904766 71 3
£3.99/$6.99